MULTI-TRACK RECORDING

MULTI-TRACK RECORDING

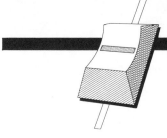

Edited by Dominic Milano
A Volume In The *Keyboard Magazine* Basic Library

From the pages of *Keyboard Magazine*
GPI Publications
20085 Stevens Creek Blvd.
Cupertino, California 95014

HLB® HAL LEONARD BOOKS
8112 W. Bluemound Road, Milwaukee, WI 53213

GPI BOOKS

Art Director
Paul Haggard

Senior Editor
Brent Hurtig

General Manager
Judie Eremo

Graphics Associate/Designer
Rick Eberly

Index
Steve Sorensen

Assistant
Marjean Wall

Director
Alan Rinzler

GPI PUBLICATIONS

President/Publisher
Jim Crockett

Director Of Finance
Don Menn

Editor: Keyboard Magazine
Dominic Milano

Corporate Art Director
Wales Christian Ledgerwood

Production
Cheryl Matthews, *Director*;
Joyce Phillips, *Assistant Director*
    Andrew Gordon, Gail Hall, Joe Verri

Typesetting
Leslie Bartz, *Director*
    Pat Gates, June Ramirez

Computer Graphics by Rick Eberly.
Photo Credits
Page 1: Paul Haggard; 30: Michael Finnigan;
55: John Sievert; all others are by the courtesy
of the manufacturers.

ISBN 0-88188-552-5

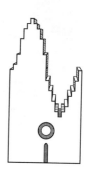
v

THE ART OF RECORDING

Music is the most evanescent of art forms. Even as you listen to it, it is flying past you at a thousand feet per second, to dissolve almost instantly into the random molecular motions known as heat. Unlike a painting or a sculpture, a piece of music can never be viewed as a whole. All you can perceive is one tiny slice of it at time; the rest must be held (perfectly or imperfectly) in memory. In a sense, attempting to capture music in any permanent form is as futile as attempting to secure absolute stability in the perpetual flux of life.

The technological marvels of the nineteenth and twentieth centuries have changed this situation not at all. Music still flies away. What technology has accomplished is to make musical sounds *repeatable*. This is what the art of audio recording was all about, in its origins. Thanks to Thomas Edison, Alexander Graham Bell, and other dedicated inventors, it became possible both to store sounds in physical form and to transmit them over long distances.

Today, recording means a great deal more than simply storing sounds. For one thing, it is a vast industry, one whose product has deep emotional meaning to millions of people. Movies may be more exciting, but they're also larger and more impersonal. Popular songs seem to speak directly to us, to our most intimate hopes and fears. And precisely because it is so important to people, recorded music has come to involve a great deal more than simply the storage of sounds in repeatable form. Recording today means enhancing, developing, perfecting sounds in ways that deepen and expand their impact on the listener.

Fifty years ago, it was possible to make a great recording by bringing a group of musicians into the studio and having them play exactly as they would onstage. In fact, no other method of recording was feasible. But recordings today are no longer simply documentations of performances, any more than films are simply documentations of stage plays. In a very real sense, what you hear on a phonograph record, tape cassette, or compact disc is larger than life. The sounds often go far beyond anything that could be produced mechanically, and they are crafted as carefully as the rhythms and pitches. The technology of recording has left Edison's wax cylinders light-years behind, and it is moving further, and faster, every week.

If you want to take chances with your music, if you care about nurturing your own ideas about what sounds good and challenging your listeners to open their ears, then you should accept the fact that you may have to learn enough about the technology to make records yourself. And if you're absolutely knocked out by Top 40 rock and plan to make millions at it—well, you'll still need to learn just as much, or more. The competition is pretty stiff. So keep a copy of this book handy. At the very least, it should help you save some money. At best, it might even help you start a revolution in the way people listen, and feel, and think. The technology is just waiting for more musicians with vision to learn to use it.

By Jim Aikin

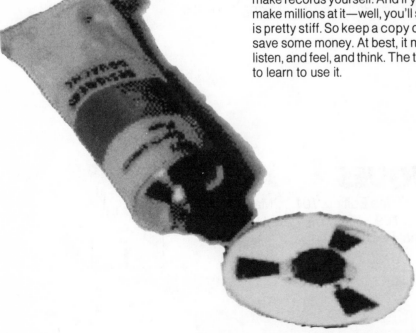

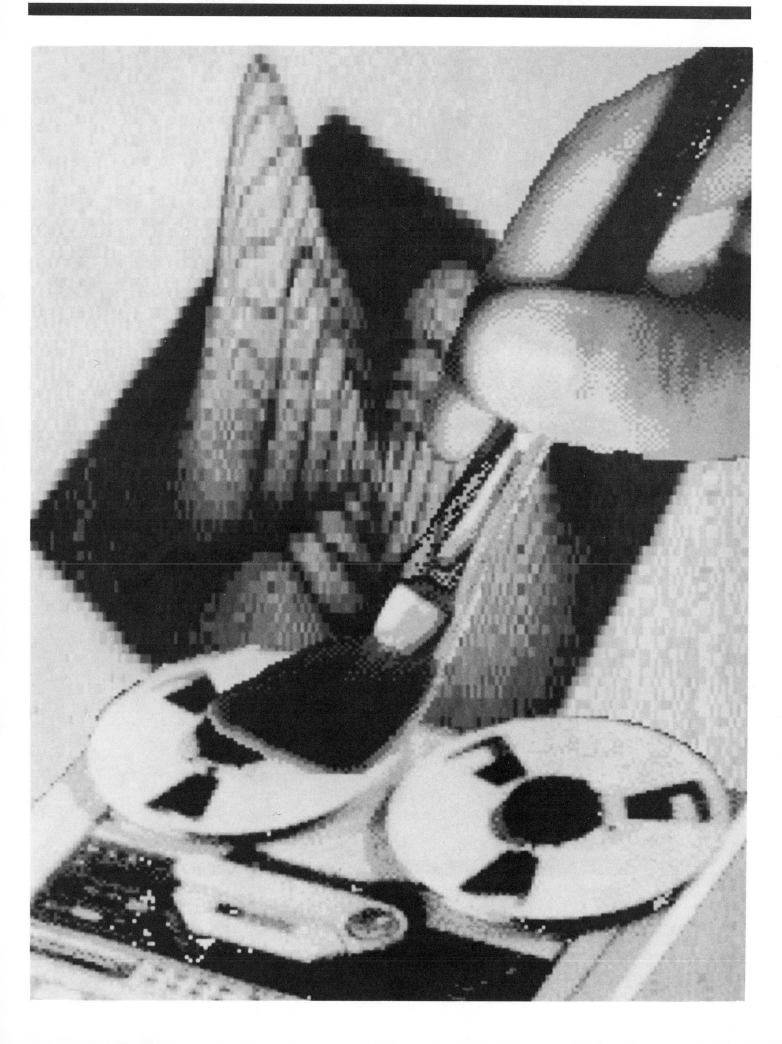

1 GETTING STARTED

SETTING UP A HOME STUDIO

June 1986. All the material in this book that has been reprinted and edited from the pages of *Keyboard Magazine* has the month and year of original publication indicated throughout.

Monstrous metallic panels, strewn with blinking LED eyes, gleam in the darkness. An imposing bank of gadgetry towers darkly in the corner, dripping with wire and cables. The only source of light is the florescent green glow of a computer's monitor screen, cluttered with flashing data displays. Its twin disk drives switch in anticipation. Could this be a top-secret air-defense installation? The bridge of a nuclear-powered submarine? The hidden headquarters of a telephone company bent on world domination? Nothing so dramatic. It used to be your living room.

Actually, you might as well have guessed that it was a professional recording studio. Never before have the flexibility and fidelity of pro recording been so nearly within the grasp of keyboard players working at home. In some cases, newly developed technologies can give you capabilities that aren't yet available at many major recording studios. The expense of multi-track tape recording has given way to the technological elegance of MIDI sequencing, drastically increasing signal-to-noise ratios along the way. Inexpensive MIDI slave modules have put textures of orchestral depth at the command of keyboard players working alone. Electronic instruments, particularly those offering sampled timbres from gong to grand piano, have freed home studios from the need for refined mike placement techniques, expensive microphones, and the space to put them in. Such signal processing units as digital reverbs, which used to play a large part in differentiating the sounds heard on popular records from those you could make in your living room, have dropped from upwards of $10,000 to well below $500. It's true, the high end has gotten higher—but the low end is falling by leaps and bounds.

This kind of equipment isn't cheap, but with a reasonable amount of scrimping and saving, a workable setup is within reach of any musician willing to go to the trouble. Home recording isn't just for players with MIDI on the brain, either. An acoustic pianist, investing a few thousand clams in microphones, a

digital reverberator, and a VCR-driven digital 2-track deck, and taking care to tailor the sound of the room, could conceivably make recordings that rival the cleanest and clearest in the world.

Furthermore, most musicians already have some of the necessary gear. The home stereo can be pressed into service as a monitoring sytem, and there's no law against mixing down to a cassette tape recorder. If you couple the equipment you already have with a rela-

tively flexible attitude about the production quality you'd like to achieve, putting together a modest but workable semiprofessional home recording studio doesn't need to cost much at all.

Keeping a flexible attitude can play large part in both the cost of your rig and the results you get from it. By adopting a "make do" frame of mind, you can kluge your way through just about anything. For example, it's not exactly the accepted practice to mix a 4-track recording to stereo by using a couple of Y-cables—in fact, electronically speaking, it's utterly wrong—but it will get you some kind of mix if there's no other way. And if it sounds good to you, *do it*. Lacking a stand-alone reverb unit? Record reverb with each track (rather than mixing it in later) by using the spring reverb in your amplifier. The same goes for outboard equalization. A spare reel-to-reel deck can be pressed into service as a delay line, and with a little feedback can produce rather crude reverberations. You can even do overdubs with a couple of cheap cassette machines and a two-channel mixer. Often what seems like a technological compromise can spur you on to creative solutions that will widen the scope of your musical con-

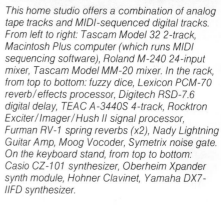

This home studio offers a combination of analog tape tracks and MIDI-sequenced digital tracks. From left to right: Tascam Model 32 2-track, Macintosh Plus computer (which runs MIDI sequencing software), Roland M-240 24-input mixer, Tascam Model MM-20 mixer. In the rack, from top to bottom: fuzzy dice, Lexicon PCM-70 reverb/effects processor, Digitech RSD-7.6 digital delay, TEAC A-3440S 4-track, Rocktron Exciter/Imager/Hush II signal processor, Furman RV-1 spring reverbs (x2), Nady Lightning Guitar Amp, Moog Vocoder, Symetrix noise gate. On the keyboard stand, from top to bottom: Casio CZ-101 synthesizer, Oberheim Xpander synth module, Hohner Clavinet, Yamaha DX7-IIFD synthesizer.

ception. While this kind of procedure rarely yields results of professional quality, it does allow you to get on with making a recording, rather than letting the limitations of your equipment stop you in your tracks.

At the same time, it's worth taking some time to design your studio and acquire the best equipment you can, weighing your needs against the limitations of finances and space. A recording studio, from the most humble to the ones that look like the bridge of the Starship Enterprise, is a system. Each component affects and depends on the others. Since the primary purpose is to capture and manipulate sounds, anything that affects what you hear is significant to your studio design. The best speakers in the world won't give you an accurate picture of your piano's sound if your amplifier's frequency response is too limited. (Then again, your piano might sound so squalid that accuracy is the last thing you're looking for.) The same principle goes for every other piece of equipment in the studio. In evaluating whether or not a certain piece of equipment or point of design is right or wrong for you, think about how it will affect the sounds your studio makes and your ability to hear them, how likely you are to upgrade that component in the future, and where it might be best to compromise now.

Space

Professional studios are generally divided into two rooms. The control room holds the bulk of the recording hardware, including the mixing console, tape machines, and outboard effects. The studio proper, or "room," is where the music is actually performed. This arrangement, developed before the advent of electronic keyboards, allows several tracks of already-recorded material to be heard in the control room along with the current take, while the microphones trained on the musicians in the studio pick up only their instruments. It also assumes that an engineer is in the control room, listening to what the microphones are picking up without interference from the actual sounds the instruments are making. Feedback would be inevitable without this isolation between the control room monitors and the microphone, and it would also be impossible to keep the current track sonically isolated from those previously recorded. If you plan to record acoustic

instruments or vocals (and you have an engineer) this arrangement is still the best, at least from a technical point of view. Unfortunately, you might have to move your bed into the kitchen in order to free up the extra room.

If this doesn't suit your taste in interior decoration, one alternative is to record and monitor in the same room, using headphones. This is by no means an uncommon arrangement. It isn't ideal for listening to the sound as it goes on tape, but at least it saves your bedroom. If you're working alone, and using microphones, headphones are the only way to maintain isolation between previously recorded tracks and the sounds currently being recorded, so you'd have to work this way even if you had a separate control room. It's not a good idea, however, to rely exclusively on headphones;

The Tascam 388 recorder/mixer is a self-contained 8-input mixer and 8-track 1/4" tape recorder. For space and convenience, many musicians prefer this "ministudio" approach—though some flexibility is sacrificed.

they can fool your ears. Always check the way things sound over speakers by recording a test and playing it back—but be sure to turn off the microphones first, or your speakers could go down in an apocalypse of feedback. If you need to use microphones only occasionally, you can simply run microphone and headphone cables into the bedroom whenever you need to.

The entire issue becomes moot if you're recording electronic instruments exclusively. The signal coming from your instrument's output jack is isolated from any of the sounds coming out of the

monitors, and there's no microphone to pick them up, so no amount of monitoring will interfere.

MIDI Vs. Multi-Track

Now that MIDI sequencers have become a viable replacement for the multi-track tape recorder, at least among keyboardists who work primarily with electronics, it's reasonable to question the assumption that you'll be needing a tape deck. Recently a number of MIDI-controlled sampled pianos have become available, blowing away the most compelling reason for keyboardists to use tape—that is, to record an acoustic piano.

Furthermore, the sounds generated by a MIDI sequence come directly from the instruments themselves, rather than from an audio recording of them. Each time the sequence plays back, the notes are being performed in real time. When an audio signal is recorded to tape, its frequency response and signal-to-noise characteristics are degraded. Each re-recording degrades the signal further, and adds some tape hiss, so that sounds recorded to multi-track and then mixed to two tracks have gone through two stages of degradation. In this case, the final mixed-down recording would be called "second generation." With a limited number of tracks, say, four or eight, it's not uncommon to add several more generations to the final mix, each causing further distortion, and adding more noise, to the original signal.

For those of you who have never suffered the agony of listening to your sounds die a slow and painful death,

2

There are still good reasons to go multi-track, though, which have more to do with budget than with the state of technology. For one thing, you may already have a multi-track deck. Since obsolescence is less an issue at home than in a commercial recording environment, there's no reason not to use a multi-track recorder if you already own one. A more substantial argument, though, is that the ability to overdub can save you the cost of a bunch of MIDI instruments and signal processors. MIDI sequencing requires that you have all of the sounding instruments on hand, and all of their signals must be processed in real time, which can run you quite a bit of money. The MIDI approach, as noted above, gives you the advantage of first-generation master tapes, but you may have to blow your inheritance to do it. In order to record eight synthesizer parts, you need to have eight synthesizers on hand, or at least four splittable instruments, either of which may cost more than an 8-track machine. (You would also need a board big enough to handle all eight inputs, plus any effects returns, while bouncing tracks of tape allows you to get away with fewer inputs to the board.) Taking the multi-track approach, you can use a single digital delay unit for the slap on your rhythm patch, for the ambience behind the snare drum, for the echoes spreading out behind your lead, and so on. That's *one* synthesizer and *one* delay unit.

You can't use MIDI to record vocals and other acoustic sources. Another more subtle point may concern musicians working outside of a steady tempo or using odd divisions of the beat. MIDI recording, as a digital medium, depends on clock resolution—that is, how finely time is divided into recorded increments. In essence, every digital medium quantizes the input, although to much smaller units than the eight- and sixteenth-notes we're familiar with from note-correct operations. Sensitive ears can detect the difference between the rhythmic aspect of the original performance and its rendering as a MIDI sequence. Virtually all other functions of tape have been either duplicated or improved upon by a number of MIDI sequencers now on the market. At least in the realm of techno-music, the choice between tape and diskette is still a toss-up.

Multi-track recorders come in a number of formats. At the bottom of the price scale, 4-track cassette decks are a very popular way to do multi-tracking at

home. These machines usually come with a built-in mixer, which kills two pterodactyls with one stone, unless you need a more comprehensive mixing facility. Since cassette tape is both narrow and thin, there's a relatively limited amount of tape to hold your four tracks, which in turn places limitations on the potential recording quality these machines can achieve. This is the general rule: The wider the tracks (tape width divided by the number of tracks), and the faster the tape speed, the more accurately the tape can record input signals. Many 4-track cassette recorders feature a higher-than-usual tape speed, which does make a difference (see Tech Talk on page 12 for more details on frequency response). Four- and 8-track machines using 1/4" tape are popular for home use, while broadcast-quality 4-

and 8-track work is usually done with 1/2" tape. One-inch width machines can be found in 8-and 16-track formats. Generation by generation, a quick explanation is in order. Imagine that you have a 4-track recorder, and you want to maintain a stereo drum mix—that takes up two tracks. The rhythm keyboard part goes on next, and after that the bass. Your four tracks are full, and you still have to put down that hip orchestral stab you sampled from a Clorox commercial. You have to do a preliminary mix of the four tracks to two (recording to a stereo cassette deck), keeping in mind that the Clorox stabs will go on top, and then re-record the mix back to two tracks on the multi-track. (This tape-to-tape trans-

With a sequencer, such as this Alesis MMT-8, all of your MIDI instruments can be recorded and played back without ever recording their parts on tape—at least until mixdown time. Sync-to-tape techniques (as described on page 55), are the key to using a sequencer in conjunction with a tape recorder, thus "expanding" your studio's number of tracks.

fer is called bouncing.) Now you have two free tracks. You record the stabs, decide the tune could use a counter-melody (which fills the other free track), and do a final mix to cassette. Listening back, you find that the snare has lost some of its punch, and the bass sounds a little dumpier than before, but all the parts are there. Of course, if the snare drum never had any punch in the first place, and you left the bass sound a little dumpy to begin with, intending to "fix it in the mix," things might not sound so rosy. Welcome to the mixdown of the living dead.

(Incidentally, there are two common variations on this scenario. First, you may decide that the Clorox stabs complete the piece. You can play them in *as you do your final mix*, which saves one generation. Second, you may decide that a monaural recording is tolerable. In this case, the drums only take up one track, and if you need to bounce from the cassette deck back to the multi-track, the mix only takes up a single track, leaving three free instead of two.)

Microphones

The wonders of electronics have made these yet another dispensable item in many recording setups. The audio signal from any electronic instrument can be connected directly to the tape machine's input, so transduction from sound waves into electricity is no longer necessary. There's no denying,

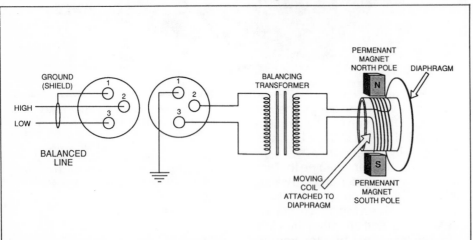

The components of a dynamic microphone.

only way to capture that on tape is to use a mike. Obviously, vocals can't be recorded without a microphone, nor can non-electronic instruments and sounds. And if you want to sample these sounds for playback from a sampling keyboard, a good microphone is indispensable.

The ambience of a room, meaning the way sounds bounce back and forth between the walls, can add a lively dimension to sounds of all kinds. In a professional situation, room ambience is either controlled carefully or eliminated altogether (to be added artificially in the mix). At home, you can mike an instrument amidst bare floors and walls to produce a sense of "liveness," although a live (that is, reverberant) room is bound to get in the way when you're listening to the mix. Room acoustics are discussed below.

If you've decided that a microphone is necessary, the next question is whether you need one or two or tons. Having two, of course, makes it possible to record two instruments in isolation at one time; with only one mike, this requires an overdub. Two microphones can record the same source in a stereo ambient field, which can be an advantage, particularly for solo piano recordings. For stereo applications, it's best to use two mikes of the same make and model. A stereo microphone—basically two mikes housed in opposite sides of a single unit—offers simplicity at the expense of flexibility in placement. There are ways, however, to simulate stereo if you only have one microphone (though they rarely sound exactly like the real thing). Some techniques for stereoizing a mono source are discussed by professional recording engineers on page 71.

Many home recordists, not to mention pro engineers, manage to get by with little technical knowledge of microphones. There are good reasons for this: If you can't spend much money, you'll use whatever is available in your price range, whether it sounds horrendous or not. If you have the resources of a well-equipped recording facility at your disposal, the engineer will pick the best mike for a given job. Chances are, he's choosing the favorite of the enginer who showed him the ropes. Nonetheless, we'll go into a little more detail on the theory that a little knowledge is a dangerous thing, and that most musicians like to live dangerously.

The job of a microphone is the opposite of that of a speaker. While a speaker

though, that direct audio sounds different from miked audio. Many musicians prefer the sound of an instrument, even a synthesizer or a drum machine, picked up from the air. For some applications, for example lead guitar simulations, the realism of the effect depends on overdriving an amplifier and speaker, and the translates electricity into sound, a mike receives sound waves, which travel through the air, and transduces them into electrical waves, which are fluctuations in the pressure of a stream of electrons. The interface between air and electrons, usually a very light diaphragm that vibrates in response to sound waves, is the basis of the three main categories of microphones: dynamic, condenser, and ribbon. Although there are differences between these types, advancements in microphone technology have made them too subtle to be worth discussing in detail here. Suffice it to say that dynamic microphones are often favored for recording high transient sound pressure levels, such as would be created by a snare drum. Condenser mikes require a power source (either a battery or "phantom power," a feature built into many mixing boards), and boast higher sensitivity and higher output levels. Some condensers, in fact, put out a line-level signal, making it possible to bypass the generally noisy mike preamp section of the board. Ribbon mikes are expensive and fragile, but you aren't likely to encounter them very often.

One aspect of a microphone that you can't ignore is its pickup pattern. The cardioid pattern is generally the most useful for multi-track applications. Cardioid mikes sense sounds in a heart-shaped pattern, with the heart's point pointing outward; that is, the microphone rejects sounds coming from directly behind, picks them up a bit better from either side, and is most sensitive to sounds directly in front. An omnidirectional pattern picks up sounds coming from any direction equallly—not ideal for isolating a single instrument from others nearby, but perfect for making a monaural recording with room ambience. A less common pattern is a figure-eight, in which the microphone's two faces are equally sensitive, rejecting sounds to either side. This is useful for picking up two sources side by side, for example a pair of mounted tom-toms, or two vocalists. The two sides don't maintain their left-right separation (you would need a stereo mike for this). High-end mikes often provide a selection of patterns.

One point of microphone technique should be mentioned. Any time you are using more than one mike at a time—for instance, when you're miking an acoustic piano—there is a possibility that you'll run into phase problems. When two identical sound waves 180 degrees out

of phase with each other reach two different microphones, the signals from the mikes will cancel each other out if combined into mono. This is a complex and dynamic phenomenon, and generally it won't be heard if the two mike inputs are panned apart. It will become audible immediately, though, if you combine the two (or more) channels; segments of the frequency spectrum will consistently be boosted or cut. Then again, if the recording you're making will never be heard in mono, and everything sounds good to you, microphone phase probably isn't worth worrying about.

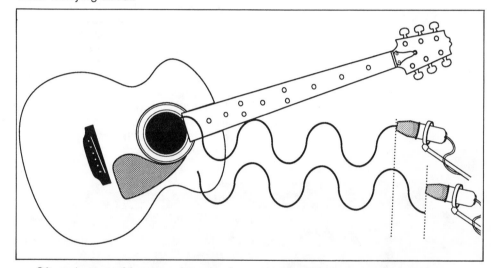

Microphone phase cancellation. When using more than one microphone, it's possible for sound waves to arrive out-of-phase with each other. When two out-of-phase waves are mixed together (particularly in mono), some signals will cancel each other.

Often phase problems can be solved by moving one of the microphones slightly. If possible, have someone else move it while you listen. If phasing is the problem, it should clear up as the microphone is moved into a better position. (You can read what the pros have to say about phasing difficulties on page 73.)

Admittedly, knowing which microphone to buy is nearly impossible without trying it out under working conditions, and without having some experience in microphone techniques so that you can give it a fair trial. A flat frequency response, the pickup pattern you need, the price, and a full sound should steer you in the right direction, but a recommendation from someone with lots of experience is the best guide.

Mixers

You might have what you need in the mixer department right in your live performance setup. A mixer is a mixer, and though some may be configured especially for live applications, they will do for recording in a pinch. Bobby Nathan's article on choosing a mixer (see page 22) explains the major features and variables to consider, so we won't go into them here.

Generally speaking, you'll need as many input lines as you have instruments, microphones, tape tracks, and outboard effects returns *happening simultaneously*. It's convenient to have even more, but it's nice to have money, too. With clever patching you can get by with this minimum number or even fewer, depending on the capabilities of your mixer. With stereo outputs becoming more common for synthesizers, and with the proliferation of drum machines boasting scads of individual outputs, the number of mixer lines you may need has increased drastically. You can cut down on them by using the optional monaural outputs, and by depending on effects, such as reverb, to broaden your stereo field. Grouping all but the most essential drum sounds (say, the bass drum and the snare) through the drum machine's stereo or mono outputs is another easy way to conserve channel inputs.

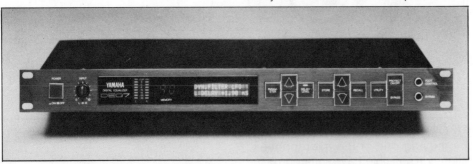

Yamaha's DEQ7 digital equalizer can store numerous EQ settings, which can later be recalled either via the front panel or through MIDI.

Equalization

Most people are satisfied with the equalization facilities supplied with their mixing boards, but keep in mind that there are alternatives. Outboard EQ can be used instead of and in addition to the board's equalizers, and it comes in handy in other ways as well. Some outboard effects, such as spring reverbs, can often be coaxed into better response by cutting troublesome frequencies at the send. In addition, a stereo EQ unit can be useful for tweaking your final mix. The ins and outs of equalization are discussed on pages 22 through 27 of this book.

Samplers

Digital sampling has opened up a new territory for amateur recordists. Why bother getting good drum sounds when the hottest engineer this side of the Top Forty has put his sounds on a chip that you can fire with your trusty

drum machine? Roland, Korg, Technics, Ensoniq, and others have opened up the same can of worms for pianists. If the sound of your recordings is a high priority, however, you would do well to estimate whether you can do better, using a pair of microphones and the real McCoy, than the piano sounds this new generation of instruments instantly puts at your disposal.

Sequencing And Sound Generators

The way MIDI is being used these days for timbral layering, there's no such thing as having too many sound generators on hand for a sequence playback. Fortunately, one instrument with a splittable keyboard can take the place of two. Split capability can be even more handy if the split points can be overlapped, and if the keyboard's regions are channel-assignable. Some synthesizers, such as Oberheim's Xpander, the Ensoniq ESQ-1 and ESQ-M, and Casio's CZ series, allow you to assign individual voices to their own MIDI channels, so that each can function as a separate instrument. These features give your MIDI studio more flexibility with fewer instruments.

Levels

The subject of level standards is a tricky one; the inquisitive reader is referred to page 14 of this book. Here's a brief overview: Depending on what kind of equipment you're using, "line level" means different things. Line-level signals terminating in RCA plugs and jacks generally have a lower level, about $-10dB$. Quarter-inch phone connectors and balanced $1/4"$ tip/ring/sleeve connectors are associated with a higher line level, around $+4dB$, and pro gear often uses XLR connectors for this level. "Mike level" varies a great deal, roughly from $-60dB$ to $-45dB$ for dynamic mikes, and from $-35dB$ all the way into the line-level range for condenser mikes. These levels terminate in XLR connectors (for low-impedance mikes) and phone plugs (for high-impedance mikes). The levels generated by keyboard instruments run the gamut from about $-60dB$, for electro-acoustic instruments such as the Rhodes piano, to $+4$ or $+8dB$ for some synthesizers. Your system's electronics will operate best if you match the levels coming into your board. You can do this by metering the input, setting the chan-

6

nel fader at 0dB, and then adjusting the mike preamp, the instrument's volume control, and as a last resort the fader, until the meter peaks at around zero.

Computers

Computers have had an established place in the recording studio since the advent of automated mixing about ten years ago, but only recently have they become useful in home setups. With the gradual appearance of low-cost, personal-computer-based automated mixers, it appears that home mixdowns won't remain in human hands for long. Right now, however, personal computers are unbeatable for sequencing and patch library management. If you're just starting out, you can hop on one of the biggest waves ever to bathe the shores of music production. If you already have some recording equipment, the integration of a computer into your setup may be a relatively easy way to maximize the power of the gear you own.

Signal Routing

Between the computer, tape recorder, mixing board, instruments, microphones, amplifiers, and signal processing units—the mere skeleton of an admittedly sophisticated home setup—you're bound to have a ridiculous number of cables snaking all over the place. Not only will they get in your way, but figuring out what's attached to what, chasing down the right cable, and then replugging everything can rob your recordings of time and spontaneity. It pays to work out an interfacing scheme that will make common connections simple to make, and at the same time allow for just about any possibility that might come up.

Patch bays are an ideal way of organizing your signal routing. The basic idea is to pre-wire all of your inputs and outputs into a single panel of jacks. Then sending signals where they need to go becomes a simple matter of plugging a jumper cable from one jack to another. For example, if your board only has six inputs, and you have four channels of tape, a synthesizer, a drum machine with multiple outputs, and a stereo reverb, you may well need to do some repatching as you overdub and mix.

An alternative to using a patch bay for the above setup would be to keep a stereo drum mix and the synthesizer semi-permanently plugged into the tape

deck's inputs, with the tape outputs and reverb feeding the mixer. This keeps things nice and simple, but it also limits you to using the reverb unit only during mixdown, since there's no way to mix it in for individual overdubs. Incidentally, a patch bay is probably not going to be practical for some items in your studio; microphones, for example, are probably better plugged into the console as you need them.

Even if your setup and style of working with it don't demand the kind of convenience and flexibility a patch bay can give you—because there aren't that many signals to route, or because you've figured out a way to plug things in so that you seldom have to repatch—organizing the signal flow through your studio is a good idea. Color-coded wires can help, and at the very least you'll want to label the functions of all plugs so that you can find them if anything goes wrong. Tying groups of wires loosely into a bunch and tailoring cable lengths to suit your setup keeps things tidy, while also cleaning up the signal. Never use a 20-foot cable where a 3-footer will do, because every inch of cable produces a tiny amount of signal degradation.

Room Acoustics

There are lots of reasons to keep the various sounds emanating from your studio contained—not the least of which is the neighbor who, inevitably, is trying to sleep whenever the muse taps you on the shoulder. Unfortunately, there's no effective way of stopping low frequencies, short of turning the room into a bomb shelter. Unless you're ready to make a serious investment in isolating your studio, or you have survivalist leanings, it's most effective to sign a peace treaty with the folks next door.

While sheer bulk is the only way to curb the bass, high frequencies can be absorbed or diffused. This minimizes the effects of sound waves bouncing around within the studio's walls. The less reverberation there is in your listening environment, the more you'll hear the sounds you are actually producing. Ditto for recording with a microphone. Unless you want to record room ambience, it's best for the microphone to pick up as much direct sound from the instrument as possible. You can add artificial reverberation in a controlled fashion later.

Materials made specifically for absorbing and diffusing sound, such as Sonex, are available, but generally they

The Atari 1040 ST computer was the first popular personal computer to include MIDI in and out ports. By 1988 the ST had firmly established itself as a powerful, yet affordable, musician's computer—with a plethora of software applications from sequencing to waveform analysis.

7

carry a hefty price tag. Fortunately, many common materials will do the job, including some that you may already have in your home. Drapes, rugs, and padded furniture are useful, though imprecise. You can hang carpet, or some other cloth material, across the ceiling for additional absorption. Acoustic instruments can be isolated by partitioning them within an enclosure of curtains, or surrounding them with baffles —absorbent vertical panels which can be moved around the room—that you can build yourself. Sound-absorbent panels can also be constructed to hang from the walls, so that they can be removed to liven up the room for recording ambience. The books listed in the Recommended Reading section on page 117 are full of tips for improving your home studio's sonic environment.

Monitoring

Pro studios usually have three pairs of monitor speakers: one set of monster cabinets hanging from the ceiling like a pair of refrigerators, one pair of bookshelf speakers, and a couple of tiny, tinny speakers that sound awful. The frequency ranges of these three speaker pairs differ, but they share a characteristic flatness across the range each reproduces. This means that there are no idiosyncratic peaks and troughs in the frequency response; within the range that the speaker can put out, no frequency is emphasized more or less than any other. A flat response is important because, in going for what sounds good to you, you will compensate for your speakers' inaccuracies. If you compensate for a particularly boomy bass response by going easy on the low frequencies, your tape will be lacking in bass when it's played back on flatter speakers. Whatever speakers you use, the first priority should be a flat response. A graph of this characteristic should be included with the manufacturer's specs for any pair of speakers you're interested in.

Once you have an adequate pair of monitors for basic listening, you can play the same game the pros do: Who's going to be listening to your recordings? If they'll be played in dance clubs, then at some point you should listen at high volume through a pair of the biggest public address speakers you can get your hands on. If your audience will be listening as they drive across town on the freeway, check your work through

speakers which simulate the frequency response of the average car radio. In most cases, music recorded at home will be listened to on a garden-variety home stereo. In this case, it's best to use the most accurate bookshelf speakers you can find. In a pinch, of course, whatever speakers you currently use at home will do for starters.

There is one danger in using home stereo speakers: They aren't designed to take the high peak levels you're likely

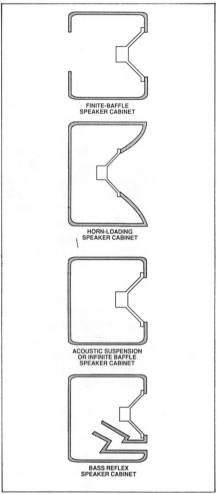

Speaker enclosure cross-sections.

to record. Commercially available recordings are heavily compressed, which squashes potentially damaging transients, while studio procedures routinely generate peaks of very high wattage. Studio monitors are built to handle this, while home speakers may blow under the stress. Whether the speakers are called upon to reproduce such transients depends on whether the amplifier you're using is capable of responding that efficiently to transient input signals, which your home stereo amp may not be. You should know, however, that you're taking a chance. Having a tech-

nician fit your woofers and tweeters with fuses will at least minimize the chances of any serious damage.

You'll want to eliminate as far as possible the effects of sound bouncing off the walls in your listening environment. This means that the speakers should be fairly close to you, and placed at about ear level. At the same time, they should be far enough away that you can hear a full stereo field from right to left (assuming you choose to work in stereo). A good rule of thumb is to place the cabinets so that, along with your head, they form the points of an equilateral triangle. The stereo field will be clearest if the speakers are placed on their sides, with the tweeters farthest to either side. In order to minimize variations in frequency response caused by uneven dispersion, the cabinets should be angled slightly inward toward your ears. This type of speaker arrangement is known as *nearfield monitoring*.

It's important to realize that, with so many variations in signal level, frequency response, transient response, noise floor, and so forth involved from component to component, nearly every home setup will have its sonic quirks. Making recordings that sound good when they're played back on systems other than your own is bound to be difficult. It's good experience to listen to your recordings in a number of other settings. This will help you learn to compensate for conditions in the real world.

Outboard Effects

Having an assortment of signal processors handy can do a lot to enhance your recordings. We've explained what they are and what they do in articles throughout this book, and specific applications are mentioned amidst the advice from recording engineers elsewhere in this book. Conventional applications break down roughly into enhancements of space (reverb and delay), stereo (just about anything that can be panned, including delays and pitchshifters), instrument definition (pitchshifters, delays, exciters, equalizers, and gates), and dynamic range (compressors, limiters, and gates). Although particular effects come in and out of fashion, the full potential of these devices for special effects has yet to be realized.

It's a truism among professional engineers that the quickest and easiest way to improve a studio's sound is to upgrade its reverberation facilities. The

8

same goes for home rigs. "Dry," or unre-verberated, sounds tend to sound un-natural, because in the real world, sounds of any significant loudness are affected by their environment. Amplified sounds coming directly from a speaker in a small room are basically environ-ment-less . Musical environments in particular, such as concert halls, have pronounced reverberant characteris-tics, and it is usual to simulate them in a studio recording. Sophisticated reverb and delay devices allow you to synthe-size simulations of unreal or impossible acoustic environments as well. Further-more, reverberations have a lot to do with how we preceive directionality (which is why most music is produced in stereo), and also contribute to sonic realism. Recently, high-quality reverb units have become portable (not long ago you needed an actual room, or at least a huge metal plate) and downright affordable. For these reasons, it makes sense to recommend that, if your studio is to have only one signal processor, it should be a reverb.

Mixdown Deck

One easy way to conserve your stu-dio's financial resources is to mix from multi-track, or MIDI, to cassette rather than reel-to-reel. The trade-off, of course, is in the potential quality of your master tape and the dubs you make from it. Another thing you give up when you forego reels is the ability to edit your final mix. Editing can be useful for any-thing from putting a number of tunes in their proper sequence (this is what stu-dio folks used to mean by the word "sequencing"), to chopping out that extra chorus at the end of the song, to spectacular musical effects like the famous stuttering "sci-i-i-i-ence" in Thomas Dolby's "Blinded By Science." With a heavy-duty aluminum splicing block, splicing tape, an ample stock of razor blades, a reel of paper leader tape, and some practice you'll be cutting together your own *musique concrète* dance mixes in no time.

Another alternative to a 2-track reel-to-reel mixdown deck is the kind of digi-tal 2-track recorder that works in con-junction with a videocassette recorder, such as Sony's PCM-701 and Naka-michi's DMP-100. Costing in the neigh-borhood of $1,000, such recorders put digital audio recording in the hands of the masses for low-distortion, noise-free mixes. Videocassettes are impossible to

edit without some pretty fancy outboard gear, but for many kinds of music, the sacrifice is well worth the gain in fidelity. For example, if you're recording solo piano performances, your entire setup might involve a pair of high-quality mic-rophones, a 2-track digital recorder, a VCR, reverberation, a small mixer, and a monitoring system.

Other digital 2-tracks, such as the new R-DAT (Rotary-head Digital Audio Tape) and S-DAT (for Stationary-head) re-corders are bound to become popu-lar among musicians, because of their low potential cost.

Synchronization

With the development of drum ma-chines, sequencers, and video, syn-chronization changed from an occa-sional problem into a daily necessity. Many sequencers come with synchron-ization facilities in addition to MIDI, allow-ing them to interact with time-dependent devices that don't understand MIDI clock commands. Pulse-based codes

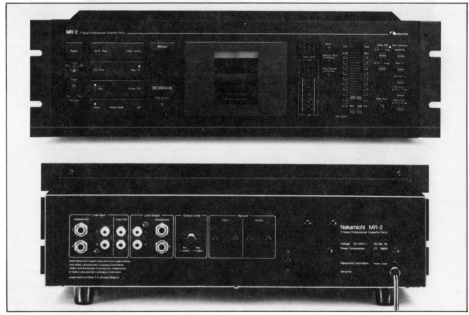

(24, 48, and 98 pulses per quarter-note) are common drum machine sync sig-nals. It is possible, however, for devices reading these codes to become con-fused by stray voltage spikes and drop-outs. FSK (Frequency Shift Key) was designed to overcome this problem. Unlike MIDI, any of these codes can be recorded to (and read from) tape, mak-ing it possible to integrate a tape deck into your MIDI sequencing system. SMPTE (for the Society of Motion Pic-ture and Television Engineers, pro-nounced *simptee*) time code was in-

While the R-DAT recorder is the heir-apparent, the cassette recorder has been the 2-track mix-down deck of choice for most home studios. Pictured is the Nakamichi MR-2 professional cassette deck.

9

vented to satisfy the needs of video producers, and has been adopted by many automated audio mixdown systems. If you've got several tracks and need to lock up to video for film or television production, and particularly if you have access to a SMPTE-based mixdown system, SMPTE is probably for you. (Outside of North America, the time code is known as EBU time code, for the European Broadcasters' Union. The two codes are functionally the same.)

There's a whole class of devices devoted to making peace between de-

Roland's SBX-80 sync box can generate and read SMPTE time code. By programming in tempos and time signatures, the SBX-80 can make a translation between SMPTE time code and MIDI measure number. This way, sequencers, drum machines, and other MIDI devices equipped with Song Position Pointer can be synced to tape, and stop and start from any position on tape (more about this starting on page 55).

vices that read different sync codes, including the Garfield line of time-base processors and Roland's SBX-80. The Chroma Polaris synthesizer can also handle some of these functions. While sync converters can provide enormous freedom in interfacing various boxes, you can probably do without them if you have a relatively uncomplicated studio.

Tape

Assuming you're using a tape deck, you have to keep a stock of tape on hand. It's tempting to buy whatever leaves your wallet with a few extra dollars in it—after all, reels of tape all look

the same. Most of us know by now, though, the difference between a good chrome-bias cassette and the ones you can buy at the drug store, three for $1.50. The situation isn't so different when the tape is wound on big metal reels.

The difference between high- and low-quality recording tape has to do with the way it handles magnetic charges—which, after all, are what your music has become by the time the tape hears it. Recording tape is covered with minute magnetic particles which are rearranged, when a recording is made, into an electrical representation of a given sound. The more densely these particles are packed, the higher the resolution of the sonic representation. If the particles tend to fall off, or if they're applied unevenly in the first place, this will distort the representation. If one particle tends to pass its charge to the ones surrounding it, this too will cause distortion. The higher the level of signal a tape will hold, the less the noise inherent in tape technology will be heard over the music. Some machines are permanently biased for a particular kind of tape, in which case that information will be listed in the owner's manual, but most offer more flexibility. As usual, your ears, specifications for frequency response and signal-to-noise ratio, and the recommendations of a professional are the best guides to buying the best tape.

Once you've decided which brand and type of tape to use, stick with it. Have an audio technician bias and align your tape deck to optimize its operation for that specific tape. The tape manufacturer can supply a reel of "tones"—a standardized set of test frequencies—which you can record and play back to check the alignment regularly. Tape decks need to be aligned often enough to make it worth your while to learn how to do the alignment yourself. The machine's service manual should outline the procedure. It may be difficult to learn, but it requires no special technical skills. Just make sure, before you start, that you really know what you're doing.

Noise Reduction

A certain amount of noise is a fact of life with analog tape. In order to be heard, the softest sounds you record must be louder than the tape's "noise floor." Thanks to modern recording technology, that floor is quiet enough that it isn't likely to drown out any of your music; nonetheless, a little background noise can be downright irritating during quiet passages. If your sounds are loud enough, they'll drown out the noise—but it they're too loud, they'll distort the electronics that are supposed to reproduce them faithfully. Whenever you use a tape recorder, you have to tread this line between too soft and too loud. Setting your levels carefully at every stage of a recording to get the hottest signal on tape without distortion, applying compression and amplification to bring the lower end of an instrument's dynamic range comfortably above the tape's noise floor, and using a noise gate to clamp down on the noise produced by the instrument itself are the first lines of defense against noise.

If it still sounds as though a stiff breeze is whistling through the studio door, a noise reduction system such as Dolby B or C, or dbx, can be pressed into service. The latter two are especially effective; you'll have to do some research to decide which you prefer. While professionals argue about whether a lower noise floor is worth the effect of noise reduction on the overall sound of their recordings, there's no denying that in a home situation, where the tradeoff for a lower budget is more noise, noise reduction of any kind can be a godsend.

Maintenance

Aligning tape machines is just one of the maintenance rituals used to placate the evil spirits that lurk in all recording studios. Another is demagnetizing the tape heads. Any decent owner's manual will tell you how to do this, but it should be pointed out that improper demagging can do more harm than good. Poor technique with a demagnetizing gun can put a charge in your heads that will never come out, and a couple of charged VU meters can make setting your levels more than a little troublesome.

Cleaning the heads, on the other hand, is difficult to do badly. You should do this as often as possible—before, during, and after sessions—to remove the magnetic oxide that rubs off the recording tape. Just a little oxide buildup can play havoc with your sound, so don't be shy about removing it. Q-Tips are perfect for swabbing fragile heads, and isopropyl alcohol is the best cleaning agent. Most consumer-grade alcohols, however, are 20 percent to 30 percent water, which doesn't evaporate as quickly and can *rust* heads and other

components. Get the highest percentage of alcohol you can find.

Cleaning dirty potentiometers is also easy. You'll need to do this whenever a dial or slider produces static when you move it. In many cases you don't even have to get behind the front panel that holds the pot, although sometimes this is necessary. All you have to do is spray the contact point liberally with contact cleaner, and work the pot back and forth until the noise goes away. (If the noise doesn't go away, you probably have some other problem.)

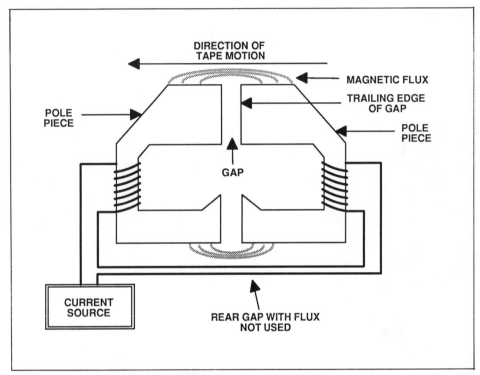

Cross-section of a record head (top view).

Depending on your technical expertise, there are hundreds of other maintenance procedures you can do yourself, from resoldering bad connections to replacing bad electrical components. It's useful to keep a table free for soldering cables. Keep a stock of wires, plugs, and jacks on hand. Cables go bad all the time, and when the need for a special-purpose cable rises—and it always does—you can slap it together yourself. For more involved operations, hire a tech to look your studio over periodically, depending on how much use your facility gets and how many things happen to be broken. This kind of regular checkup tends to forestall unpleasant surprises—was that an earthquake, or did the reverb just blow up?—and allows your equipment to give you the best sounds it possibly can.

By Ted Greenwald

TECH TALK

June 1986

A Simplified Guide To Specs, Levels, And Tape Formats

Before you buy a piece of gear for your studio, you'd naturally like to know how it's going to sound. One solution is to run from store to store trying out the various items you're considering. Listening tests are invaluable, no doubt about it—but there are so many variables that they can't ever be truly definitive. What type of monitor system is being used? Does the salesperson understand the equipment? Can you hear it in a quiet enough room to really judge? And can you remember just how much distortion there was in the highs with the XYZ Transfabulator you listened to last week, compared to the ABC Audio Blending Confusatron you're hearing right now?

Fortunately, there is a way around this problem. All manufacturers of audio gear publish lists of specifications (specs) for each unit in their line. Assuming that the specs are accurate (which they are in most cases), they can tell you a lot about how an audio device will sound under normal operating conditions. But only if you know how to read specs. It's impossible to get any real feeling for an audio product's performance without listening to it, but the specs will often give you a good idea whether you should even bother.

In the following pages we'll introduce you to the basic units of measurement that you'll find in a spec sheet. You don't need a degree in electrical engineering to understand the jargon, just a little patience and a logical way of looking at things.

Frequency Response

How many times have you run across ads that read like this: "The new ultra-advanced Mondophlegm console has a frequency response of 4Hz to 5,000,000Hz to catch all the subtlety of your music"? What does this mean? And why should you care?

For those who don't remember what frequencies are all about, here's a quick review: Instruments create sound by generating pressure waves in the air. If you could see these waves, you'd see that the molecules in the air are packed together more tightly in certain areas

(the peaks) and are spread slightly further apart in other areas (the troughs). The peaks and troughs are not stationary; they move through the air at about 1,000 feet per second, which is the speed of sound. While the waves move at a constant speed, they are not evenly spaced. When lots of them are packed close together, hundreds or thousands may pass a stationary point (such as your ear) every second. When they are spaced further apart, the number reaching your ear every second may only be one or two, or a few dozen.

The *frequency* of a sound is the number of waves that pass that stationary point in a single second. (Don't confuse this with loudness, which is determined by the difference in density between the peaks and troughs.) We hear these perturbations in air pressure as sound, provided that they fall between 20 peak/trough cycles per second and 20,000. (The unit used to measure cycles per second is called Hertz, abbreviated Hz.) This region between 20Hz and 20kHz (kiloHertz, or thousands of Hertz) is the range of human hearing. Some animals can hear higher frequencies.

The lowest *A* on a piano keyboard vibrates at 32.5Hz, while the top *C* vibrates at 4,186Hz. However, sounds in nature rarely consist of simple vibrations at a single frequency. In addition to the basic, or *fundamental*, frequency, most sounds contain higher frequencies called *overtones* or *harmonics* that are multiples of the fundamental. While few instruments produce fundamental frequencies that are above 5,000Hz, the harmonic spectrum of many instruments contain overtones for higher than 20kHz.

When you're looking into audio gear that's going to be asked to reproduce the sound of an instrument or performance without coloring that sound, you need to look at the device's frequency response specs. Frequency response is a measure of how well the device handles inputs at a wide range of audio frequencies.

Audio gear frequency response specs are often given in graph form, representing the output amplitude of the device given an input of constant amplitude over the range of frequencies from 20Hz to 20kHz. If you haven't seen these graphs, check out an audio cassette—there are a couple of brands that put the frequency response graph right on the wrapper.

One expression you'll run into is "flat out to . . . ." This means that the system will reproduce the entire frequency range presented to within a narrow tolerance up to the device's high-frequency limit. The "flat" expression comes from the shape of the frequency response graph—a flat line with a minimum of undulations in it until it drops off at the low and high limits of the frequency range.

Of course, the way you'll see frequency response listed most often is in numeric form. For example, the frequency response of our imaginary Mondophlegm console is stated as 4Hz to 5,000,000Hz—way outside the range of what anyone could hear, even if you happen to be of the canine persuasion. More realistic examples of frequency response ranges would be 20Hz-20kHz, 80Hz-12kHz, and so on. Accompanying the frequency range would be a spec for the output variation tolerance, expressed in decibels (dB, see below for details). This would appear as something like $\pm3dB$ after the frequency range spec. Following that would be the input level (or output level for amplifiers) that the test was performed at, expressed in watts, VU, or some other form. An entire written frequency response spec for an amplifier might read something like "30Hz-15kHz, $\pm1dB$ at one watt into eight ohms."

In general, a smaller number in the $\pm dB$ column means that the device has a flatter frequency response, which is good. $\pm3dB$ is a fairly large amount of slop. This is 6dB of variation: 3 up and 3 down. A company that reports frequency response to within $\pm1.0dB$ is probably saying more about their product's ability to reproduce an audio signal.

The range of frequencies which the device can accept within tolerable limits is called the *bandwidth* of the device. In most cases, this can be thought of as the flat portion of the frequency response curve.

We don't have space to go into specifics on each piece of audio gear you might be considering for your studio. For the most part, learning to interpret frequency response specs is a matter of common sense. Different pieces of audio equipment will have different frequency responses due to the limitations of their particular technology. It's important to consider the device type when assigning significance to the spec. Tape recorders, amps, outboard gear, speakers, and mikes all have specific,

non-overlapping uses. Therefore, their performance requirements will be different.

Here are a few things that may not be obvious to some keyboard players about tape recorders. Their frequency response is very dependent on the input level at which the device is tested. If a cassette deck boasts a frequency response of 20Hz-20kHz, $\pm1.0dB$ at 0VU, make sure the company doesn't also sell plots of land in the Everglades. The fact is that magnetic tape has level-dependent response with severe attenuation of high frequencies at high recording levels at slower tape speeds, and usually exaggerated low frequency response due to "head bump," which is compensated for in most pro machines and neglected in most inexpensive semi-pro decks. Most semi-pro tape decks (especially systems using cassette tape) are thus tested for frequency response at relatively low recording levels—*i.e.*, -10 or -20 VU. The standard conventions are that cassette decks and open reel decks operating at or below 3¾ ips are tested at -20 VU input level, decks running at 7½ ips are tested at -10 VU input level, and decks operating above 7½ ips are tested at 0 VU input level.

Tape speed also has a direct effect on the frequency response of a tape recorder. The faster the tape moves, the more tape will pass the record/playback head during a single cycle of a tone of given frequency. The more tape, the more faithfully that frequency will be recorded. This adds up to better high-frequency response at higher speeds. For example, a cassette deck running at 3¾ ips instead of the standard 1⅞ ips will show an increase in high-end response by as much as 2kHz in some cases. This is why pro studios don't even think twice about using rolls of 2" tape at $150 each every 15 minutes by recording at 30 ips.

When comparing decks operating at the same speed, verify that they were tested with the same fluxivity level—that is, check that the same amount of magnetic flux was being applied to the tape in each case. (Fluxivity is measured in nanowebers.) Tape type *does* make a difference in frequency response, but you can rest assured that the manufacturers are all using the best tape they can find.

On the subject of multi-track cassette decks, some companies are providing separate specs for the electronics and the recorder sections.

Sometimes the difference will be as much as 6kHz. If you plan to use the recorder as a recorder, pay more attention to its spec than the electronics spec. If the recorder is going to wipe out everything above 10kHz, who cares if the electronics section is flat out to Mars and back?

The Decibel

Most of us think of decibels (dB for short) as a measure of volume. After all, everyone knows that 0dB is the threshold of hearing and 120dB is the threshold of pain—bleeding ear drums, jet planes taking off, and all that. There are at least three other types of decibels that you'll run into very quickly if you're reading through the spec sheets of audio gear. These are dBm, dBV, and dBu. Here's a bit of history:

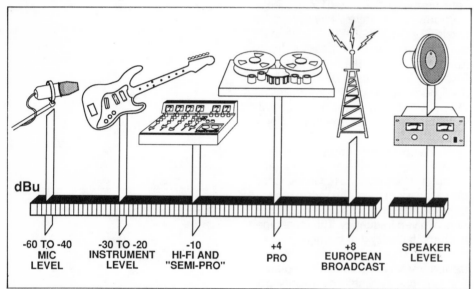

The dBu scale allows comparison of all the common levels we encounter. (Diagram not to scale.)

Decibels are numbers that in themselves are meaningless. They are used to express the relationships between two values, one of which is a reference of some sort. Unless you know what the reference is, the number is meaningless. That's why it's important to know that when you're using dB to talk about volume, 0dB is *referenced* as the threshold of human hearing and all other numbers are in comparison to that reference.

Decibels were developed out of a need to express the relationships between the power of various signals in telephone systems (deci means ten and bel is named for Alexander Graham Bell). To make a long and confusing

story short, it was decided that one milliwatt (one thousandths of a watt) would become the reference for decibels when they are used to talk about power, and that the decibel that used this reference level would be called the *dBm*.

At the time, pocket calculators hadn't been invented yet, so it was decided to base the decibel around the logarithmic scale—a scale which allowed you to add relatively small numbers rather than multiply huge numbers together to get comparisons in signal levels.

The dBm scale works in such a way that a doubling of the power results in a 3dB increase. If the power is increased tenfold, then there is a 10dB increase. If we go all-out and increase the power by a factor of 10,000, we have only realized a 40dB increase. Confused? Such is the nature of logarithmically based numbers. Large numbers are scaled down to easier-to-manage smaller numbers. The equation, if you're interested, looks like this:

$$dB \text{ above referenced level} = 10 \times LOG \text{ (power/reference power)}$$

Sticklers for detail will want to know that dBm for audio is always based around input and output impedances of 600 ohms, which makes 0dBm equal to 0.775 volts into 600 ohms, or, to put it mathematically,

$$dBm = 20 \times LOG \left(\frac{\text{measured voltage}}{.775V} \right)$$

This equation tells us what the difference is between some output voltage and our reference of .775 volts, provided

that both voltages are measured at the same 600-ohm impedance. Now, because we're talking voltage instead of power, and because there's a 20 before the LOG in the equation, a doubling of *voltage* corresponds to a 6dB increase (not 3dB as with power), and an increase fo 10,000 times the input voltage realizes an 80dB increase (not 40dB as with power). Are your eyes crossing yet? If not, just wait 'til you wade through this next bit.

Since not all audio gear is created equal, and more importantly because not all audio gear is based on 600-ohm input and output impedances, yet another dB scale was invented. This one isn't based on power, since power-based scales are dependent on the impedances of the system. This new dB scale is referenced to voltage only—one volt, to be exact. The reason we can get away with this is that most gear these days uses extremely high impedances, which do not load the output of the equipment driving it. This dB referenced to one volt is called the dBV.

Naturally, most people confuse dBm and dBV (didn't you?). If we calculate what one volt gives us in dBm, we find that there is a 2.2dB difference between the dBm and dBV scales, such that 0dBV = 2.2dBm. That's a less than ideal situation, so some bright soul came up with an equation that would give both dBm and dBV the same zero value by making the reference voltage .775 volts. To make matters more confusing still, they called decibels referenced to .775 volts dBv—with a lower case 'v'! As you might expect, this drove a lot of tech types crazier than it's driving us explaining it to you, so the 'v' was changed to a 'u' to avoid confusion. Note that 0dBu is equivalent to 0dBm at 600 ohms.

So now we have three basic conventions for decibels: (1) **dBm** = decibels referenced to 1 milliwatt (in audio equipment it refers to .775 volts into 600 ohms, which is 1 milliwatt); (2) **dBV** = decibels referenced to 1 volt, so 0dBV = 1 volt (this type of dB tells you nothing about power; it only gives you the relationship between two voltages, one of which happens to be 1 volt); (3) **dBu** or **dBv** = decibels referenced to .775 volts, so 0dBu = .775 volts (used to eliminate the 2.2dB difference between the dBV and dBm scales). The dBu scale is independent of impedance.

So what's all this used for, and why should you care about any of it? We turn now to the wonderful world of levels.

14

Levels

Anyone who has looked seriously into studio gear specs has run into the expressions "+4dB inputs and outputs," "-10dB inputs and outputs," and "-20dB inputs and outputs." All of these refer to audio gear signal levels. It's important to understand that there are differences between these levels and that the levels determine whether item A will be compatible with item B.

Why isn't there one standard level for all audio gear? Who knows? The idea for +4dB gear started way back in the days of vacuum tubes and monaural recording, when the VU meter (we all know what those are, right?) was selected as a handy way to measure audio signals. Without going into the pros and cons of different types of metering, the VU meter was designed so that the average audio level of the incoming signal would be displayed by the little needle; 0 VU was designated as the highest level the incoming signal could achieve without distortion (remember, tape headroom wasn't what it is today).

Of course, it would have been ideal to have designed a meter where 0 VU = 0dBm, but unfortunately, such a meter would have had such a low impedance that it would substantially load the circuit whose level it was measuring, thereby reducing the output of the circuit (for details on loading see the section on impedance below). As a result, the impedance of the meter circuit was raised so that the presence of a meter would not disrupt the actual signal levels, which meant that the meter would read 4dBm too high when registering 0 VU. This was in the days before inexpensive op amps and FET circuitry, which could have been used to achieve parity between 0 VU and 0dBm. So the standard became such that 0 VU would represent +4dBm of level into 600 ohms.

Time passed, stereo came to be, and a new standard was born: 0 VU = -10dBV, the level of most home recording gear. Now, it would seem safe to assume that if you had a piece of gear with an output level of +4dB and another piece of gear with an input level of -10dB, you'd have to come up with some way to reduce the +4 signal by 14dB—the difference between +4 and -10, right? Wrong. That old varying dB reference level comes back to haunt us with this one. +4 gear is referenced to the *dBm* scale (0dB = .775 volts into 600 ohms), where -10 gear is referenced to the *dBV* scale (0dB = 1 volt)! Since 0dBV = +2.2dBm, there will only be an 11.8dBV difference in level between the two pieces of gear.

Why should you care? If you try to connect two pieces of gear with different levels, you could either get massive distortion, or not enough signal level (and consequently lots of noise), depending on which way you were trying to make the connection. Mismatched signal levels are one of the most common problems in a home studio, especially when it comes to matching outboard gear with your mixing console.

Solutions to these level mismatches vary depending on the equipment you are using. You need to either pad (attenuate) or boost (amplify) the signal, again depending on the direction you are connecting the devices. When connecting a +4 input and a -10 output, the ideal (and some might consider expensive) solution is to use one of the +4 to -10 converters available from a number of manufacturers. The other solution is to try to miminize the difference in levels as much as possible without overloading the input of one device, or pushing the output of the other too far. Sometimes, it's simply impossible to find an optimal solution without the use of a level-matching device. A word of advice: Always consider the levels of your gear before selecting any piece of outboard gear, since not everything is as standardized as we'd all like.

A lot of outboard gear manufacturers are starting to include switches on the back of their equipment that allow you to select a +4dBm, -10dBV, or -20dBV operating level. Wise use of these switches is necessary for proper gain structuring. Since there are plenty of possible combinations of these levels, we'd suggest consulting the owners' manuals. If all else fails, experiment.

There are basically four different levels you'll run across in dealing with audio signals—mike, instrument, line, and speaker levels. Microphone level is the lowest on the totem pole. It's around -60dBV, or 1 millivolt—not much. This is why microphones are so susceptible to picking up noise in long cable runs and require good shielding (not to mention balanced lines) to reduce the chance of stray noise messing up the signal.

Line levels are produced by a variety of audio devices, including some synthesizers, tape machines, most mixing consoles (at the output stage; many boards also have inputs for all three levels), and most outboard gear. Line levels are based on two references: -10dBV and +4dBm. Signals at -10dBV have .316 volts (316 millivolts) associated with them. Levels at +4dB are at 1.23 volts. As mentioned above, special considerations must be made in connecting -10 and +4 gear due to this large difference in operating level.

Speaker levels will vary with the volume settings of the amplifier. An 8-ohm speaker driven with 10 watts of power is seeing approximately 9 volts. This is why you should never connect a speaker output to a line-level input—chances are you'll melt down the input amplifier of the line-level input. Not a pretty sight.

The fourth, and somewhat elusive, level is the so-called instrument level. This level is normally associated with

The motions of the needle of a VU meter (its ballistics) are designed to represent an averaging of overall levels. Instantaneous peaks—such as those produced by the attack of a snare drum—are not followed accurately by a VU meter, but may trigger the blinking of an LED peak indicator, if the meter has one.

what might come out of a guitar pickup, a Rhodes piano, or a Clavinet. Some home recording gear offers switchable level controls labelled mike/instrument, but the fact is that the range of instrument levels can be anything from -60dBV (in the case of some guitar transducers and mikes) to -10dBm or +4dBm. In other words, it can be anything from mike to line level. Check the instrument's manual for specific details. If that fails, experiment until you find a setting that works.

Awareness of these different levels is important if you intend to interface different pieces of equipment and expect optimal performance. A good understanding of the decibel and its different incarnations will also serve you well if you intend to interpret the mound of specs that accompanies every piece of audio gear.

Balanced And Unbalanced Lines

One very important factor to consider in addition to a piece of gear's input and output levels (see the section above on levels) is whether it has *balanced* or *unbalanced* inputs and outputs. In general, balanced lines carry hotter signals and are less noisy than unbalanced lines. That's why pro audio gear features balanced XLR connectors 99 percent of the time.

An unbalanced line has two wires in it (or a central wire surrounded by an electrically conductive shield). One wire carries the audio signal and the other (the shield) provides a ground connection between the two devices. The cable used in a balanced system has three wires in it. One is connected to ground, one carries the in-phase or hot signal (commonly referred to as +, though engineers will tell you it has nothing to do with positive or negative), and one carries the anti-phase or cold signal (-). The only difference between the hot and cold signals is that they are 180 degrees out of phase with each other. In case you're not familiar with the idea of phase cancellation, suffice it to say that when two signals that are exactly the same are 180 degrees out of phase, they cancel each other out when added together.

Why is this important? Well, as an audio signal travels down a cable, noise accumulates equally in the hot and cold signal paths. When the two signals arrive at their destination, they are *subtracted* from each other electronically, which means that the signals that are similar (i.e. the noise) get removed, since they are found equally in both wires. The audio signals, since they are subtracted (not added) actually get boosted, since subtracting out-of-phase signals is the same as adding in-phase signals.

A great majority of balanced equipment is sold with XLR connectors; however, some manufacturers offer balanced 1/4" connector systems. In these, a stereo headphone plug is used, with the tip and ring providing the pair of out-of-phase signals, and the sleeve providing the ground. You shouldn't automatically assume that a device is balanced just because it has XLR inputs and outputs. Always check the specs or the owner's manual.

When interfacing unbalanced equipment with balanced equipment, the balanced line must be converted to un-

balanced by tying the negative line to ground. The internationally agreed-to standard for 3-pin XLR connectors is pin 2 hot (with pin 3 negative)—though a lot of gear out there is pin 3 hot (with pin 2 negative)! Always consult the owner's manual or the manufacturer in order to determine which pin is hot and which is cold.

Impedence

Most people, if they know a bit about electricity, think of impedance as just another name for resistance, the opposition, to current flow in an electrical circuit. That's only partly true. What's left out of the picture is that impedance is the sum of resistance *and* reactance, the latter being the effect that capacitors and inductors have in an electrical circuit. Resistance in a circuit will always be constant, no matter what the frequencies passing through the circuit are. Reactance, on the other hand, is frequency-dependent. So, strickly speaking, resistance and impedance are not interchangeable terms! Despite all that, however, at 'low' frequencies like those in an audio range (20Hz to 20kHz), most impedances act like resistances and are treated in the same way.

Impedance is measured in ohms, and one thousand ohms are called a kilohm, abbreviated k ohm (or simply k, in a parts list where it's clear that the numbers refer to the values of resistors). Some audio devices, particularly speakers, do not have fixed impedances. An 8-ohm speaker's impedance can vary between 2 and 10 ohms, depending on the audio frequencies being put into it.

Before we go any further, we should establish a few definitions. (1) Outputs plug into inputs. A microphone has an output, just as a speaker has an input. Almost all other pieces of audio equipment have both inputs and outputs. (2) A piece of gear that provides a signal to another piece of gear is called a *signal source*. (3) The gear that receives the signal from the source is called the *load*. A speaker is a load to an amplifier. (4) Both sources and loads have impedances.

Audio equipment usually has two impedances—one for the inputs, and one for the outputs. The lower an impedance, the less opposition to current flow; the higher the impedance, the more opposition to current flow. This is important stuff! Let's look at an ideal amplifier

to see why.

An ideal voltage amplifier has extremely high input impedance (preferably infinite) and extremely low output impedance (preferably zero). If you're new to electronics, this might look backwards to you. Shouldn't a high input impedance prevent the incoming signal from getting in? In fact, the input impedance must be kept high to keep the load from overloading the source. When the input impedance falls too low, the connection starts to look to the source like a short circuit, which means that the load draws current from the source. An extremely high input impedance, on the other hand, will look like an open circuit to the device that is driving it, which means that it will not require much in terms of signal. A low output impedance is desirable to maximize the voltage transfer from the output to the input of the next device (the load) in the chain.

Consider the example of some outboard device connected to a recording console. Recording consoles have low--impedance outputs and high-impedance inputs (except for microphone inputs, which will probably be low-impedance also). The source for the outboard gear input is the console, and the outboard gear acts like a load to the console. In order for the coupling of signal to occur with a minimum of loss, the source impedance should be much lower than that of the load impedance. The equation, for those of you who must know, looks like this:

$$V\ output = V\ source\ x\ \frac{Z\ load}{Z\ load + Z\ source}$$

Z is used to denote impedance, *V source* is the output voltage of the source, and *V output* is the actual voltage delivered to the load. Going back to those wonderful days in high school math class, you might remember that as the denominator of a fraction gets larger, the number gets closer and closer to zero, while as the numerator and denominator get closer to the same value, the fraction gets closer to a value of 1. Ideally, we would like the voltage delivered to the load to be equal to the source voltage, so we would like the fraction in the right half of the equation to be close to 1. What the equation shows is that as the source approaches zero impedance, the actual output approaches the value of the source voltage. If the two impedances are identical, on the other hand, only 50% of the voltage will reach the load.

This is why almost every piece of audio equipment you are likely to find in the studio world has very low output impedances and very high input impedances. Typically, values one finds at an input range from 10k ohms up to 200k ohms. Output impedances might range from 200 ohms down to 2 ohms.

But what happens if we try to drive a low-impedance input with a high-impedance source, such as you'd get connecting the output of a high-impedance piece of outboard gear to a mike input with a low impedance? Looking at our equation, we find that very little voltage will be delivered, since the source impedance is much greater than the load impedance. In other words—*don't!* This condition is called an impedance mismatch, and will cause terrible results. In some cases you could lose all the low-frequency information in your audio signal.

Another thing to consider when connecting gear is what happens to impedances when you connect things in parallel, as you would if you connected a bunch of speaker cabinets to one output of your amplifier. This effectively lowers the total load impedance seen by the source. This can have absolutely disastrous results especially when multiple speakers are connected to one output, since the total load impedance can fall below the minimum load impedance the amp can handle, causing the amp's output section to melt down (or at least blow a fuse).

On the subject of speakers, some of you may be wondering why the most common output impedance of amplifiers and input impedance of speakers is 8 ohms. The reason is that in driving a speaker, the prime concern is that power, not voltage transfer, be maximized. The reason for this is a little beyond the scope of this article, but it is important that it be possible to maximize the efficiency of either voltage, current, or power by simply selecting the proper input and output impedances. The same thing is true for mikes—you want to maximize power transfer between the mike and the mike input, so you want equal impedances.

Low-impedance lines are much less susceptible to the effects of the capacitance of the wire, which acts like a low-pass filter in very long runs of cable (50 feet or more). High-impedance lines should be kept as short as possible because they are very susceptible to high frequency losses.

When you want to interface a high-impedance output (from an instrument, for example) to a low-impedance input (such as a mike input on a board), you'll use a direct box.

Tape Heads

Most people understand that an audio signal can be recorded onto magnetic tape, but probably not everyone understands just what mechanisms make that process possible. Basically, a tape recorder converts incoming electrical signals to magnetic impulses, and transfers these impulses onto tape (just how the tape is able to accept and store those impulses is discussed below in the section on tape). After the impulses are recorded on the tape, the recorder

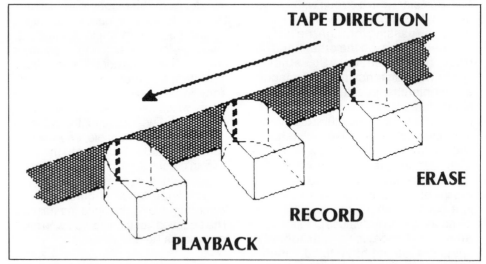

Figure 1. The headstack. All 3-head recorders have separate erase, record, and playback heads. Two-head recorders use a combined record/playback head, as well as an erase head.

must be able to reprocess them in the other direction, turning them back into electrical signals so we can listen to what was recorded. Both recording and playback functions are performed by the recorder's *record head* and *playback head*. In addition to these two types of heads, there is also an *erase head*, which is used, not surprisingly, to erase or wipe out signals on the tape to make room for new signals. On multi-track decks, each head will actually consist of multiple heads. For example, an 8-track recorder's record head will actually be split into eight electronically independent sections, making it possible to record eight separate tracks onto one piece of tape.

Figure 1 shows how erase, record, and playback heads are positioned in a typical recorder's *head stack* (the assembly that holds the heads). Notice that there is considerable space between the record head (which puts the incoming signals on the tape) and the playback head (which reproduces those signals after they're on the tape). This means that there will always be a time delay between signals being recorded by the record head and those being played back by the playback head (that's how tape delay got invented).

Think about that for a second, and you'll realize that *overdubbing* (where a musician goes in and adds a part to an already existing recording) would not be possible with such a system, since the newly recorded part would always be offset in time (out of sync) relative to the parts being played back.

The innovation that made multi-track recording with overdubbing possible was the ability to turn the record head into a playback head at the flick of a switch. This feature (called Sel-Sync, Simul-Sync, Sync, and so on) allows you to listen to tracks and record on other tracks simultaneously. Without it we wouldn't have multi-track tape recordings.

Sounds simple but it's not without its technical problems. How well those problems are overcome in any particular machine is what determines if that machine is a mouse or a moose. Here's the catch: It takes a lot of energy (measured in nanowebers) to get a recording to stick to a tape. It also takes a high sensitivity to be able to sense that recording on a tape in order to reproduce it. That gives you a condition where a lot of power is being generated by a record head, and a lot of effort is being made by the playback head to 'hear' the track it's supposed to reproduce. When those two

18

heads are right next to each other (as they very probably are in a multi-track machine), there exists the possibility that you get *crosstalk*, where the signal from one track spills over to another.

The headstack pictured in Figure 1 is a 3-head configuration. Most cassette decks, as well as many personal multi-track machines are of a 2-head design; with this design there is an erase head and a combination record/play head. While less expensive than 3-head design, a 2-head machine does not allow you to hear the tape while it's being recorded.

Technical terms you will hear bandied about when people talk about head assemblies include *azimuth*, *zenith*, *height*, and *head gap* (Figure 2). Azimuth is rotation in the left-right plane. The azimuth of the head must be adjusted so that the head gap is exactly 90 degrees perpendicular to the tape. The head gap is a very thin vertical slit in the front of the tape head. In record mode, the gap is where the magnetic field comes from; in playback mode, the gap is what senses the magnetic impulses on the tape. Zenith is the forward/backward alignment of the head at one side of the tape compared to the other side. The head gap must be exactly level with the tape in order for the tape to make complete contact with the head. Height is the up-and-down orientation of the head in the plane of the tape but perpendicular to the direction of the travel. It too must be set just right, so the tracks will line up with the tape properly.

Heads *must* be aligned properly in order for you to get the most bang out of your recorder. We recommend regular annual servicing for your decks even if you think they're in perfect shape. Bad head alignment can cause loss of high-frequency response, variations in level between tracks, phase distortion, and incompatibility between one deck and another.

Magnetic Tape

Rolls of magnetic tape are made up of trillions of microscopic magnetic particles slathered onto a non-magnetic backing material. Subjecting these particles to a magnetic field will cause them to become polarized so that their magnetic field is oriented in the direction of the field created by the head. When you open up a new box of tape, the particles are all randomly oriented with no particular pattern to them; that is, the tape is blank. When you expose the particles to a magnetic field (which is what happens when they pass across the record head), they become oriented in new patterns that are analogous to the pattern of the magnetic field (hence the term *analog* recording). When the field fluctuates, different segments of the tape become magnetized in different directions.

This might make recording on magnetic tape sound easy. Run the tape over the record head, and bingo, instant Top 40 hit. Would that it were so simple. The problem (to simplify things a bit) is that the tape's magnetic particles can be belligerent. They don't like being reoriented. In fact, unless they are forced to behave, they make a fuss in the form of signal distortion. The solution (found by accident) is what is known as *bias*.

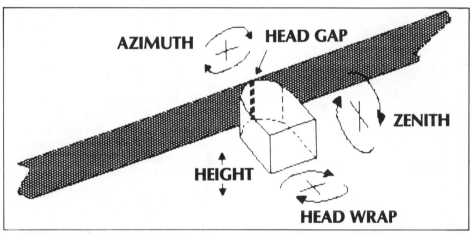

Bias is a high-frequency signal, usually five or more times higher than the highest audio frequency a tape deck can record. Bias is added to the record signal to reduce distortion and increase *headroom* (the amount of signal you can record above the average recording level without distortion). A typical tape deck has a bias frequency of 100kHz—well beyond audibility.

Biasing is the act of adjusting the amount of ultra-high frequency bias signal that gets mixed in with the recorded signal. The optimum amount of bias will vary depending on the formulation (or physical makeup) of the tape being used. Bias is usually adjusted either to minimize third harmonic distortion or for equal output at low and high frequencies. Tape manufacturers will often recommend a certain bias point, such as "3dB over at 10kHz." What this means for you techno-types who like to do everything yourselves is that you increase the bias of the deck while monitoring the output from the playback head

Figure 2. Proper tape head alignment is critical to a recorder's performance. While this depicts the parameters which a technician must consider when performing a complete head alignment, azimuth adjustment is the most common.

19

while recording a 10kHz tone. At one point, the output level will reach a peak and then start to decrease gradually due to a condition called *overbiasing*. If the spec is 3dB over, then you keep increasing the bias until the output drops by 3dB from the peak value output level. For you non-techno types, just make sure the engineer knows what he or she is doing. For optimum performance in home recording, your deck *must* be biased for the particular type and brand of tape you use. Some machines make it easy to adjust the bias for different tape types with a front-panel or rear-panel control. On others, the owner's manual may recommend one specific type of tape for which the deck has been adjusted at the factory.

Everyone has encountered the different types of cassette tape that are available, but not everyone knows the difference between them. There are four classes of cassette tape, based on the type of particles in the magnetic tape formulation. Type I cassettes are what we know as *normal* or *standard* bias tapes. They are made from iron oxide particles (better known as rust), and can vary in quality from 'the pits' to 'mighty fine,' depending on various factors such as uniform thickness and the evenness of the oxide coating. Type II tapes are called *chromium dioxide*, *CrO2*, or *chrome* tapes because they use chromium dioxide particles. These require much more bias than Type I tapes and have a different record equalization standard because they reproduce high frequencies better than normal bias tapes. Type III tapes are called *ferrochrome* tapes. These were very popular once, but are now almost extinct. The category, however, lives on. Type IV tapes are the *metal* tapes. They are formulated from actual metal particles instead of oxide particles. They require more bias than any other tape formulations, and provide the best performance, especially at high frequencies.

Those of you using cassette decks have probably seen the terms 70-microsecond and 120-microsecond mentioned. These refer to the playback equalization time constants, which, put simply, determine what kind of filtering is done to the tape on playback. When you align or adjust the record/play response of your deck, you are adjusting the record equalization so that the playback response will be flat with respect to one of these two equalization curves.

Equalization exists because, up to a

certain point, as the frequency being recorded goes up, so does the tape output. At another point, other factors take over and this natural boost in higher frequencies ceases. Using normal tape, it was found that the increased output effect levels off at 1,326Hz, which corresponds to the filter time constant of 120 microseconds. Since chrome (Type II tapes) have naturally greater high-frequency output, the filter frequency for chrome tape was set to 2,273Hz, which corresponds to a 70-microsecond time constant. Record equalization allows you to flatten out the response of the deck by changing the amount of high frequencies recorded on the tape. The playback equalization is fixed with one of these two EQ curve time constants.

One recent development you'll run into is Dolby's HX Pro. This has nothing to do with Dolby noise reduction; rather it's a process that is designed to increase the tape's high-frequency headroom. It's a process that monitors the high-frequency level being recorded on tape and reduces the amount of bias as the high frequency level increases. This is done because high frequencies can act as bias by themselves, and can cause overbiasing. Overbiasing reduces the amount of tape headroom, which causes the tape to distort earlier than normal.

Digital Recording

These days, digital is certainly the buzzword in pro audio. Multi-track digital decks are still extremely expensive propositions, and the details of how they work are beyond the scope of this article, but no book on recording would be complete without a word or two on the subject. The advantage of digital recording is that, if the digital encoding and decoding are done properly, tape hiss (background noise) is eliminated, while the dynamic range (the difference in level between the loudest and softest sounds that can be accurately recorded) is increased.

Converting audio signals into digital information is a science all its own. Recording digital information on tape poses some additional problems, because a single pop or dropout on the tape can cause whole chunks of data to be read incorrectly, resulting in garbled sound. To work properly, a digital tape recorder must store the data about each millisecond of sound in several different physical locations, so that when an error is detected, an averaging process can estimate what the missing bits ought to be.

Because of this *interleaving* of data, it's not normally a good idea to chop and splice chunks of digital audio tape. Sophisticated editing systems are required to move the sounds around.

While multi-track digital is still beyond the reach of most musicians, adapters are now available that will turn any moderately good video cassette recorder into a two-track stereo digital audio recorder for in the neighborhood of $1,000. Either for mixdown of home multi-track, or for direct-to-stereo recordings of live performances, this type of system offers the best possible sound quality.

Track Formats

Tape comes in lots of different widths. Just to make matters more confusing, there's no guarantee that two tapes the same width will have the same number of tracks recorded on them. It depends on what machine they were recorded on.

For any given tape width there may be many different recorders and track configurations available. For example, a recorder that uses quarter-inch tape might have one track, or two, or four, or as many as eight. Since the tape width remains the same, the physical track width (the area that a particular track can record and play on) must get smaller as the number of tracks increases. This is not a trivial thing, since the more area you record on, the greater the signal-to-noise ratio, and the lower the crosstalk (where signals on one track bleed through to adjacent tracks). Noise reduction is often used to diminish the noise that results from narrow track widths. Indeed, systems that have high track density are often so dependent on noise reduction that they may not allow you to turn it off, even if you want to!

The two-inch tape machine is the most favored by pro studios (at least those that haven't made the switch to all-digital technology, which is another story altogether). Two-inch machines offer either 16, 24, or 32 tracks. Many of these machines allow you to change track formats by simply switching the head block (the assembly that contains the record and playback heads). Even so, the most popular format is the 24-track. The spacing between adjacent tracks on a two-inch 24-track is some-

thing like .037 inches. Most of these decks move tape at speeds of 15 ips (inches per second) or 30 ips, although some may be configured for 7½ ips. The tracks are laid out on the headblock in such a way that the first track is on top and the last is on the bottom of the tape.

One-inch tape formats usually feature 8 or 16 tracks. The spacing between the tracks on one-inch 8-track is the same as the spacing on two-inch 16-track, which is .070 inches. Both the one-inch 8-track and two-inch 16-track formats provide the best performance possible in multi-track tape formats, since they have greater track width and wider spacing between adjacent tracks than other analog formats. Tape speeds on one-inch machines range from 7½ ips to 30 ips. As in 2-inch format, the tracks are laid out with the first track on the top of the tape and the last track on the bottom.

Half-inch tape format machines have from 2 to 16 tracks on them. Half-inch two-track stereo (also called half-track) is the highest quality standard for recording studios that haven't made the jump to digital. Pro decks feature tape speeds of 15 ips or 30 ips. Half-inch 8-track is the favorite for semi-pro decks. Typical speeds are 7½ ips and 15 ips. Spacing between adjacent tracks is .037 inches.

Quarter-inch formats have anywhere from 1 to 8 tracks on them. The speeds are usually 3¾ ips, 7½ ips, or 15 ips, though, 30 ips 2-track stereo (half-track) is the common studio mastering configuration. These tracks are .080 inches wide and are recorded in one direction. The standard home stereo deck features quarter-track format; that is, there are four tracks, two for one side of the tape and two for the other. When tape is recorded or played back in one direction, two of the four tracks are active. When the tape is flipped over (which changes the direction of the recording), the other two tracks are active (see diagram). Track spacing is .043 inches. Full-track (mono) occupies .24 inches of the total .25-inch width. If you're doing any non-stereo film work, this is the format you'll probably mix down to. Quarter-inch 4-tracks record on .037-inch wide tracks in one direction only. Quarter-inch 8-tracks have very narrow tracks on the order of .021 inches, with noise reduction built in.

**By Bryan Lanser
and Dominic Milano**

The Tascam Porta Two 4-track cassette recorder/mixer is typical of many "mini-studios"—the most popular home recording format.

21

Yamaha's DMP7 digital mixer can store and recall different settings, including levels, equalization, panning, and even reverb and other effects. By dumping level and other changes into a sequencer via MIDI, and then playing back the sequence, full automation—complete with moving faders—is possible.

Cassette recorders use eighth-inch wide tape and operate at $1\frac{7}{8}$ or $3\frac{3}{4}$ ips. The standard stereo cassette deck has .021 inch track widths, organized such that the top two tracks are one side of a stereo program and the bottom two tracks are the other side, so that when the tape is flipped over, the 'B' side is played. Most cassette decks have noise reduction built in. Dolby B (see the noise reduction section of page 10 is the most common, although Dolby C and dbx are gaining in popularity. Home cassette decks usually allow you to bypass the noise reduction, whereas multi-track cassette decks often do not, although you may be able to disconnect one track in order to record a sync tone on it for driving a drum machine or sequencer. Multi-track cassette decks are different from home stereo cassette machines in that all four tracks operate in one direction. Tape speed is usually $3\frac{3}{4}$ ips, although some are available that can be switched between $1\frac{7}{8}$ ips and $3\frac{3}{4}$ ips. Dolby C and dbx are the most common types of built-in noise reduction on multi-track cassette decks.

So you can see that as you cram more tracks onto smaller tape widths, track width goes down and you lose some quality. However, what you gain is increased accessibility to affordable multi-track recording facilities of a type that just 15 years ago were reserved for pro studios.

CHOOSING A KEYBOARD MIXER

February 1986

A mixing console is at the heart of any multi-keyboard rig. Choosing the right mixer for your keyboard setup, however, is no easy task. How many effects sends will you need? What kind of equalizers should you look for? What other considerations are important in a mixer? It is possible to match a board's features to your particular needs; but in order to do this, you have to be familiar with the basic components of mixing consoles, and how to evaluate them.

Inputs And Equalizers

In any console the input stage is the starting point in the signal path, and that's a good place to begin our review of mixing boards. The input stage, or "front end," contains a console's mike- and line-level amplifiers. The mike pre-amplifier has to work harder than any other section. It deals with the very low signal levels generated by microphones and, more importantly for keyboardists, direct boxes—and amplifies those low levels by great amounts. The technological trick is not to add noise (hiss) in the process. Listen to the mike preamps in any console you're considering. Make sure the level of noise they introduce is tolerable. The microphone preamp pot usually can be found toward the top of each individual channel section.

Find out whether the console provides on-board phantom power, which is used to power active direct boxes as well as condenser microphones. This can save you money later; a single phantom power supply alone can cost a few hundred dollars. (Some consoles don't even have provision for interfacing external phantom power supplies, so you might want to check on that too.)

Direct boxes (also called DIs, for "direct inputs") allow you to take a line level, such as that from a keyboard, and plug it into a mike input. Active direct boxes are preferable tp passive DIs for three reasons: Active DI boxes can handle transients better; they are generally quieter; and they tend to preserve the rich harmonics preset in complex waveforms, whether from analog or digital sources. Phantom power is generally supplied for each mike input. Be sure that the voltage of the phantom power

supplies is somewhere between +12V and +48V. Although +12V will work, I prefer the higher voltage swing of a +48V phantom power supply, especially when I'm driving a number of active direct boxes.

Whether you're using mike or line inputs, the front end's transient response is an important consideration. Transients are severe peaks in audio level. They happen too fast to register on most VU meters. They are most commonly encountered when you're working with percussive sounds, such as drums or acoustic piano. A rating called "headroom" can help you to evaluate transient response. If a transient's level exceeds the headroom of a console's mike or line amplifiers, distortion will result. The greater headroom a console offers, the wider the range of transient response. An overload indicator LED can help you to keep input signals within the mixer's headroom range. The overload indicator will flicker whenever transient peaks overload the front end.

Input pads for each channel can help you tailor input signals to the console's headroom. A pad is a switchable device, placed between the signal source and the mike preamplifier or line stages, which cuts input level by some predetermined amount. The fanciest pads are selectable for -10 or -20dB of cut, with a trim potentiometer to fine-tune levels in between. By using a pad correctly, the input level can be trimmed to match the console's headroom range. A pad is rarely necessary for line-level inputs. This is because line level is relatively consistent compared to mike level inputs, which cover a much wider range of levels.

Be aware of what type of input connectors are supplied. The standard configuration calls for balanced female XLR cannon jacks for mike-level inputs, and unbalanced 1/4″ phone jacks for line-level inputs. Looking for this configuration can save you money by eliminating the need for costly interface boxes. Don't choose a console with phone jacks for mike inputs—an unbalanced mike input is totally unacceptable! Unbalanced cable runs are susceptible to RF (radio frequency interference) and other sources of noise. Since a mike preamp has to boost the input signal by great amounts, inevitably adding some noise in the process, it's important to ensure that mike-input signals are as clean as possible to begin with.

Most keyboards with 1/4″ phone jack outputs generate a signal hot enough for line-level inputs. A direct box, however, is recommended for line-level signals sent along unbalanced cable runs of more than 20 feet. The direct box connects to the console's balanced, mike-level XLR inputs. Keep unbalanced cable runs between instruments and direct boxes as short as possible.

Even keyboards with balanced XLR output connectors often generate a signal at line, rather than mike, level. This kind of output is too hot for a microphone input, and requires a pad to keep it from distorting. The line-level inputs on most mixers are fed from unbalanced phone jacks. These unbalanced signals are acceptable because line-level signals are less susceptible to noise and RF. Ideally, however, even line-level inputs should be balanced. Incidentally, on top-of-the-line mixers, both the mike and line inputs are accessible from custom connectors. These multi-pin connectors allow you to configure your own connector scheme.

The equalizer is the next component we'll scrutinize. It is usually next in the signal path, too—that is, after a signal passes through the mike or line input stage, it enters the EQ section. Correspondingly, each input channel's EQ section usually can be found just below the mike preamp on the board. It's important to have an EQ in/out switch, so that you can compare the equalized signal with the original. Another useful feature is a center detent for the EQ's boost/cut knobs. At this center point the pot is neither cutting nor boosting frequencies in fact, it's no longer even in the equalizer circuit. This is most useful when you need only to EQ a certain frequency and the EQ section has three or four bands, since you can quickly dial out the bands you're not interested in. Once they are out of the circuit, they won't contribute to the noise floor.

Most consoles come with some form of parametric, as opposed to graphic, EQ. A true parametric EQ has three separate controls. The first is the control that selects the amount of cut or boost, measured in decibels. The next is the frequency sweep knob; this control selects the center frequency, the frequency at which the boost or cut (selected by the first control) is applied. The third control selects the bandwidth affected, or "Q." Despite this odd terminology, the Q control is pretty easy to understand: The Q value determines how frequencies on either side of the

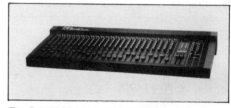

The Roland M-240 is a 24-input line-level mixer, perfect for many keyboard applications.

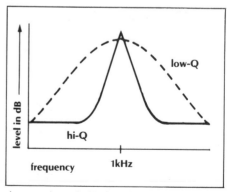

A comparison of wide (low-Q) and narrow (hi-Q) bandwidth.

center frequency are affected. A "high Q" is a narrow bandwidth—that is, the amount of boost or cut will decrease drastically as you get farther from the center frequency. A lower Q affects a greater range of frequencies on either side of the center frequency. A low Q, represented graphically, looks like a very wide bell curve. (The Q control on a parametric EQ has a similar function to the Q, emphasis, or resonance control found on analog synthesizer filters.) An equalizer is not truly parametric unless it has these three basic functions, controlled by three separate knobs.

Some manufacturers offer "semi-" or "quasi-parametric equalizers." These have either a fixed or a switchable Q. So-called "sweep" EQ has a fixed Q, a

ical EQ applications, such as taking the ring out of a house P.A. system without affecting the overall mix.

As you probably know, graphic-type equalizers provide boost/cut control over several bands, but a graphic EQ is rarely found on each individual channel input of a mixer. Nonetheless, the number of bands an equalizer divides the frequency spectrum into is perhaps the most crucial consideration. A band EQ, consisting of sweepable low and high bands and a parametric midrange, is quite powerful. A band with selectable-frequency low and high bands and sweep or parametric midrange is also a good choice. And, just to make sure that all bases are covered, make sure that the frequency range of each band over-

leaving the EQ's high band (if there is one) free to work on other frequency characteristics. A highpass filter does the opposite, shaving off frequencies below the cutoff frequency. It can be used to filter out unwanted rumble, leaving the low band of the EQ section free for more specialized work. The simplest type of low- or highpass filter offers a preset cut, usually somewhere between –12 and –18dB. The cutoff frequency is almost always variable, either by a fully sweepable dial or by a selective rotary switch.

Effects Sends

Figure out how many different effects you will need for your sound, and then get a mixer with the appropriate number of effect sends. If you don't have a clear idea of your needs, four sends will handle most situations.

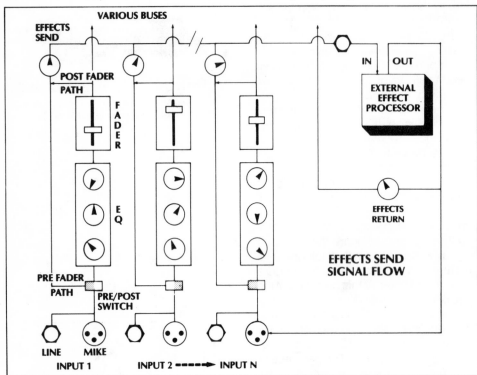

This block diagram show how effects sends are routed through the typical mixer and to an effects device. For most applications, effects sends are ideally post-fader. This way, bringing down the overall level of a channel's fader will also bring down that channel's level to the effects.

full-sweep selectable center frequency, and a separate cut/boost control. There is yet another type, called "selectable" EQ, with a boost/cut control and either a click-stop control (a pot graduated in discrete steps) or a three-way switch to select preset frequencies. Which type is better? That is truly up to your ear. Just because an EQ is parametric does not mean it sounds musical. Besides, parametric EQs can be great for non-mus-

laps that of the bands above and below it.

Because a parametric EQ allows you to be very selective regarding what frequencies you affect, it is also called a notch filter. This term will be familiar to users of Oberheim synths, many of which have notch filter capabilities.

Parametric equalization isn't the only kind to consider; low- and highpass filters can also be useful. Most readers will recognize the lowpass filter from analog synthesis. As the name implies, a lowpass filter screens out high frequencies, allowing frequencies below the cutoff point to pass unaffected. As part of a mixer's EQ section, such a device may be used to trim off hiss, for example,

For keyboard applications, it is best to have post-fader sends. This means that the signal level presented at the send's own level control is that set by the fader. A pre-fader send receives its signal before the fader, so that the level set by the fader does not influence its operation. If you use a pre-fader send for an effect, then the effect will continue to receive the channel's signal even after the fader has been pulled all the way down. Although this can be useful in some special cases—for example, if you're using reverb, fading all of the dry signal out and leaving only reverbed signal for treating keyboards, post-fader effect sends are much more useful. Some four-send mixers automatically assign two post-fader, and the other two pre-fader. If you own one of these, ask the manufacturer whether the pre-fader sends can be modified to come after the fader level.

It's nice if the effect sends have mutes. This is useful for checking out the effect of a particular send over the mix without having to mess with its level, and it can be used for many interesting effects as well, like dub-style momentary echoes. For example, the lead vocal's reverb send could be muted all of the way through except for a single word, which would be given its own special reverberation. The ability to EQ the sends is another useful feature. Certain reverbs and delays sound better if their input signal is equalized.

"Insert" patch points are used for sending individual channels to their own individual effects, as opposed to some multi-channel effect such as reverb. Insert points are used primarily for compressors, noise gates, outboard EQ, or any other effects which are better applied on a channel-by-channel basis. For reverb or delay the insert points, just like effect sends, should be post-fader.

Inputs

The number of inputs you need should equal the total number of audio outputs from your keyboards. A keyboard with stereo outputs should count as two channels, even if you're not planning to use both right now. You should always allow an extra channel or two to serve as spares. The number of effects you will be returning to channels (rather than to effect returns) will have to be considered as well. If you bought a console because you are happy with its EQ section and effect sends, it would be a shame to have to replace it just because of the number of inputs. One way to avoid this is to purchase a console with a larger mainframe than the total number of channels needed (including spares), and then buy extra modules as needed.

Be aware of how many effect returns are included. If there aren't enough for all of your effects, you are going to have to use more channels. Check out whether they have panning, and whether they are returned to the buses as well as the stereo mix. If the reverb returns have EQ, then they are really the same as extra channels. Having EQ on effect returns is always a plus.

Mutes And Solos

Ideally, each fader should have its own mute switch, and it should be noiseless. If a cable from a keyboard goes bad while you are onstage, you or your technical assistant are going to have to mute that channel; and if the mute makes a loud pop or click, that could take out the house system! Having mutes on the effect returns is also important. They really help in tracking down noise sources caused by reverb, delay, and other signal processors.

A solo button is another nice feature, but you should investigate how it affects the stereo mix and the buses. A solo is designed to mute all other channels except its own. (If you solo more than one channel, all the others except those will mute.)

Faders

Take a little time to push the faders up and down. They should feel smooth to the touch. One unavoidable problem with sliding conductive faders is that they get dirt and cigarette ash in them, and eventually they wear out. You can clean them every day, but they always seem to wear out just at the spot you need for the right balance. As long as you can get replacements, you'll be okay. If you are on the road a lot, buy some spares.

Fader travel distance is important too. Short travel faders wear out faster,

The Akai MPX820 mixer can store and recall 99 different settings. These settings can be recalled as program changes by a sequencer. Unlike the Yamaha DMP7, the MPX820 doesn't have moving faders, internal reverb, or other effects.

and often they develop problems at the bottom of their range. For example, it is common for such faders to allow some signal through even when they are pulled all the way down. During a live show you might want to fade a whole group of MIDI instruments up or down, so your faders are too important to ignore. To an engineer, in fact, the faders are his keyboard. Having excellent faders on the buses and the stereo mix is imperative!

Meters

Three basic kinds of meter are commonly found on a console's meter bridge: VU meters, LED meters, and plasma meters. Each kind has its own advantages, depending on the instrument you are monitoring. In addition, there are two kinds of meter ballistics: VU and peak. Ballistics determine how the meter reacts to changes in signal level. It is possible to have a VU meter set to peak ballistics, although you won't come across one of these very often. There are also VU meters that have a peak-reading LED for detecting transients that VU ballistics are just too slow to pick up. To use this type of meter properly, you must find out what level the LED represents, and also whether it can be recalibrated to your specifications.

Find out what type of meters and ballistics the console you are interested in has. It may or may not matter, depending on your attitude toward meters in the first place. To me, meters are for mixdown engineers without ears—ideally, an engineer should know whether the levels are right by listening. (If I had to express a preference, it would be for VU meters with VU ballistics.) Meters are a necessity when aligning a tape machine to a console and vice-versa. Then—and only then—does the 0 VU point on a meter have total validity. If the console is properly aligned to the tape recorder, you only need to look at the meters to find out how much signal you're trying to put on the tape.

Meters are installed on what is called a meter bridge. This makes it more convenient to see the meters on the console than the meters on the tape machine, especially when the tape machine is behind you. It is rare that the 0 VU point is the optimum level for the buses and stereo mix on any console. Some mixers are noisy unless you really push the levels into the red. If you are not using your mixer with a tape recorder, find out

whether you can recalibrate the meters to reflect the level at which the console sounds good. If your console has insert points for the buses and stereo mix, find out if the meters come after the patch point. At least then you will know that the meters represent the signal after any effects you may have added.

Bussing And Automation

Professional consoles have a set of outputs, or buses, to which each channel may be selectively assigned. These buses feed two further buses, collectively known as the stereo or two-channel bus, which handle the console's final output. For the moment we will be discussing the first set of buses, which usually comes in configurations of four, eight, or 16. The set is often referred to by this number; for example, the 8-channel bus. In general, though, they are known as the output buses.

Usually the output buses are normalled to the input channels of a multitrack recorder. Although it is convenient to have a separate output bus for each track on your tape machine, it is also significantly more expensive. In fact, it is commonplace in many recording studios with 48 tracks of tape (twin 24-track recorders locked via SMPTE) to find a console with only 24 output buses.

An external patch bay makes this discrepancy less problematic by giving you separate access to both the console's output buses and the inputs to the multi-track recorder. This is fine if you don't intend to record on more tracks than you have buses at any one time.

If you have to record simultaneously on more tracks then your console has output buses, you need the direct output option. A direct output allows an individual channel to be routed directly, without assigning it to one of the buses. A channel's direct output can be wired to its own patch point in the patch bay. If all of the output buses, individual-channel direct outs, and inputs to the multi-track show up in the bay, it is a simple affair to record on more tracks at once than you have output buses.

For example, if your console has 16-channels and four output buses, and your tape machine has eight tracks, you could use a combination of buses and direct outputs to get all 16 channels onto all eight tracks in the following way (see Figure 2). Channels 1 through 4 (four individual instruments or two pairs of

The Electro-Voice BK-1632 16-input mixer.

stereo instruments) could be routed, via their direct outputs, to tape tracks 1 through 4. Channels 5 through 12 (perhaps all of your drum machine's outputs) might be routed, via buses 1 and 2 (that is, mixed to stereo), to tape tracks 5 and 6. Channels 13 and 14 (a pair of MIDIed synthesizers creating a composite sound) could be sent, via bus 3, to tape track 7. And finally console channels 15 and 16 (another composite synthesizer mixture) could be routed, via bus 4, to track 8. The basic understanding is that (1) buses are used for merging any number of channels of the console to any one track of tape, or (2) for mixing any number of channels to any two tracks (for stereo imaging).

In live mixing applications, whether in the studio or onstage, the buses can also be used to create sub-groups. A sub-group consists of any two (or more) channels sent to an output bus. A console with four buses is ideal for sub-grouping stage mixes. The four buses can be used to group your MIDI instruments according to the MIDI channel they are receiving. This way you can control the volume of an entire MIDI channel/subgroup.

Having a separate level and pan for each of the four buses feeding the stereo bus is very useful. By sending the individual output buses to the house (the club's own mixing console), you can set up your own mix onstage via your console's stereo bus. If the sound technician receives four individual bus outputs, each sending a group of instruments, he or she can add effects and balance the different instrument groups without affecting your stage mix. Of course, if you adjust the level or EQ of the buses themselves, it will affect the house mix. If you adjust the stereo bus, though, it won't affect the output of the four buses.

If four buses aren't enough, shoot for eight or 16. Unfortunately, the more buses a mixer provides, the more it costs. If the house sound man requires so much individual control over the keyboards that you need a whole bunch of output buses, and you're not ready to mortgage your house, try using a few mike splitters. Insert these into the signal path before the mixer's mike/line inputs. Sending individual channel signals to the house P.A. from the post-EQ insert points (if your mixer provides them) will serve the same purpose. Remember, though, that if you send the house post-EQ signals, the house will have to work with your EQ settings.

Whether you intend to use the output buses for sub-grouping during live performances or for multi-track recording, having a separate VU meter for each bus is a must! Overloading the output bus is pretty easy, especially during live mixing. An overloaded bus out will

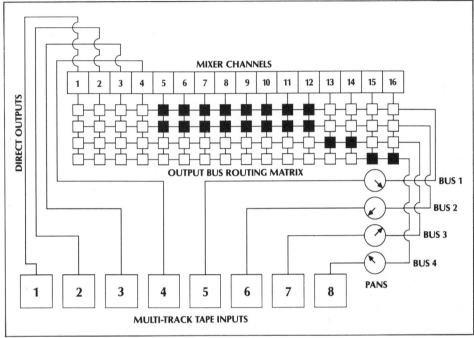

If you have a 4-bus mixer with direct outputs, it's possible to record more than four tracks at once. In this example, 16 inputs are assigned to eight tape tracks by using a combination of direct outputs and busses.

sound as bad as a distorted mike preamp, possibly worse. Seeing the signal level on the bus meter tells you instantly whether distortion is coming from the mike pre-amp or the bus. If you solo a bus and hear some serious distortion, but you don't see the meter levels going well into the red, chances are the mike pre-amp or the EQ section is running hot enough to fry an egg. Many consoles can switch the bus metering to read either the output bus or the tape return (from the corresponding normalled track). The added flexibility you get with this feature helps to justify the additional expense of separate VU or LED meters for each bus.

By Bobby Nathan

PATCH BAYS

June 1986

If a console is the heart of your keyboard setup, then a patch bay is the circulatory system. It can give you quick, convenient access to all the signals your equipment is putting out, and to all of the inputs you might want to send them to. Patch bay panels have jacks on the front, and most of the time you have to solder the leads (also called pins) behind those jacks to create the signal paths you need. Some bays, however, come complete with jacks on both the front and the back, which makes connecting them up a lot easier. Patch bays of the prefab variety aren't cheap, though, so it makes sense to look into wiring the rear connections yourself. This calls for good soldering skills, proper planning, and patience, but whether you solder all the connections or simply plug them in, after you have a patch bay you'll wonder how you ever lived without it.

There are three basic types of patch bays, depending on the kind of jacks you want to use: RCA, phone, and bantam. A bay with RCA jacks is the least expensive to produce. For this reason, RCA bays are available pre-made, which will save you time and effort (if not money). If you're not into soldering, this is definitely the way to go! The main disadvantage of the RCA-type bay is that RCA connectors are unbalanced, which can lead to unwanted hums and buzzes. Also, RCA plugs are generally lacking in sufficient strain relief. This means that the molded plastic patch cords you'll probably be using are bound to break pretty often. They tend to fit into the jacks so snugly that pulling on the cable causes a break in electrical contact at the molded plug. This can be avoided by grasping only the plug itself, rather than the cable—a good habit to get into regardless of what kind of cables you use.

The phone jack bay uses 1/4" guitar-type patch cords. This is handy for plugging keyboards directly into the bay. Strain-reliefed phone plugs are more rugged and last longer than the molded kind. They are also more expensive, but strain-reliefed cables can be found more readily and in various lengths. Some companies make pre-wired 1/4" patch bays terminating in either RCA or phone jacks at the rear. Balanced (tip/ring/sleeve) phone-jack bays can be ordered to allow longer cable runs without inducing radio frequency interference (RFI). Generally there are 24 jacks to a row, or 48 to a double-row bay.

Many phone-type bays offer normalling as an optional feature. Normalling is having your most-used patches hardwired into the bay; the normal connection can be broken by using the patch points if you need to. For instance, most consoles have an "insert in/out" patch point for each channel, usually found on the rear of the board. If you connect these insert jacks to two jacks on a patch bay, the channel won't pass a signal unless a patch cord is used to bridge the gap between the insert in and the insert out. Normalling makes this connection without the patch cord. Then, if you want to actually use the insert points, say, to route the channel's signal through an outboard effect, plugging a cord into either jack will break the normal connection. The only catch is that you have to wire it up (that is, solder together the normal connections).

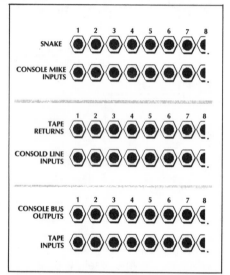

Figure 1. A suggested patch bay configuration. Note that adjacent rows form pairs of inputs and outputs that would usually be patched together. A normalled connection may be appropriate.

In my estimation, the third type, bantam, is the best. Bantam plugs, also know as TT plugs (for "Tiny Telephone"), look like balanced phone plugs, but smaller. Because of their size, they allow for the most jacks per row, as many as 56 across. Thus a double-row bantam bay can hold up to 112 patch points total—many more than you'd get with phone jacks. The immediate advantage over RCA jacks is that they come balanced. In addition, bantam bays can be purchased with or without the normalling option. Bays with bantam jacks are the most expensive of the three, and generally they are not available with TCA or phone plugs on the back. If you can't stand to solder one up yourself, you can probably find someone in you area to do this work for you. Don't expect it to be inexpensive, though; tech time usually doesn't come cheap. They are available in various sizes (18" lengths are the most common). Since they are made of brass, bantam connectors tarnish and require regular cleaning with the proper solvents and utensils. Pipe cleaners do the job admirably.

Now for the fun part. After you've selected which type of bay is most convenient for your purposes, the planning begins. One of the reasons for using a bay in the first place is to avoid going behind the console every time you want to change a connection. For stage use, the best setup is to get a snake box that will sit near your keyboards. Pro-Co and Whirlwind are two manufacturers of these boxes, though Belden or Connectronics supply good multi-conductor cable if you wish to build your own snake. If your console has 16 or 24 inputs, then you are going to want a snake box with 16 or 24 inputs. Then allot one jack in your patch bay for each connection on the snake box. This keeps things as tidy and flexible as possible. In building your snake box, incidentally, you may want the inputs to be all 1/4" jacks, or XLR, or even both. If you are plugging unbalanced keyboard outputs into balanced inputs, you will need to install balancing transformers (the kind found in direct boxes) inside the snake box. Whirlwind makes transformers of this kind, called 20k-ohm-to-200-ohm direct box transformers.

Figure 1 illustrates one way you might configure a patch bay for this kind of setup, with the addition of a multi-track tape recorder. Note that adjacent rows form pairs of inputs and outputs which would usually (read "normally") be patched together in conventional situations. For example, for basic recording applications the console's bus outputs would be fed into the multi-track tape deck. I've laid it out this way for maximum convenience. These connections—snake to console inputs, tape outputs to console line inputs, and console bus outputs to tape inputs—might be normalled in your setup. This would make all of the signals accessible, and at the same time require a minimum of patching. Also, note that the numbers all line up: snake input 1 and console input 1, tape out 2 and console line in 2, and so forth.

Effect sends and the inputs to your signal processors could also be arranged in the same fashion for flexibility and convenience. Ditto for signal processor outputs and console effect returns, and for the stereo mix outputs and a two-track recorder (or power amps, if you are working onstage).

To solder your own patch bay, you

will need a 30-watt soldering iron with a relatively small tip, a roll of 60/40 rosin-core solder, a wire stripper, a wire cutter, needle-nose pliers—and patience! Make sure you have enough wire and shrink-wrap (plastic tubing used to dress the ends of wire), and a heat-shrink gun (like a hair blower, but much more powerful). You will need the appropriate type and number of patch bays, an adequate number of plugs (to connect the bay to all the jacks on the rear of your console and outboard gear), and of course zillions of patch cords. For wire, you can again use Connectronics multi-conductor cable or the equivalent. You'll probably want one snake for each major set of signals; say, one for your console's inputs, another for its direct outputs, one each for the multi-track tape deck's inputs and outputs, one for your outboard effects, and so forth. Connectronics wire is color-coded, and the coding follows the standard coding for resistor values. You can match the color-coded values to various input and output channels, which will make it easier to track down problems if they occur. Make sure the wire has two conductors and a shield (braided or bare wire, used for the ground). Before plugs are put on the console's or outboard gear's end of the snake, the wire should be measured to the desired length and then dressed.

To prevent the possibility of a short circuit, the bare shield should be dressed with 3/64" clear shrink tubing. Shrink tubing comes in four-foot lengths, so cut it into 1½" pieces ahead of time. Strip the wire 1½" at both ends of the snake (see Figure 2). Put the shrink over the shield and carefully melt the shrink-wrap over the top with the heat shrink gun (Figure 3). Be extremely careful—the heat shrink gun can burn your skin off (which may or may not make your keyboard riffs hotter). After you have dressed the shield, put a piece of 3/16" black shrink over the wire right where you've stripped it, covering the dressed shield about 1/16" (Figure 4). Now the end is dressed. For added neatness, 3/32" black shrink-wrap can be cut into 1/4" slivers and placed on the wire before soldering it to the bay.

Once the wires are properly dressed, it's time to make some connections. The bay should come with a diagram of its jacks, telling you which pins are which. Unbalanced jacks give you only two pins, high and ground (also called shield). Balanced jacks come with an additional pin, called low. We'll look at jacks with the normalling option later. Here's how to identify the corresponding pins on the patch cord's plugs: The lead, or protruding metal tongue, attached to the plug's tip is high. The lead from the plug's sleeve is always connected to ground. If the plug is balanced, it will have a ring between the tip and the sleeve. The lead coming from this ring should be connected to the low pin. After

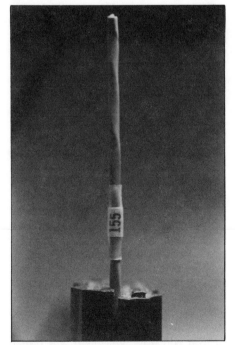

Figure 2. Stripping the multi-conductor cable.

Figure 3. The individual conductors stripped of insulation and shrink-wrapped.

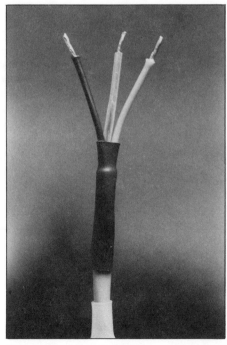

Figure 4. Conductors "dressed."

29

Once your wires are dressed, they can be soldered to the patch bay. Note how the wires are held between the thumb and ring finger, and the solder is held between the index and middle fingers.

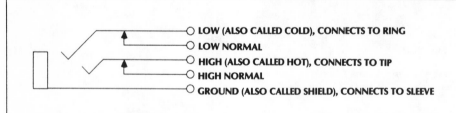

Figure 5. The pin connections for a balanced and normalled jack.

should be tinned as well. Then you are ready to solder the wires to the jack connections. Holding the wire in place at the same time you're applying both the solder and the iron can be a problem if you're not used to it. A simple clamp can work wonders here. Some come with little adjustable arms with alligator clips on the ends to hold things in place. Experienced techs develop a way of holding the wires and solder in one hand, like chopsticks, while holding the iron in the other. Everybody has his own technique, so I'll just suggest that you experiment to find what feels most comfortable—and hope none of you burn yourselves. However you do it, hold the iron to the tinned jack connection and place the tinned wire in position. When the solder on the wire begins to flow, put a dab more solder on the connector. When it flows, hold the wire steady and remove the iron quickly. Congratulations! You've just completed your first solder connection. Now get on with the hundreds of other connections you'll have to make.

If you opt for normalled connections, you must start with a dual-row bay that has normalling jacks. Once again, it is most convenient to keep each pair of jacks involved in adjacent rows, so that, for instance, the output of tape track 1 is normalled to the console's line input 1 in the row directly below. For neatness, the two functions you wish to normal should be in the same dual-row bay, as indicated by Figure 1. This also makes your connections neater, since the connecting wire doesn't need to be very long, and it makes it easier to service the connection, since both ends are on the same panel. Balanced normalling jacks have two extra pins in addition to high, low, and shield (see Figure 5). These are called high-normal and low-normal. Here's how to wire them up: In the case mentioned above, the tape output's high-normal (track 1/jack 1/row 1) should be connected to the high-normal of the console's line in (channel 1/jack 1/row 2). Do the same with the two low-normal pins. The two shields do not have to be connected unless there is a grounding problem. Now there's an invisible patch cord connecting the two jacks at all times. When a patch cord is plugged into either the tape output or the console input, however, the normal between the two will be broken and the signal will flow wherever the patch sends it. If you do not want the normal to be broken (thus allowing the tape output

each connection has been soldered to the bay, the 3/32″ slivers can be shrunk over each wire where it meets the connector. When using the heat shrink gun be careful not to give the shrink tubing too much heat. It may crack or, worse, melt the wire!

Some of you have never touched a soldering iron, right? Well, that's not a good reason to forgo the pleasure of a patch bay, and there's a first time for everything. Give it a try. If you are clumsy with a soldering iron, one of two things will happen: Either you'll get better, or you'll waste your money. So, you neophytes out there, listen up. To make a

good solder connection it is important that the tip of your soldering iron be kept clean. An old sponge, slightly moistened, makes an excellent cleaner. Tinning all wires in advance makes for easier and more reliable connections. To do this, first twist the wire. Touch the tip of the iron to the wire, and then touch the solder to the wire. Never put solder on the tip itself. When you see the solder flowing down the bare wire, the wire is tinned. Remove the iron immediately, or else you might melt off the plastic covering.

The connections to the bay's jacks

30

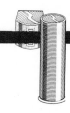

to continue to return at the line input, while also being fed elsewhere, say, to another channel or an effect input), then connect the tape output's high and low leads to the console input's high-normal and low-normal leads.

Your work will be easier if you make a chart of the individual wires in each snake. Label each snake (i.e., console mike inputs, keyboard snake, outboard effects, etc.). Before you start soldering, be sure you have the proper connections diagrammed out. Patch bay manufacturers often place the bottom row of jacks in upside down, so the pins are configured differently. It's easy to make a mistake—don't be fooled. It's a real pain to unsolder all your hard work and start over again. Also, take a break from the solder's lead fumes every hour or so. If you're not used to them, they can make you dopey. (Some musicians seem to enjoy this, but I don't recommend it.)

By Bobby Nathan

TUNING YOUR TAPE RECORDER

August 1986

There are some important tips for tuning up your tape recorder and making sure it stays in shape.

Cleanliness

All tape recorder maintenance begins with routine cleaning. This means that at the beginning and end of each recording session, the tape path must be cleaned properly. This keeps oxide that rubs off the tape from coating the recording heads and other parts, ensuring the best frequency response and accurate feeding of the tape along its path. You will need the following supplies: a box of Q-Tips (I recommend the plastic kind, because the cotton fibers stay attached to the plastic better than to the wooden shafts), isopropyl alcohol (91 percent pure or better), and rubber cleaner (Friends and TEAC are two good brands). The first two items can be purchased from any drugstore, and the latter can be purchased from the manufacturers or from any music store with a pro audio department.

Specially-made head cleaner fluids are made by Ampex and other compa-

nies, but in inexperienced hands these can cause great damage to your deck. Certain manufacturers coat their heads with a plastic that can be removed by these strong head cleaners (which can also melt plastic Q-Tips!), so stick with the alcohol—it works just fine. Never use alcohol to clean the rubber parts such as the puck (the rubber wheel that pushes the tape against the capstan, also called the pinch roller). Certain parts on professional decks look like rubber, but really ought to be cleaned with alcohol. Check with your deck's manufacturer if you are in doubt about which parts can take the alcohol.

The Technique

First dip a Q-Tip into the alcohol. Start with the tape guides and the capstan (the shaft of the motor—the metal part that spins). Even if your deck is of the cassette variety, it probably has tape guides. They can usually be found near the heads. Be sure to observe this next rule: Always clean in the direction of the tape's motion. This means that if the tape moves from left to right, clean with left-to-right motions, not up-and-down ones. Q-Tips are abrasive. Rubbing too hard and in the wrong direction can scratch the heads. They may be made out of metal, but they're delicate, so be careful. Use each Q-Tip till it looks dirty. It will usually turn brownish (the color of the tape oxide). Once again clean only the metal parts with alcohol! Alcohol will clean the rubber nicely, but in a short while your puck will get hard and slick, and eventually it will crack. Also, be sure to leave behind no trace of the Q-Tip's cotton fibers when you have finished cleaning. The tiniest of fibers can hinder the record and playback frequency of your deck if it dries and sticks to one of the heads.

Next, inspect the rubber puck. If it has a slick or discolored band around its middle, you are in for some rubbing. That band can cause irregular tape speed, and thus a recording that wavers in and out of tune. If the manufacturer recommends using a rubber cleaner, then grab a fresh Q-Tip and get to it. Be sure you have adequate ventilation. Rubber cleaner produces some pretty mean fumes, so unless you enjoy the high, open a few windows.

Your recorder should be cleaned before and after each session. At first this may seem like a royal pain, but once you make it part of your routine, it soon

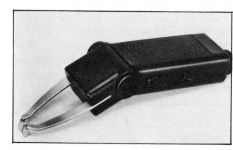

A hand-held head demagnetizer.

31

becomes painless.

Here's a little test that will check your deck's frequency response. A 1kHz tone is one of the standard alignment frequencies for record and playback level calibration. If you don't have a test-tone generator, one of your synths will do just as well. Play the C two octaves above Middle C—this is actually 1.045kHz, but that's close enough. The waveform should be a sine wave, and use only one oscillator without any modulation to eliminate frequency beating and fluctuations in level. Patch the synth into your recorder so that the test tone shows up on one of the VU meters. If the needle stays steady and solid, you are ready to proceed. Set the synth's output level to measure 0dB on the meter. If you can patch your synth into more than one channel of your recorder simultaneously, you can check all of the channels at once.

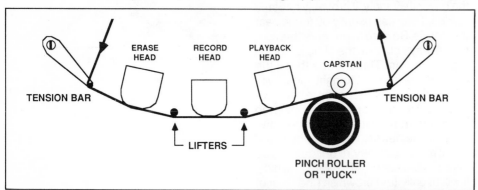

A typical tape transport assembly.

Record about 30 seconds of the tone, using the brand of tape you normally use. Rewind the tape and play it back. If you have a three-head deck (erase, record, and playback heads), first observe the level on the VU meters of both channels in sync mode, and then in repro. If your deck is properly aligned, the tone will play back at exactly the same level at which it was recorded (0dB). If the meters indicate a variation of more than 1dB in either mode, it would be wise to have the deck serviced.

It's also a good idea to try the same test with a higher frequency (around 10kHz) and a lower frequency (around 100Hz). That way you test over a broad range of the frequency spectrum. The 100Hz tone represents the bass response, the 1kHz tone represents the midrange, and the 10kHz tone represents the treble. A properly aligned recorder/reproducer will reproduce exactly what it records.

Trouble Shooting

If you've tried the test and your recorder did not pass, here are some possible reasons why: (1) You are using the wrong kind of tape. This occurs when you haven't read the part of the manual where the manufacturer recommends a particular brand of tape. Read it. (2) The heads are dirty. Well, we've already gone over the head cleaning procedure—so swab that deck. (3) You dropped your recorder, or it was jarred in shipping. In this case, the playback, record, or bias (the current for the type of tape used) alignments may have been knocked out of kilter. They probably need to be adjusted—by a qualified technician, of course. (4) The guy at the factory who originally aligned your deck sniffed too much rubber cleaner—or not enough! (5) The VU meters themselves are out of calibration, or the monitor calibration is off. This causes the meters to respond inaccurately to the signal in various ways, so the alignment can look wrong even when it's right. If you depend on your meters, have them calibrated, too. (6) The last and most painful: Your heads are old and worn, and need to be relapped. Relapping is a process in which the heads are repolished. This revitalizes their performance, and once this is done, the entire deck ought to be re-calibrated to make the most of this upgraded performance.

Here's a rough outline of the alignment procedure: First the VU meters are calibrated, so that all reference levels can be read accurately. Then the playback amplifiers are aligned to a reference tape, to make sure that the deck reproduces a wide range of frequencies accurately. (The reference tape has a number of test frequencies, including the 1kHz, 10kHz, and 100Kz tones we simulated above.) After that, the bias is set by recording test tones onto the type of tape you'll be using. And finally, the record amplifiers are aligned to the test frequencies, so that your recorder will not distort the frequency content of the material as it is recorded.

Be sure that whoever is going to repair and/or align your deck is qualified. He or she ought to be an authorized service representative of the manufacturer of your recorder. Always make sure the work is guaranteed, but above all, trust your ears.

By Bobby Nathan

HUMS AND BUZZES

January 1986

Whether you are using your equipment in a live or a studio situation, the following tips will help you to arrive at a good interfacing scheme. With a little care, many of those annoying hums, buzzes, and background noises can be eliminated entirely, or at least located and dealt with quickly when they do occur.

AC Grounding

If you have a fixed rig of gear, including a mixer and outboard effects, it is important to establish a permanent grounding scheme. A permanent arrangement for all your electrical connections can make it simple to overcome grounding problems, both on stage and in the studio. The first step is to plug all your gear into one large multi-outlet box. Make sure this box has the third prong (ground) connected from all the outlets to its plug. A number of manufacturers supply ten-outlet boxes. If one of these isn't enough, get a few. Next, plug all of them into one main AC extension box. A heavy-duty 20-amp-rated quad box with a 20-foot extension is usually perfect. Check the ratings of your gear: In most cases, the total amperage of your keyboards, mixer, effects, and power amp won't exceed 15 amps. This box can be extended when a longer run is needed. On many stages the AC hookup is pretty far away, so keep an extension handy.

Next, hook up your stage monitor amps, mixer, and console. If you hear any AC ground hum or buzz, try unplugging the different components until you find out what's causing it. If a piece of gear is humming, make sure that its audio cables are good by swapping with tested cables. If a cable-swap doesn't cure the problem, try a third-prong AC ground-lift adapter. They're inexpensive and you never know when you'll need one, so keep plenty on hand.

Turn all of your keyboards on and plug them into the mixer one by one. If you notice any noise, try additional ground-lift plugs on the keyboards that cause problems. Once all your gear is hooked up, note for future reference where in the chain you had to use ground-lifters. If you experience any grounding problems in a new environment, the solution should be a simple matter of lifting the third pin of your master AC extension cord.

[*Ed. Note: When lifting grounds, be 110 percent sure that all of your gear is in perfect electrical operating order. Equipment grounds are for your safety; when you lift a ground you run the possibility of electrical shock, should there be any AC problems with your gear. Often, signal cables will serve as grounds (if one central piece, such as a mixer, is grounded), but not always. If in doubt, consult an electrician!*]

Voltage Regulation And Spike/Surge Reduction

You'll keep your microprocessor keyboards a lot happier by using a spike/surge-protection filter on their AC lines. This keeps the AC clear of transient fluctuations in voltage, and many filters reduce 60-cycle hum, too. Computer stores sell a variety of filters from about $30.00 up. It's also a good idea to use a voltage regulator, which helps to maintain a steady overall voltage level. Although regulators are expensive (a couple of hundred dollars), they're well worth the cost. They will help to keep your gear out of the repair shop, especially if you play large arenas where the AC lines are full of spikes and surges. Incidentally, older analog synths will also stay in tune longer with filtered and voltage-regulated AC lines. Check and see how much amperage is drawn by the keyboards you're using, and then buy an appropriate model.

Direct Boxes

Most of your keyboard audio outputs probably terminate in 1/4″ phone jacks. If any have balanced cannon (XLR) connectors, use them instead. In fact, you should use balanced lines wherever possible. Phone plugs are convenient,

but they're also unbalanced and will add noise to your system if you use cables over 15 feet long. In addition, running unbalanced lines near AC cords can cause them to pick up 60-cycle hum. If a balanced output isn't available, a direct box can provide one. The unbalanced input cable between the direct box and your instrument should be kept as short as possible—as long as you're spending the $30.00 to $150.00 it costs for a direct box, you might as well get the quietest possible response. A direct box can allow you to run balanced lines as long as 50 feet, and even longer if you're using an active, rather than a passive box.

A passive direct box has nothing more than a transformer inside, while active models use more involved electronics which require a power source. The frequency response of an active direct box far surpasses that of most passive boxes. Many active boxes are phantom-powered (48 volts DC). Consoles often have phantom powering built in just for this purpose. If your console doesn't have phantom power, don't worry; a number of active direct boxes offer a nine-volt transistor battery option. Almost all direct boxes have an AC ground-lift switch that lifts the ground (pin 1) in its balanced output cable. This is meant to compensate for the use of third-pin AC lifters. When your system is working, take note of the quietest position for each box's ground-lift switch.

If you use a volume pedal, it must be placed before the direct box. To my knowledge, there are no balanced volume pedals on the market. Once again, keep the unbalanced cables to and from your volume pedal as short as possible. Like direct boxes, there are passive and active pedals. The active ones are quieter, and have circuitry to keep the signal at unity gain (no signal loss at full volume). If your active pedals require AC, be sure to figure out a grounding scheme for them, too!

Mixers And Power Amps

Your mixer actually adds more noise than anything else. In order to drive a power amplifier, it multiplies the signals you feed it many times over. At the same time, it has to pad down (attenuate) many input signals. Some keyboards put out a hot signal, called line level. Direct boxes put out a low-level signal, called mike level. The board has to equate line and mike level instruments, and all of that cutting and boosting adds noise. There are a few ways you can compensate, so that your mixer doesn't have to work so hard at juggling all those levels. Make sure that the volume on all your mike level instruments is turned up—low levels will have to be amplified greatly, adding noise. Make sure that your line level instruments are sufficiently padded, too. Insufficient padding will result in distortion.

You can pick up an incredible amount of 60-cycle hum by placing your mixer too close to power amps, or near AC outlet boxes. The bigger the amp, the bigger its power transformer, and the bigger the hum. Try to keep your power amps in a separate rack, away from your mixer. Outboard effects generally produce little hum, but check them out anyway. If an effects box seems to introduce hum, move it!

Again, if your mixer has balanced outputs, use them. Using unbalanced cables between your mixer and your power amp will increase noise. The same holds true for any equalizers between your mixer and power amp.

Cables

Even though the next suggestion will not reduce noise or hum, it will improve your sound: Never use an instrument's audio cable to connect speakers to an amplifier. Guitar cords were not designed for this purpose. Get some zip cord (the stuff that runs between a lamp and the wall outlet) and make your own, or have them made for you. If you invest in heavier gauges of wire, your speakers will sound even better. Try not to run long wires between an amp and speakers; this will insure a better sound by improving the "damping factor" (control over subsonic speaker response). And don't let the ground from your amplifier's speaker outputs make contact with the audio ground. This can cause a tremendous ground loop which could harm *you* along with your equipment.

Cheap guitar cables are exactly that: cheap. You know, the type with the molded plastic plugs that you buy in order to save a few bucks here and there. As many musicians have discovered, molded plugs work fine in the beginning, but after a short while they invariabley become intermittent. I've gotten my best results using cables that incorporate a low capacitance wire, such as that manufactured by Beldon, Mogami, Connectronics, Monster Cable,

Canare, and others. This kind of cable is shielded better to reject RFI (radio frequency interference), 50-cycle hum, and other causes of noise. Also, check to see if the phone jacks are strain-reliefed. This can prevent the cable from breaking at inopportune moments during a performance. Brass 1/4" phone plugs are great, but they tarnish and need to be cleaned on a regular basis. Fine emory cloth or Polysand will do the trick. And keep all of your cables away from moisture, especially Coca Cola!

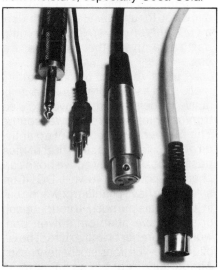

From left to right: 2-conductor 1/4" (phone) plug, RCA (phono) plug, 3-pin XLR connector, 5-pin (DIN-type) MIDI connector.

Watch That Shock!

Guitar players know—all too well—what a shock caused by improper ground polarity feels like. You, too, may experience this exquisite pleasure, if one of your hands is touching a metal keyboard casing at the same time your lips come into contact with the microphone. Save yourself some pain and embarrassment. Buy a small AC outlet tester, the kind that has two probes for inserting into AC wall outlets. Touch your keyboard's audio output jack with one probe, and the metal casing of your microphone with the other. If you see the test light flicker, then you've just spared yourself a fried lower lip. Try reversing your master AC extension with the aid of a third-prong ground-lifter.

The above tips should make your gear more manageable. The only thing I can't stress enough is the importance of having spare AC outlet boxes, third-prong adapters, and audio cables to repair or modify in emergency situations.

By Bobby Nathan

SOUNDPROOFING

August 1987

The best way to ensure your freedom of musical expression is to choose the right location for your music room. This can save you thousands of dollars in soundproofing right from the start. If you live in a house, the basement is good, since usually it's surrounded by a healthy slab of earth. Likewise, the end apartment in a one-story building is preferable to one with neighbors on all sides. Lofts and apartments in commercial buildings have some advantages over residential buildings; commercial tenants usually go home at five P.M., which is when most musicians seem to get creative. Put some space between your music and other people's ears—at least before the record is released.

If possible, find a space with concrete floors and ceilings. Having ample amperes of electricity and enough outlets is a must. Also, the fewer the windows, the better. If you plan to go first-class with your soundproofing, look for high ceilings and few columns. For a heavy-duty studio, you are also going to need a heavy floor-load capacity.

The most effective way to soundproof a room is to "float" the room's surfaces. As you can see from the diagram, a floated room is actually a room within a room. The idea is to create a buffer of air and other materials between the inside surfaces and the outside surfaces, so that sonic vibrations aren't transferred from inside the room to the outside world. The best way to handle a particular soundproofing problem varies with the situation, so before you take any elaborate steps of the kind outlined below, I'd recommend speaking to an expert. An acoustic consultant can analyze the construction of your building to determine the routes by which sounds travels through it. Here are a few general guidelines, so you can get an idea of the options available to you.

The first rule is: Keep the music off the floor. Whether you're recording an acoustic piano or amplified synthesizers, all sound sources should be isolated from the structure of the building, which can carry vibrations to other rooms and to the outside walls. A simple way to float sound sources is to use machinery isolators. These handy little items are intended to keep things like large air-conditioning compressors from vibrating themselves out of existence, and consist of a heavy-duty metal spring sandwiched between two thick rubber pads. Incidentally, they fit nicely under an acoustic piano's legs. Keeping the speakers off the floor is a good idea. Resting them on closed-cell foam can help.

In many cases, the most effective single step you take is to float your floor. This won't help if the only neighbors you have are directly above you, but otherwise it's a good bet. The simplest formula is to cover your floor with two layers of 5/8" plywood with oak planking or carpeting on top. The plywood should rest on Neoprene donuts, about one per square foot. These are circular pieces of dense rubber material. Just where can you get Neoprene donuts? No, you don't buy them at Dunkin' Donuts. They're a specialty item, so you may have difficulty finding them. Look in the yellow pages under acoustical contractors, call one, and ask where you can get them or some other material that does the same job. Rubber bottle stoppers of the kind used in chemistry labs work great, too. Get the kind with two holes in them— sizes 7½ to 10. They're much cheaper than the Neoprene donuts, if you can find them.

A floating floor can do wonders. Unfortunately, a floating floor often isn't enough, particularly when live drummers and bass players are thumping away. To keep that kind of noise from escaping, you'll need to float the rest of the room. Float the walls by building new ones, leaving at least two inches of air space between the new and the existing walls—a sufficient air gap between sufficiently massive structures will go a long way toward stopping sound vibrations. Filling the space with a Fiberglas-like material can help. (Incidentally, if you're going to take it this far, the walls should be floated before going to work on the floor.) Use two or three layers of 5/8" sheet rock, resting them on a two-inch layer of felt (the new walls should be built from the existing floor, not the floating floor). A two-inch felt strip should be glued to the ceiling, so that the wall can butt up against it. Then, when the walls vibrate, they won't pass the vibrations on to the ceiling. Building isolators, which are kind of like the machinery isolators mentioned above, can be placed between the new and the existing walls for extra strength.

The ceiling should be suspended from building isolators. Black iron beams

make a sturdy frame for the structure. Attach metal studs to each of the four corners, and then fill out the frame with lines of studs. Two or three layers of 5/8" sheet rock attached to the metal studs complete the ceiling. Wherever the ceiling would touch the walls, two-

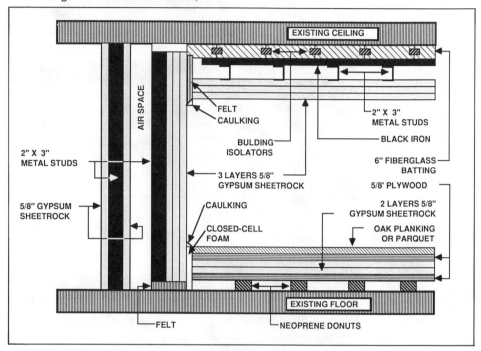

inch felt is used to isolate the ceiling from the walls. As a final precaution, caulk all floor/wall and floor/ceiling joints. Remember, if air can get in or out, so can sound!

That's your basic floating room. Of course, there are other things to consider, such as air-conditioning vents and electrical outlets. Arrangements for such things should be made before you break out the hammer and nails.

Now that the police have gone back to the station and your neighbors have gone back to sleep, I'd like to explode a soundproofing myth. First, a word about carpeting. Carpet will not stop sound from bothering your neighbors. You'd be better off buying your neighbor a Walkman and a good set of headphones! Carpeting only keeps high frequencies from bouncing around inside the room. It won't keep the vibrations from escaping. Besides, a room with carpet on the floors, walls, and ceiling sounds awful. To my ears, it's too dead. The same thing goes for covering the walls with Sonex, egg cartons, or acoustic tile. All these materials do is deaden the room—it takes mass to lessen sound transmission.

A cross-section of a "floating" room. By physically isolating all surfaces from each other, external noises can be kept out of the room—or internal noises can be kept in.

By Bobby Nathan

2 *OUTBOARD GEAR*

SIGNAL PROCESSING

June 1986

"If only I can get my hands on the same kind of equipment that Steve Superstar is using in his records, I'll sound just like him!!"

Goaded by this myth and their dreams of greatness, thousands of musicians spend millions of dollars every year on pro-quality equipment that they haven't the faintest hope of getting pro-quality sounds out of.

There are two reasons why these people are bound to be disappointed. One is that Steve Superstar just plain plays better than they do. He'd sound better on a battered spinet, and he sounds a hell of a lot better on a Fairclavier, because he knows what to do with it. The other reason is that Steve is not running his Fairclavier through a Sears Silvertone. When he goes into the studio, every keyboard he owns is being processed through about a zillion bucks' worth of outboard effects devices.

We're not going to try to con you that you'll sound exactly like Steve Superstar if you not only buy all the keyboards he has but also fill up five or six floor-to-ceiling racks with state-of-the-art processing gear. What we will do is try to give you some idea what Steve's engineer is using to give Steve that zillion-dollar sound. Once you understand how it all works, all you have to do is learn to play good. And get a hip haircut.

Delay Lines

Delay lines are devices that electronically create echoes and other time-based effects (including chorusing, flanging, and so on). There are digital delays, tape delays, analog delays, and even MIDI data delays, all of which accomplish essentially the same thing —they delay an incoming signal by some variable amount of time and the spit it out again.

The first delay lines were your Grand Canyons, Carlsbad Caverns, and the like. The first electronic echo was produced when someone found that you could mount a playback head after the record head on a tape recorder, record a signal, and play it back a fraction of a second later, producing a time-delayed signal. The amount of delay depended on the tape speed and the distance between the record head and the play-

back head. Then someone thought to mount the playback head on a movable arm, so you could change the distance between the playback and record heads, thereby changing the amount of delay between the original and playback signals. Then someone thought to feed a small amount of the delayed signal back to the record head, generating a delay of the delayed signal (feedback, in other words). Thus tape echo devices like the Maestro Echoplex and Roland Space Echo were born.

More recently, ways have been found to create delays without the use of tape. The first of these was the analog delay. Analog delays used bucket brigade devices to store an incoming signal for a variable amount of time before spitting it back out again. Analog delays were soon eclipsed by digital delays, which digitally sample the incoming signal, hold onto it for some variable amount of time, and then spit it back out. The result can be anything from discrete echoes to very tightly spaced doubling, to chorusing or flanging, depending on the delay setting. The benefits of electronic delay over tape delay are increased reliability, decreased noise (tape introduces hiss), and added flexibility. Digital delay lines (DDLs) are much less noisy when compared with analog delays. Of course, some people still swear by their old tape delays, claiming that their warm sound is unattainable by digital, analog, or other means.

The MIDI data processor is a device which produces delays by intentionally holding onto the MIDI data stream for some variable amount of time. MIDI delay devices offer a superb signal-to-noise ratio, since the effect is happening in real time (as if you had some phantom keyboard player following your playing on another instrument). The disadvantage is that you have to use up as many additional synthesizer voices to create the echoes as you used to play the original part.

Delays can be used for a variety of things. One very popular use is to delay an instruments's signal by between 15 and 40 milliseconds to produce a doubling effect. It's also common for engineers to place the original non-delayed signal in one channel of the stereo field and the delayed signal in the other channel, creating a stereo effect from a monaural source. There are also a number of stereo digital delays on the market which will bounce a delayed sound around in the stereo field.

37

Yamaha's SPX90-II can perform pitch shifting, reverb, and many other signal processing functions. Programs can be recalled and certain parameters changed via MIDI.

By modulating the amount of delay time and mixing the direct signal with the delayed singal, you can use a delay line to create flanging and chorusing as well as discrete echoes.

Pitch Shifters

Ever wonder how Laurie Anderson creates those neat effects where she sounds like a bass vocalist in the Metropolitan Opera? No, it's not done with mirrors. The magical devices that change the pitch of their input are called pitch shifters. They are more commonly referred to as Harmonizers, a name that happens to be a trademark of the pitch shifter made by Eventide. Those of you who feel sympathetic toward the Xerox, Kleenex, and Leslie speaker people in their Sisyphian struggle to keep their trademarked names from becoming generic terms will doubtless want to stop referring to pitch shifters by any other name.

Pitch shifters begin by digitally sampling their input. If a sampled sound is played back at a rate different than the original sampling rate, then the original pitch will be shifted or transposed. But there's more to pitch shifters than this. With a sampling machine, playing back a sample at a higher or lower pitch causes the entire sample to be speeded up or slowed down. In a pitch shifter, on the other hand, the overall length stays the same.

This is accomplished by cutting out some of the samples (if the sound is being lowered in pitch) or adding new ones (if the sound is being raised). In order to minimize the harmonic distortion introduced by this process, the more expensive pitch shifters use algorithms that search for the best places to add and subtract samples.

Other features you'll find on some pitch shifters include delay, feedback of output to input, a freeze function that allows a recorded segment to be played back repeatedly, and multiple simultaneous outputs at various pitches.

Probably the most popular application for pitch shifters is to fatten the sound of a synthesizer, a vocal line, or even a drum. This is accomplished by selecting a very small amount of pitch shift and perhaps adding a very slight delay to the transposed signal, which gives an effect similar to double-tracking. Another application is to create parallel harmonies without the use of other instruments. When this process is applied to vocal lines, it should be used sparingly, since the pitch shifting process does color the sound and it can be unnatural-sounding when used too heavily. You can also correct pitch to a certain extent, so if your singer is flat on an important note, you can throw that one note onto a new track with the proper pitch, and (dare we say it?) fix it in the mix. By cutting out some of a sampled input and then slowing the output down to the original pitch, some pitch shifters can shorten a sound without otherwise affecting it; this is often used with spoken lines in commercials, to tighten them up.

Reverb

Reverberation is yet another time-based effect; however, compared to echoing, chorusing, and flanging, the process that produces reverb is much more complex. Instead of a few discrete repetitions of a sound, in reverb there are many repetitions spaced so close together that the ear can't distinguish them from one another. The repetitions blend together into a continuous wash of sound. This is what you hear when you're making noise on the stage in a concert hall or a gymnasium. The sound goes out to the walls, bounces around, and comes back at you from lots of different angles with lots of different time delays, depending on how far the individual sound waves happened to travel.

There are a number of ways to create reverb effects in the studio, some of which work better than others. The method most of us will remember from our garage-band days is the *spring reverb*, the kind you find in guitar amps, inexpensive P.A. boards, and home organs. The spring reverb works like this: An incoming electrical signal is turned back into sound waves with a transducer (essentially a miniature

speaker) and fed through a pair of springs (usually about 12″ long). Two springs of slightly different lengths are used in order to minimize the acoustic resonances of the springs themselves. As the sound passes along the springs, time delays and reflections are introduced by the coils of the spring itself. The signal at the other end of the spring is then reconverted to an electrical signal and passed on to the amplifier. Spring reverb works pretty well with pitched sounds, but not very well with percussive sounds with sharp transient peaks, or sounds that have lots of noise in them. When you feed noise or sharp peaks into a spring reverb, what you get out is no longer a pitched echo, but simply the tone color of the spring itself—*boinggg*!

Many recording studios feature *live chambers* to create reverb. In these, a speaker is placed in a room with highly reflective walls, floor, and ceiling. The signal you want to add reverb to is run through the speaker, and the room is miked to return the reverberated sound to the mixing console. Home recordists can recreate the live chamber effect in their bathrooms—many a tiled shower stall has been pressed into service for some great sounding reverb.

Up until recently, the most popular device for creating reverb in studios was the *plate reverb*. These devices operate in a way similar to the spring reverb, the major difference being that the incoming signal is fed into a plate of sheet metal stretched taut in a frame instead of into a spring. The plates are relatively large and require very delicate adjustments, which is what kept this style reverb out of guitar amps.

Digital reverb is fast becoming a favorite in both professional and home studio environments. A digital reverb samples the incoming signal and then processes it through complex mathematical algorithms designed to mimic the multiple reflections of various sized rooms and plates. High-end digital reverbs give you control over virtually every aspect of the reverberation, from room size and shape down to the density and delay time of the early reflections.

Chorusing And Flanging

There are a number of other time-based effects besides delay and echo. These include chorusing, double-tracking, and flanging. These effects can be produced by most digital delays, but there are also dedicated devices designed to produce each effect exclusively. Let's look at what distinguishes each effect from the others.

Flanging gets its name from the way it was discovered. An incoming audio signal was being recorded onto two tape decks and monitored from both playback heads simultaneously, in an attempt to create a doubling effect. It was found, however, that small changes in the tape speed between the two decks created a whooshing sound. It was later found that this could be enhanced and controlled by leaning on the flanges of one of the tape reels to slow the tape.

Flanging is created when two identical signals are offset from each other by small, constantly varying amounts of time between .25 and 20 milliseconds). This offset creates phase cancellations and reinforcements between the two signals at various frequencies, an effect called *comb filtering* because the peaks and troughs in the frequency spectrum resemble the teeth of a comb. When the time delay changes, the in-phase and out-of-phase frequencies move up and down in the harmonic spectrum. It is this movement that we hear as flanging.

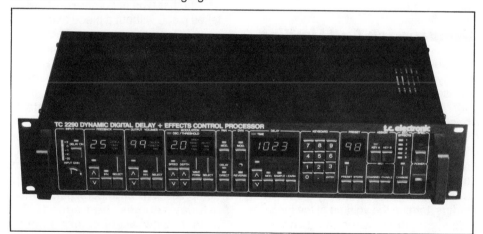

In an electronic (as opposed to tape-based) flanger, the variations in delay time will usually be introduced by a low-frequency oscillator (LFO). This LFO's frequency can usually be controlled with a parameter called "sweep rate" or something similar. A control called "sweep depth" will determine how much the time offset changes during an LFO cycle. The greater the sweep depth, the farther the peaks and dips of the phase cancellation effect will travel. Flangers usually offer some kind of regeneration control which feeds the input signal back to the device after processing. This feedback intensifies the effect. One popular use of flanging during the '70s

From Denmark, the T.C. Electronic TC 2290 digital delay allows you to store and recall a number of different settings. As with the SPX90-II pictured opposite, the TC 2290 has MIDI implementation.

39

was to give pianos an out-of-tune honky-tonk sound.

Everything said so far about flanging applies equally well to chorusing. The difference between flanging and chorusing is that in chorusing the delay time is usually longer (10 to 30 milliseconds), which brings the comb filtering down into the fundamental and low harmonics of the sound. Chorusing is used to thicken sounds. It's hard not to get carried away with chorusing, since it works great on just about any synth sound, drums, vocals, and anything else. Flanging is not electronically the same thing as phase shifting, though it sounds similar when you listen to it. Phase shifting is not a time-based effect, but rather an electronic process that rotates the electronic phase of a signal in relation to itself.

Automatic double-tracking devices create delays that are between 15 and 80 milliseconds long, which gives the impression that two identical lines were played instead of one. The effect is exaggerated as the delay time is increased. A dedicated double-tracking device will not have an LFO for modulating the time delay, as this would introduce flanging.

Compression And Limiting

Question: What do you use to smooth out dynamic peaks that are so high they cause distortion? Answer: A compressor/limiter. These devices were created back in the days prior to rock and roll, when the loudest peaks of orchestras far exceeded the capabilities of tape to record them without considerable distortion. Before compressor/limiters, recording engineers simply 'rode' the faders, turning the volume of the incoming signal down when things got too loud, and back up when they quieted down again. A sensitive engineer who knew the score of the piece that was being recorded could do a lot with this method, but for best results some sort of automatic system was clearly needed.

Compressor/limiters (comp/limiters for short) made life much easier. Basically, a compressor is a voltage-controlled amplifier (VCA) that begins to reduce its gain below unity (equivalent to pulling down a fader) only when the incoming signal goes beyond a certain variable threshold. A ratio control lets you adjust the amount by which the gain will be reduced in comparison to the input level. For example, a 2:1 ratio indi-

cates that for every increase of 2dB in input, the output gain will be reduced by 1dB. With this setting, the peaks will still be louder than the threshold, but their sharpness will be reduced by 50 percent. A ratio of 1:1 means no compression. Generally, ratios between 2:1 and 6:1 are the most effective, although you should let the situation dictate the needs.

Compression of greater than 10:1 is for all practical purposes indistinguishable from *limiting* (thus compressors that offer greater than 10:1 compression are called comp/limiters). In limiting, the output level is never allowed to exceed a set value, no matter how high the input level is. Whether you use compression or limiting is a matter of personal taste.

One result of compression and limiting is that the overall signal on the tape can be made louder, since there will be no peaks to cause distortion. Another, less desirable effect is that with low threshold settings, the background noise in an instrument's signal will be boosted relative to the loudest sounds coming out of it. For this reason, you'll sometimes see a comp/limiter followed in the signal chain by a noise gate.

Another type of compression, which takes place without a piece of outboard gear, is *tape compression*. This occurs when magnetic tape reaches saturation —all its oxide particles are being used to record the signal, leaving no particles free to take a louder incoming signal. This condition naturally prevents the signal from getting any louder, hence the term tape compression. You'd think from the description that tape compression would be completely undesirable, since it would produce distortion, but tape compression is an integral part of many of today's coolest drum sounds. Just goes to show where breaking the so-called rules can get you.

Exciters

Exciters are used to enhance the 'presence' of an audio signal. A signal that has been excited is perceived as having more high-frequency brilliance and presence, even though the level (amplitude) of the high-frequency energy has not been substantially raised. With a speech signal, an exciter can produce increased intelligibility without increasing the signal level. If this sounds like magic, it's because these processors play tricks on the brain, causing it to think it perceives one thing

when in fact something slightly different is occurring—kind of like doing it with mirrors.

There are many different exciter-type processors available today. The best known of them, the Aphex, fools the brain into thinking there is more high-frequency information in the audio signal than actually exists by introducing frequency-dependent phase shift into the signal. This psychoacoustic phenomenon is only possible due to the way

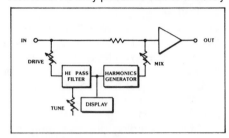

A block diagram of the Aphex Aural Exciter Type C, showing the procesing chain.

in which the brain interprets sound. Some exciter manufacturers get a similar effect by introducing slight amounts of second-harmonic distortion. The actual level of the effect is 20dB below the nominal signal level, so the overall signal level does not change substantially during processing. The excitement works as well in mono as it does in stereo.

Exciters are sometimes applied in-line with the stereo bus during mixdown, during tracking of individual instruments, and in live performance to improve voice intelligibility. One interesting use is for restoring old recordings: These can be given new life by using single-ended noise reduction to eliminate excess noise, and then an exciter to regenerate the lost high-frequency information.

Equalizers

Next to tape itself, equalizers are just about the most basic component of a recording system. They don't do anything fancy, but without them most recordings would be a muddled mess. In order to understand what an equalizer does, you need to know a bit about the physics of sound. A single sound, such as a bass guitar note, contains vibrations at many different frequencies. The equalizer's job is to boost certain of these frequencies and/or cut other frequencies so as to change the tone color.

Equalizers come in several different

types, the most common ones being the graphic equalizer, the parametric equalizer, and the fixed-frequency equalizer. Some form of equalization (EQ) is built into most mixing boards, but outboard EQ is often used as well.

The parametric equalizer is the most versatile. A semi-parametric equalizer is similar to a parametric, but lacks one of the types of control found on the true parametric. A parametric equalizer usually divides the frequency spectrum into two, three, or four wide bands. For each band, you'll find controls for center frequency, bandwidth, and amount of boost or cut. In a typical semi-parametric, the bandwidth control is missing. Other quasi-parametrics may offer switchable center frequency or switchable boost/cut amounts in place of full control. When shopping for a parametric, make sure that the bands overlap—for example, that the low band can be set anywhere between 20Hz and 500Hz while the mid-band can go as low as 400Hz or as high as 5kHz and the high band from 3kHz up to 18kHz.

The bandwidth control is useful because it allows you to zoom in on very narrow frequency areas, such as a 60Hz hum, or to give a slight coloration to a much broader area. Another term you'll see used for bandwidth is Q; a high Q setting produces a narrow band with a sharp peak.

Graphic equalizers get their name because they use banks of sliders for their boost/cut controls. The setting of these controls gives you a visual, graphic representation of the resulting equalization curve. The graphic equalizer is actually a bunch of fixed-bandwidth, fixed-frequency filters. When you hear terms like 10-band, 15-band, or 31-band graphic EQ, you're hearing a description of how many different bands the frequency spectrum is divided up into. Obviously, the more bands, the narrower each band will be, giving you more precise control over the spectrum. Graphics often give you frequency bands placed half octaves (two bands per octave) or third octaves (three bands per octave) apart. Graphics are often used to correct frequency response problems in studio monitoring setups.

Fixed-frequency equalizers are found in most semi-pro consoles, home stereos, and your basic guitar-type amps, where they are referred to simply as tone controls. They will boost or cut entire regions of frequencies—lows,

mids, and highs—but they can only operate on broad bands of frequencies, which limits their usefulness. Low and high fixed-frequency equalization are sometimes referred to as *shelving*, because the frequencies at the edge of the audio band are pressed down or raised up as if by a shelf.

EQ is used to correct problems with the sound of certain instruments, to fit an instrument or vocal into a mix by limiting the frequency band where it is heard, and so on. Boosting the highs coming from a noisy source will have the effect of increasing the hiss in your sound, so use equalization with care. And watch your output levels. Equalizers can be thought of as frequency-dependent amplifiers/attenuators. As such, they change the volume level of different frequencies. Massive amounts of EQ may boost the overall level of a signal to the point of distortion. Likewise, cutting unwanted frequencies may pull the overall level down below the optimum level for recording. Remember that you can cut as easily as boost with an equalizer; this has the effect of boosting the relative level of whatever frequency band(s) you leave uncut.

Noise Reduction

Public enemy number one in the recording environment is noise. Noise can come from an electronic instrument itself, from an outboard device, or from the cable connecting them. In any of these cases the tool of choice is a noise gate or single-ended noise reduction. Noise also resides in the magnetic tape itself. Here, a different system, called noise reduction, is the preferred method of dealing with it. As the moniker implies, noise reduction is a process designed to eliminate those unwanted typhoons blowing out of your tape decks.

What we're discussing here is complementary, or two-ended, noise reduction. The complementary noise reduction systems we've all come to know (though some of us hate 'em and some of us love 'em) are Dolby and dbx. Both of these are two-step processes. The first step is called *encoding* and the second step is called *decoding*. In the Dolby encoding process, the level of the high frequencies is raised far above what you're hearing in the monitor speakers. On decoding, the encoding process is reversed. The high frequencies are lowered to their normal level, and at the same time the *noise floor*,

41

which was on the tape to begin with, is pushed farther down, often into inaudibility. In dbx, a slightly different scheme is used. All the frequencies are compressed during recording and expanded during playback, again driving the noise floor down toward inaudibility.

No noise reduction will occur in complementary systems unless both encoding and decoding are performed! Playing back Dolby B-encoded tapes without decoding them does nothing

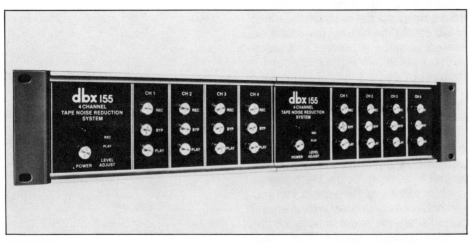

The dbx 155 was one of the first affordable outboard noise reduction systems, and helped popularize dbx noise reduction as a small-studio option in the late 1970s.

except give you an exaggerated high-frequency level. We really don't recommend playback of dbx-encoded signals without decoding, because dbx uses some extreme signal compression, which will give you a somewhat objectionable sound when not decoded. Dolby A (the pro audio version of Dolby) and Dolby C (found on many consumer tape decks, 4-track cassette machines, as well as open-reel 8- and 16-track recorders) must also be decoded in order to be listenable, due to their extensive decode/encode processing.

Many people feel that noise reduction colors the sound by reducing the amount of high frequencies in the audio program. This may be due to the fact that the presence of noise is often associated with the presence of high-frequency information. It is *crucial* that a noise reduction system be properly aligned, since the encoding/decoding process is a level-dependent process and that should not alter the frequency content of the original input signal.

Noise Gates

If your keyboards or effects put out hiss and hum along with their signal, the first thing to do is check for grounding problems. (If you don't understand grounding, we recommend consulting a

technician to make sure your system is free of ground loops.) If you've grounded everything properly and still have noise, it's time to look into getting a *noise gate*, a device that only lets a signal through when the level of the input rises above some variable threshold.

Let's say you're miking a piano and for some reason there's a lot of low-level background noise (someone talking in another room, for example) that you'd rather not hear. When the piano is being played, it completely masks the low-level noise, but when there is a rest in the music, all you hear is the background noise. With a noise gate, you can set the threshold to just above the level of the background noise. Now when the piano signal crosses that threshold, you will hear the piano. As the piano's notes decay and cross back under the gate's threshold, the piano will cut out, as will the noise.

Gating has its uses. It's great for noisy guitar amps and cutting out room noises. However, be aware that the gate can shut down rather suddenly. With the acoustic example above, a long sustained chord held by the damper pedal is liable to be chopped off in a very unnatural way when the volume level drops below the threshold. If the threshold is set too high, the sustained chord will drop out too soon. If it's set too low, the background noise will be heard.

Of course, there are times when this abrupt gating is not only desirable, it's great. Take the infamous Phil Collins/Hugh Padgham drum sound, where the ambience of the room is intentionally cut off by a noise gate. Many noise gates allow you to trigger them with signals other than the input signal. This lets you produce effects where you only hear something (maybe a synth chord) when something else (maybe a bass drum hit) triggers the gate. Some noise gates feature envelope controls that let you set the cutoff slope, so instead of getting instantaneous gating off, you can get a smoother decay.

A more complex type of noise filtering is offered by single-ended or non-complementary noise reduction systems like the Symmetrics 511-II, the Rocktron Hush, and others. These have something in common with tape noise reduction systems, but they act without the encode/decode process. They are remarkably effective in reducing noise in outboard gear and keyboards. For those of you who complain about the DX7's signal-to-noise ratio, try a single-ended noise reduction unit on it; they work wonders.

Single-ended noise reduction can be accomplished a couple of different ways. One is to use a dynamically controlled lowpass filter. Because the filter is dynamic, the high-frequency content of the input signal is sensed and the filter will open up to let this through if it is above a certain threshold volume. When the highs are below that threshold (i.e., they're noise), they get filtered out. Another way singled-ended systems can act on noise is to perform downward expansion on the input signal. For every dB the input signal falls below a (usually variable) threshold the output signal will fall by an even greater amount. This means that the lowest level, which is usually residual noise, will be attenuated into inaudibility.

**By Bryan Lanser
and Dominic Milano**

ECHO AND DELAY

July 1985

Long before there was MIDI, keyboardists and other musicians were fattening up their sound with echo, delay, flanging, and chorusing. Part of a good engineer's reputation, to say nothing of a keyboard player's trademark sound, was based on the subtle—and sometimes not so subtle—use of these effects. For the most part, they were obtainable only in the studio. Later, as devices like the Echoplex, the Binson Echorec, the Guild Copy Cat, and the Roland Space Echo became available, musicians could afford to use effects onstage as well. Even though reverb was on the scene as a standard feature on many guitar amps and organs, reverb never excited players and listeners the way echo units did.

Let's look at the differences between echo and delay. I've always thought of a single echo as a replication of the original sound but with a distinct frequency curve or coloration. In this curve, many of the low-mid and midrange frequencies are boosted, and the highs are attenuated. A delay, on the other hand, is the original sound duplicated exactly, without any coloration. A delay can be much more flexible than an echo. It is a good starting point for synthesizing ambience, because it is relatively flat in frequency response. Also, I have always

thought of echo as having more than one repetition, while delay has primarily one.

The early echo units were in reality tape recorders. They had a movable head, either the record head or the playback head. The length of time between the original sound and the echo depended on the distance between the two heads divided by the speed at which the tape was moving. Mastering the use of echo with a mechanical system like this required a good ear. Today, most good digital delay units display the length of the delay in milliseconds, which makes it much easier to set the correct timing.

Knowing the right length of delay to use is essential for creating the right effect. For example, if your delay is timed to the length of the quarter-note in the song, but is slightly faster than the quarter-note, this will produce a very "anxious" type of psychological effect on the listener. Good for high-tension music. On the other hand, a delay slightly longer than the quarter-note will create a more laid-back feeling suitable for ballads. Delaying an instrument perfectly in time with the track will have no other effect than to create ambience. As you can see, knowing the right and wrong ways to use echo and delay can definitely have advantages.

At Unique Recording, we use a simple formula to calculate the length of various musical delays. This was conceived by one of our senior engineers, Frank Heller. It works as follows: There are 1,000 milliseconds in a second, or 60,000 milliseconds in a minute. So dividing 60,000 by the number of beats per minute gives the length of the quarter-note in milliseconds. For example, if the tempo is 120, we calculate:

$$60,000/120 = 500$$

So the delay setting for quarter-notes should be 500ms. Other note values can be calculated by dividing or multiplying the length of the quarter-note. Once this is done, it's a simple matter to set your digital delay to the appropriate delay time.

Creating echo with a digital delay unit is another matter. As I said earlier, an echo has a distinct frequency curve of its own. Because a digital delay is close to flat in its frequency response, digital delay makes very unnatural-sounding echoes. Unnaturalness definitely has its place in today's music. But to synthesize a natural ambient environ-

Like the Space Echo, Roland's Chorus Echo used a continuous loop of tape to create delay effects. Today's digital delays have supplanted these and other tape echoes.

ment with a digital delay, one needs a good ear, a good understanding of the relation between delay time and room size, and a good idea of what frequencies are boosted and attenuated in various environments. A basic formula for calculating the length of delay in relation to the distance of the far wall in the room, which the echo is supposedly bouncing off of, works as follows: On the basis that sound travels at 1,100 feet per second (that is, per 1,000ms) we can divide 1,000ms by 1,100 feet, which gives us .91 ms/ft. So if you multiply the distance in feet by .91, you'll have the amount of time in milliseconds that it takes the sound to reach the far wall. It will take the same amount of time for the sound waves to return to you, so multiply this figure by two to determine the echo setting.

In rooms with carpeting and upholstered furniture, the echo, if any, will be lower in amplitude and will have very little high-frequency content. Rooms with bare wood floors and walls will have more echo and more highs. Other things

The Roland SDE-2500 is a programmable digital delay, with presets that can be recalled via MIDI.

being equal, the resonant frequency of a space (the pitch at which standing waves tend to reinforce themselves) is lower in a larger room and higher in a smaller one. For this reason, a large wood and concrete gymnasium will have a boosted low-mid and midrange curve with slightly attenuated high frequencies.

What this means is that to synthesize a natural echo, equalization must be used. Many digital delay units have high-frequency rolloff settings but these are limited in their ability to create a natural echo. With natural echo, which has more than one echo in the room sound, each additional echo has fewer highs than the one before it. To synthesize these types of ambience successfully, you'll need a mixer. If you are using a keyboard mixer, try returning the output of your delay unit to an unused channel on the mixer. Turn the mix control on your delay unit to the 'delay only' setting

and use the equalizer in the echo return channel to contour the frequency spectrum of the delay. Use an echo send from the echo return channel as your feedback control, sending part of the already delayed signal back to the delay on the same echo send channel that the direct keyboard signal is going out on. With this hookup, each additional repetition will have less high-frequency content than the one before. A spiraling effect can be created by adding highs instead, but be careful: You can easily get serious feedback this way, as with any feedback loop.

Whether you're using echo, delay, or any other time-related effect, balance is the key to realism. When trying to synthesize a natural ambience, keep in mind that the echo is never louder than the direct signal. If your keyboard mixer is stereo and your stage setup is too, try panning different instruments left or right and their echo and delay returns to the opposite side. This can best be achieved on a mixer that has two different effects sends, and only if you have two different echo or delay units. If you've got the gear, try setting the delay time of each unit differently. If you are returning your echoes into mixer channels, try this: Send one feeds delay one, send two feeds delay two; when you return delay one into a channel, pan it to the left, return delay two and pan it right; send some of delay one to delay two via send two; send some of delay two back to delay one via send one. This makes for a great ping-ponging effect.

All this boils down to fattening up the sound of your keyboards. Some of the newer MIDI delay units have presets so you can recall you favorite echo and delay patches as well as changing delay patches to go with program changes on your MIDI synthesizer. This allows you to do things like getting a standard chorusing effect on your Rhodes patch and then instantly switching to a repeating quarter-note echo for the solo synth patch.

By Bobby Nathan

REVERB

November 1985

The discrete reflections of a sound heard in echo are important in establishing ambience, but they're only half the story. In a real auditorium, the multitude of reflections quickly blur together into a continuous wash called reverberation.

The first reverberation devices used in recording studios were sealed rooms with highly reflective walls, a speaker at one end, and a microphone at the other. Building such a chamber costs money! Plate reverbs, in which the sound was driven by a transducer into a large metal plate, were less bulky, but they were still beyond the reach of the average musician. Spring reverbs are both portable and affordable, but they tend to color the sound, and are not often used in studios. Today's digital reverbs simulate the action of reflective walls using mathematical algorithms.

Simply patching a reverb unit between your synthesizer and the tape deck won't necessarily give you the realistic coloration you want. If you think for a moment, you'll see why. When you play a note in a real room, it takes some time for the sound to travel to the far wall and bounce back to your ear. Sound that hits the far wall and then the side wall or ceiling before returning takes a bit longer (see Figure 1). As multiple echoes build up, they turn into reverberation. But the first echo occurs after some slight time delay, and it is not smeared by reverberation but quite distinct.

This first sharp echo in a reverberant sound is what I mean when I use the term "pre-delay." Pre-delay is essential to natural ambience. If you have been using reverb from a guitar amp or even a keyboard mixer, you've probably noticed that it doesn't really create a natural ambient sound. In a natural environment you first have the direct signal. Then comes what is called the first early reflection—the sound of the direct signal bouncing back off the opposite wall. In most natural environments there will be second and third early reflections as well. The difference between these and the dry sound is not only the delay time but the altered frequency response. This depends on the hardness of the surface that the sound is reflecting off of, but in general there will be fewer high frequencies in a reflection than in the dry sound.

After the early reflections come many shorter echoes tapering in their envelope, and finally there is reverb (see Figure 2). Reverb consists of so many finite echoes so densely packed that it is impossible for the human ear to distinguish between them.

There are environments where reverb is not preceded by any perceptible pre-delay. An example of this would be your bathroom. It's a small room, and the reverb decay time (the time it takes for the reverb to die out) is short. In a bathroom, the midrange frequencies of the direct signal are retained in the reverb and therefore have a longer decay time. This decay time factor gives a bathroom a definite mid-range quality. Our ear can recognize this, and most of us can identify a bathroom sound when we hear it. In a concert hall, on the other hand, there is a long pre-delay before the beginning of the reverberant sound. The decay time is longest for the low frequencies. Knowing what frequencies are boosted and cut in different environments is essential to anybody who wants to be good at synthesizing reverb.

Another parameter you will want to consider when synthesizing reverb is presence, which is the relative loudness of the dry signal as compared to the reverberations. If the reverb is fully as loud as the dry signal, you will seem to be listening from the other end of the auditorium, while a strong dry signal with a low reverb level will make it seem that you are onstage—perhaps with your head inside the piano.

Many of the newer digital reverb units have a pre-delay section that precedes the reverb section. By delaying the time before the reverb starts, they simulate the early reflections. Some of the other controls, such as the rolloff section, will help contour the frequency response of the reverb's decay. Rolling off certain higher frequencies will change the apparent decay time.

To synthesize a more natural-sounding reverb, though, you're going to need a separate delay unit to feed your reverb chamber. When using a separate delay to simulate the early reflections, a careful use of feedback, as well as equalization in the feedback loop, will help make the reverb more natural. This system will come close, but with a single delay you cannot actually achieve the distinct differences in symmetrical timing of the early reflections.

Nevertheless, the cost of most professional digital reverbs with excellent pre-delay capability is well above what most musicians would care to spend.

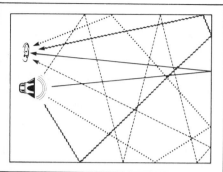

They average in the $10,000 price range. This is not to say that good reverb can't be created with lower-priced digital reverbs in the $1,000 range. In the studio, with careful adjustment, just about any reverb unit on the market can yield great effects.

Delaying the input to the reverb can add clarity to an instrument while giving it depth, whereas just adding reverb by itself may only muddy the sound. The trick is not to add the same amount of pre-delay to all the instruments in a mix. You may have only one reverb chamber, but if you delay each instrument differently before you send it to the chamber, each instrument will have more of its own dimension. Be sure to set the delay unit to delay only, and combine the reverb's output with the dry signal.

Having several different delays and reverbs will yield even more clarity and depth. In live performance, you can send some instruments to the delay only and others to the reverb only. If you send the same instrument to both effects simultaneously it can take something away from the whole mix, but it can be done if you do it carefully. If you have enough channels on your mixer, try putting an instrument into two channels and equalize them differently. Then feed one channel direct to the output mix and the other, heavily EQ'd, to the reverb chamber. This technique is called pre-chamber equalization.

Most mixers have at least two sends. If you add more effects they will have to be assigned to a specific instrument and patched before that instrument enters the mixer. Some mixers have effects loops on every channel, allowing patching at that point.

Use the decay of your reverb unit to suit different instruments. For a bass sound, stay away from long reverb decay times. With thin sounds and primarily high-pitched sounds, long reverb times can be most unpleasant for the listener. In general, if you would like to use a long reverb decay time, use a

Figure 1. Sound bounces around a room in many different directions. Some of the paths are longer than others, causing the echoes to reach the listener at different times.

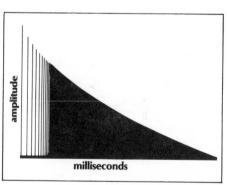

Figure 2. Natural reverberation. The first echoes to reach our ears are known as "early reflections," and are followed by a wash of overlapping echoes which gradually decay in level.

45

decent amount of pre-delay. This is especially true with fast passages. Otherwise, the notes may tend to melt into one another.

With digital reverbs that have a separate decay rate for low and mid-range frequencies, setting the decay times too far apart will give a less natural effect. Set them both to approximately the same length and then nudge one or the other just a bit to give the room a characteristic.

By Bobby Nathan

COMPRESSION

December 1985

Compression was introduced in the pre-rock and roll days to help recording engineers cope with the problems of recording live music. Because the volume of a symphony orchestra could easily exceed 100dB while tape could only handle around 75dB of dynamic range, an engineer had to be awfully quick at the faders (his keyboard) or be lucky enough to have a compressor and know how to use it.

It should be easy for synthesists to understand what a compressor does, since it's basically a VCA. A compressor's VCA, however, reacts only when a certain input level, or threshold, is reached. When the input level reaches the threshold, which is adjustable on the compressor, the VCA starts to reduce its own output level, continuing the reduction for as long as the input signal exceeds the threshold. An adjustable ratio control determines the amount by which the signal is decreased. The ratio in question is the amount of input signal in excess of the threshold to the amount of output signal in excess of the threshold. Let's say the threshold is set at 50dB. If an input signal suddenly lurches to 60dB, or 10dB greater than the threshold, and the ratio is set to 2:1, the VCA will restrict its output level to 55dB, 5dB above the threshold (see Figure 2).

The threshold control is a good place to start adjusting your comp/limiter. For instance, if you want to soften the peaks of an acoustic piano, play your loudest passages and set the threshold to react only to those high levels. Check the setting by playing softer passages, making sure the threshold indicator (usually an LED) isn't being triggered. If it is flickering, your threshold is too low and you'll be compressing the whole program

rather than just the peaks. Next you have to find a good compression ratio. Notice that when the ratio is 1:1, nothing audible happens to the program. If you turn the ratio up to 2:1, you should hear the compressor working slightly when the input is above the threshold.

In the case of a solo synth you might take an entirely different approach, flattening out its overall dynamic response. This allows its overall volume in the mix to be greater, since incidental peaks won't stick out so much. A solo instrument should be loud and dramatic, but not so undynamic or dominating that it's offensive. Instead of affecting only the peaks, we want to compress the synth's overall dynamic range into a narrow span. The threshold should be set so that almost all of the notes played are above it. A higher ratio, say 4:1, will keep the dynamic range under control.

In general, ratios between 2:1 and 6:1 are effective for compression. Higher ratios, especially above 10:1, are no longer considered compression—at these extremes you've stepped over the line into limiting. Limiting is best defined in relation to compression. A compressor, as we've already seen, is a VCA whose output gain decreases as its input level increases. A limiter is a compressor whose output level never exceeds a set value, regardless of the input level (see Figure 3). Knowing whether to use compression or limiting is a matter of taste. Percussive sounds, either from a synthesizer or from an acoustic instrument such as a piano, sometimes create harsh peaks that can be removed entirely using a limiter. On the other hand, they may just need the gentler effect of a compressor, as in our example above. The better comp/limiters have adjustable attack and release times that allow you to tailor their operation to suit situations like this. If your unit doesn't have these controls, you'll just have to experiment with different threshold and ratio settings. But beware: If you set the threshold too low, you'll squash the percussive quality of the initial attack (although you may come up with some interesting effects).

Besides threshold and ratio controls, most comp/limiters have an independent output gain pot. This function is more than incidental; if you've reduced the input signal strength by setting a low threshold or a high ratio, you'll have to bring it back up at the output. This control can add a lot of noise, however, if it's used improperly. If the instrument itself

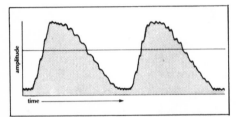

Figure 1. An unprocessed input signal.

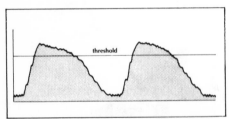

Figure 2. The same signal's output, with some mild compression.

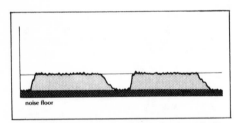

Figure 3. The output signal after hard limiting.

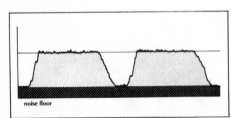

Figure 4. Amplifying a limited signal to compensate for gain losses will also raise the background noise level.

is particularly noisy, we're going to amplify that noise along with the useful part of the signal (see Figure 4). So the threshold needs to be set carefully, sufficiently above the noise level but below the general instrument output level. In tight situations, a noise gate placed before the comp/limiter will allow for lower threshold setting. It's best to get an optimal signal-to-noise ratio from the instrument itself, and then adjust threshold and gain settings. Whenever you have to amplify a signal excessively, you're going to add noise in the process.

A bass, either synthesized or electric, is one of the best sounds to work with in learning about compression effects. In the studio, it's common practice to record bass sounds with compression in order to add punch and definition. Experiment with high and low ratios, listening to the differences they make on the lower, as opposed to the higher, frequencies. Also, try different threshold levels. Note the settings that make the bass line really jump out at you, and also those that take the edge off of its attacks. After a little experimentation it will become clear how threshold and ratio settings interact. If your unit has attack and release settings, try a slower attack; this can help bring out bass lines too.

One side-effect of compression, known as "pumping" or "breathing," is usually a problem at higher ratio settings. Remember: the higher the ratio, the greater the gain reductions imposed by the compressor when the input level rises. As the input level falls, the compressor reduces its gain reduction. At high input levels and high compression ratios, these fluctuations may range over 10dB or more. Pumping is the sound produced by such drastic fluctuations in gain reduction. Furthermore, if the compressor is set for a slow release time, notes directly following a peak will also be gain-reduced, even though their level is below the threshold. The only way to reduce the pumping effect is to know your unit's capabilities and set it properly. Of course, you can use this effect to your advantage: With a high ratio, very fast attack, and a slow release time, you can create a sort of backwards effect that is most effective applied to crash cymbals.

Where's the best place in the signal path to insert a comp/limiter? If you only have one unit, it might be best to use it for all of your keyboards. In this case it's most common to place it between the

mixer output and the amplifier input. Keep in mind that in this configuration, the compressor comes after any equalizers and effects. Changes in the setting of these devices will, of course, affect the compressor. If you need compression only on one keyboard, patch it in

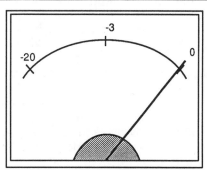

(A) When the input signal to the compressor is below the threshold the gain is normal.

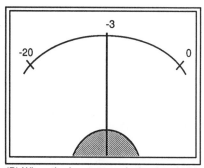

(B) When the input exceeds the threshold level, there is a reduction in gain. Here the meter indicates the gain is 3 dB below normal.

between the instrument and the mixer's line input. A pre-EQ insert point is preferable, if your mixer provides one. If you have a few instruments to compress and your console has more than one bus, assign them to the bus and patch the comp/limiter at the bus' patch/insert

An output level meter, such as this one, can show the amount of gain reduction taking place by showing the change in output level. These meters can be found on many compressor/limiters, either as a mechanical meter (pictured), or more commonly as an LED meter.

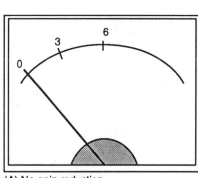

(A) No gain reduction.

(B) A gain reduction of 3 dB.

point. If the console lacks a patch/insert point, make sure that the bus isn't assigned to the main mix bus, and then send the bus output to the comp/limiter, returning its output at any unused mixer channel's line input. *Be sure not to assign that channel to the bus you're using for the comp/limiter—serious feedback will occur.* And if you have a stereo unit, you can use one half for a separate stage setting and use the other for your sound man's house feed. This way your sound man will love you, and your overall sound will be smoother as well.

The same 3 dB gain reduction. These meters, however, show the actual amount of gain reduction, rather than the change in output level. Modern gain reduction meters most commonly use LEDs rather than mechanical needles.

By Bobby Nathan

47

STEREO

March 1987

Much of the depth and "bigness" in the sound of modern records is achieved by the right-left separation of various components of the total sound—that is, stereo. When stereo was new, it was as simple as putting the bass and drums on one side, and the guitars and vocals on the other (get out your collection of 45 rpm singles, rock and roll fans). That didn't sound very natural, though, and over the years recording engineers and producers have worked out other ways of doing it. Many of these techniques are simple, very effective if used properly, and don't require a lot of equipment to put to use.

If you don't have access to a Harmonizer or a digital reverb unit don't worry. Just about any stomp box—delay, phaser, fuzz-tone, or whatever—can be applied in exactly, or nearly, the ways we'll be talking about, and none of these effects requires more than a few mixer channels and one or two effects sends. Remember, there's always room for a little more creativity in the studio, so if anything here sparks an idea, don't hesitate to try it out with whatever gear you own. You're bound to discover something useful.

Delay

One of the most popular ways to stereoize your synthesizer sound is to use a delay unit. Long before digital delays there were tape delays; which of the two you prefer is a matter of taste. Either way, the technique is the same. It's most effective if the dry (unaffected) synthesizer sound is panned to the right and the delayed signal is panned to the left, or vice-versa. Most delay units have a mix control to balance wet and dry versions of the signal. If you've panned the direct synth to one side, you can pan the delay output to the other and adjust the mix control to add the desired amount of delayed signal.

You want to start with a very short delay time. We're talking really short here, folks, so short you don't even notice that the sound is repeating (repeats become noticeable when their delay time is greater than 40 or 50 milliseconds). This is what gives the effect subtlety. You can make it more obvious by increasing the delay time.

The delay unit's feedback control can be useful for enhancing the stereo effect. By adding some feedback, you can make the delayed side of the stereo field linger a bit longer, which gives a feeling of movement from one side to the other. Using higher feedback settings, you can produce reverb-like effects.

Setting the delay time to produce a rhythm in time with the music can create a subtle but powerful effect. For instance, setting the delay to be just slightly shorter (faster) than a quarter-note will cause an anxious sort of feeling. A quarter-note delay slower than the tempo of the song will produce a sluggish effect. If you're in doubt about the exact timing of the quarter-notes for a given song, but you know its tempo in beats per minute (bpm), use this formula: 60,000/bpm=delay time (in milliseconds). Obviously, to get the time for an eighth-note delay, divide the answer for quarter-notes in half. For sixteenth-notes, divided by four, and so on.

Another interesting delay effect is what we in the studio biz call Bobby Nathan's World Famous Ping-Pong Echo—well, at least that's what I call it. To produce this effect you need a mixing console with two effects (or auxiliary) sends and two delay units (see the diagram). Don't use any feedback for now. Return your synthesizer to mixer channel 1, and pan it up the middle (center). Patch send #1 to delay unit 1, and send 2 to delay unit 2. Now comes the tricky stuff: Return delay #1 to mixer channel 2 and pan it to the left. Return delay 2 to channel 3 and pan it to the right. Set all three channel faders to the middle of their travel.

Start by setting both delay units to a quarter-note delay, although any delay time will do. Send a little of the synthesizer to delay 1 (that is, turn up channel 1's effects send 1). You should hear the synthesizer in the middle and the delay on your left. Now send a little of delay 1's output to delay 2 (turn up channel 2's send 2). You'll hear delay 2 coming in on the right. Finally, feed delay 2's output into delay 1 (*carefully* turn up channel 3's send 1).

In case you hadn't noticed, you've created a feedback loop here, with delay 1 returning to itself after being delayed by delay 2—that's why it's important not to use the units' own feedback circuits, or at least to be careful if you do. If you've set it up right, you should hear the synthesizer delay ping-ponging back and forth whenever you play it. Try some staccato notes and adjust the send and return levels until the effect is audible and balanced on both sides. Be extra careful setting the sends, though, because runaway feedback can damage your speakers as well as your hearing.

A useful variation on this technique is to use different delay times for the two units. Try setting one for a quarter-note delay, and the other for an eighth-note.

pet? Go to it, electronic keyboard players.

Flange, Phase, And Chorus

Monaural flanger, phasers, and choruses can all be stereoized in the same manner as delays and pitch shifters: Dry synth to one side or up the

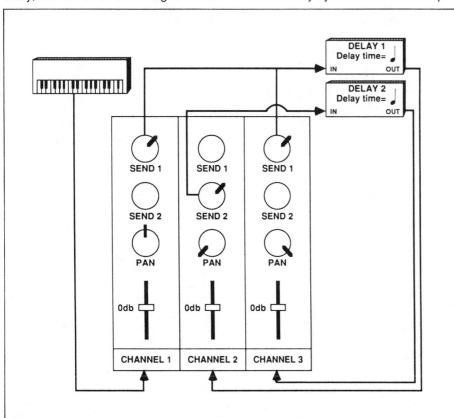

The ping-pong echo effect: The synthesizer feeds the first delay unit via send 1. The delayed synth signal is heard on the left side (channel 2) and simultaneously sent to the second delay unit via send 2. The output of delay 2 is heard on the right, and feeds back into delay 1. The synthesizer, originally heard in the center of the stereo field, bounces back and forth with each repeat. The send level settings are critical to avoid runaway feedback, and to balance the effect on either side.

Pitch-Shifting

A very popular stereo effect is to pan your synthesizer to one side and run it through a pitch shifter (using either a Y-cable or a send from your mixer) set to either 1.01 or .99—a very small amount of pitch shift, in any case—on the other. Again, if the pitch shifter (also called a Harmonizer) has a wet/dry mix control, set this to your own taste. The effect is a bit like that of a chorus unit.

A variation on this is to pan the dry synthesizer in the middle, and use two Harmonizers, one on the left set at .99 and one on the right at 1.01. It's not three-part harmony (although you can set the Harmonizers that way if you're really outside), but it sure fattens things up. You can use this technique to create an out-of-tune honky-tonk sound by using settings farther away from 1.0. Ever hear a honky-tonk guitar or trum-

middle, effected signals to the other or, if the effect has two outputs, both sides. The widest effects, generally, are produced by setting the effect unit's mix control fully in the wet position.

Reverb

When using reverb, it is customary to pan the direct synthesizer sound up the middle, and pan the stereo reverb returns hard left and right, respectively. If you have a spare reverb unit to dedicate to a single synthesizer, try this effect instead: Pan the dry signal hard left, and pan both the left and right returns from the reverb to the right (or just use the one reverb return). This gives a sense of motion to your synthesizer, and in a busy mix can give more clarity to that particular instrument.

Using pre-delay with the above effect (if your reverb unit has it, or by patching a delay before the reverb) is most effective in making the synthesizer appear to travel across a larger space. Most modern digital reverb units have pre-delay built in. Try setting the pre-delay for a quarter-, eighth-, or sixteenth-note delay, so that it's in time with the tempo of the song.

Auto-Panning

Automatic panning was very near and dear to the hearts of all of us Fender Rhodes suitcase-model players. It was called vibrato, and sometime tremolo, but one thing it definitely was was stereo. The Rhodes sound ping-ponged between the front and back of the suitcase speaker cabinet, and we dug it. This same effect can be achieved with an auto-panner. For this effect, patch the output of the synthesizer directly into the auto-panner, and pan the left and right outputs of the device accordingly. Presto, it's 1975 all over again.

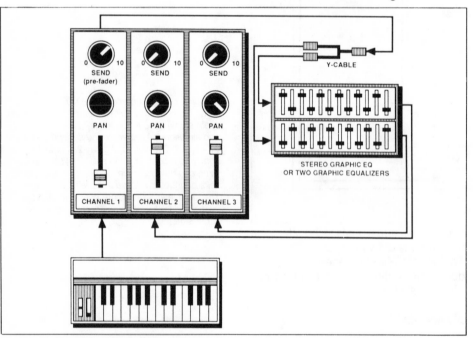

A do-it-yourself stereo comb filter for "stereoizing" any mono source. The synthesizer's direct signal is not heard, but is sent to two equalizers with opposite boost and cut patterns. Their outputs are then panned to opposite mixer outputs, and the result is a simulated stereo synthesizer.

Most auto-panners have an internal LFP that, try as you may, you never can match to the tempo of your tune. Instead use the auto-trigger function, if there is one. You can send a quarter-note click from your drum machine (or eighth-note, sixteenth-note, or whatever—even triplets) to the unit's trigger input. You can even feed a live drummer's kick or snare to this input, if you want to pull this off live. Now the auto-panner will pan from right to left (or vice-versa) perfectly in time with your tune. Some auto panners even have a counter function that will pan every four triggers.

Those of you who have an old modu-

lar synthesizer collecting dust in the closet can produce auto-pan effects if the instrument has two VCAs. Just route the audio signal into both, modulate the amplitude of one by a low-frequency sine wave, and modulate the other by an inverted version of the same sine wave. Congratulations! For the price of a little dusting, you've saved yourself the cost of an auto-pan box.

Equalizers

The technique of using an equalizer to widen mono sounds has been around for quite a while. A lot of early monaural records have been converted into stereo using a comb filter, which is a specialized kind of equalizer. This was especially true on some of the early Beatles albums that were mixed only to mono.

You can make your own comb filter with the aid of a stereo EQ unit, or two mono equalizers (see diagram). A stereo graphic with ten or more bands for each side is ideal, but you can approximate the effect with just about anything. On one side of the EQ, boost every other slider to the maximum amount of gain, and cut the rest to the minimum. Set the sliders the other way on the other side, with every other slider at the minimum, and the others maxed out. Next, multiplying your synthesizer's output using a Y-cord, two pre-fader effect sends from your mixer, or an effect send and an insert point on your mixer, send the synth to both the right and left inputs of the stereo EQ. Bring up the EQ outputs on two channels of your mixer and pan them opposite each other. The effect is subtle but definite: The synthesizer will sound more animated and spacious.

The effect can be useful, if less pronounced, if you only use one equalizer and pan it opposite the synth's dry signal. You can also experiment with parametric equalizers; even though they will not produce comb filtering, you can get interesting frequency splits. For example, if you boost the low frequencies (and perhaps cut the highs) on the left channel and boost the high frequencies (while cutting the lows) on the right, your synthesizer will give a vague impression of moving from left to right as you play up the keyboard (see diagram).

MIDI Applications

Here's one that anyone with two MIDI synths can try—no fuss, no muss,

50

no fancy gear. Just MIDI them up, pick two similar patches, maybe two brass sounds, pan them right and left, and behold. If you happen to have two of the same synthesizer, load the same patch into both, give them opposite panning, and set the envelope of one with a slightly longer release time, or perhaps a slower attack time. Simply using different envelope settings with this setup will produce a most interesting stereo effect.

With MIDI, my favorite stereo combos are percussive sounds teamed with slow-attack/long-release sounds—Rhodes and strings, acoustic guitars and voices, Clavinet and brass. The combinations, as you know, are endless: sampled sounds with synthesized sounds, digital with analog, peanut butter with mayo, you name it.

Whenever you use a stereo effect for a recording, center the panning and listen to the effect in mono. In the studio, stereo effects are always checked in mono, often by pushing the mono button on the console, and preferably while listening through a single Auratone speaker (the ones with the car radio sound). If what sounded so great in stereo still sounds great in mono, you're on easy street. If a certain part of the frequency spectrum, usually the bass, seems to be missing or is exaggerated, you have phase problems and should consider tweaking the various parameters of the effect, especially if your recording might be broadcast on AM radio someday. If the effect sounds stronger in mono, try panning your left and right channels at nine o'clock and three o'clock, or eleven o'clock and three o'clock, or thereabouts. That usually clears up the problem without messing up the stereo effect.

By Bobby Nathan

NOISE GATES

December 1986

Ahhh, the bliss of a totally quiet recording. It's a nice concept, but electronic keyboard outputs are seldom free of hiss: hiss that is equalized into more hiss, and then amplified into still more. Electronic keyboardists who cut their chops during the '70s were well aware of the hiss from their Rhodes pianos and Hohner Clavinets, and when we added those phasers, flangers, and chorus units, it became—let's face it—intoler-

able. Yet on records by our favorite players, that hiss was absent, or at least reduced to a reasonable level. We have our recording engineers to thank for that. You know—the folks who fight that never-ending battle against hiss, clicks, pops, and buzzes.

How did they do it? Often with a nifty little signal processor called a noise gate. These devices are so much a part of the modern recording process that most major recording consoles include one with every channel. A noise gate is a different beast from a noise reduction unit. While most noise reduction processes actually alter the signal you feed them, a gate simply blocks out hiss whenever your instrument isn't playing.

The gate is like a drawbridge for the audio signal presented at its input. It stays closed—that is, the drawbridge is down so that boats can't get past it—until the signal reaches a predetermined level. When that level is present, the gate opens and the signal is allowed to pass. Since the noise in an instrument's output is normally much softer than the sound of the instrument itself, it's usually a simple matter to set the gate to shut out the noise until the instrument plays a note, at which point the higher signal level pushes it open. (Of course, while the gate is open, the signal passes through noise and all; often, though, the instrument's own sound is loud enough to mask the noise.)

Those who spend more time onstage than in the studio might remember MXR's Noise Gate/Line Amplifier. This box provided a solution to the hiss produced by the Rhodes and Clavinet. It had only a single knob called "threshold." The threshold knob, as you may have guessed, sets the input level that will open the gate. For example, if the threshold is set for 1dB, the gate will not open until the instrument level reaches 1dB. As long as the sound level stays above the 1dB threshold, the gate will remain open. If the noise you're trying to get rid of is loud relative to the instrument's sound, the threshold must be set pretty high. If the instrument puts out less noise, the threshold can be lower. The threshold should be set as low as possible, because otherwise the gate may not open until your instrument's sound is well into its attack (particularly if that attack is slow, as it would be in a string patch).

All of you true synth people know how useless a synthesizer is without any envelope controls. Well, in the one-knob

51

noise gate design, the envelope was preset. The envelope section of the gate takes effect whenever the input level is below the threshold. The envelope control most commonly found on noise gates is release time. This determines how fast the gate's output will taper off after the input falls below the threshold. The release should be slow for a ballad, or any time when piano-like chords are likely to be allowed to die away, so that your instrument's decay isn't cut off abruptly when it reaches the threshold.

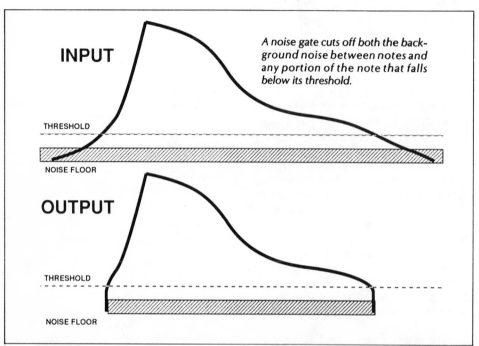

A noise gate cuts off both the background noise between notes and any portion of the note that falls below its threshold.

The black lines in these graphs represent the signal entering and leaving a noise gate. When listening to the input, we hear both the complete signal and the noise floor; when listening to the output, we hear only what's above the threshold level.

At the other extreme, a funky Clavinet riff requires a lightning-fast release setting, so that the gate will close between those staccato riffs. If the gate isn't fast enough, the hiss you're trying to gate out may actually be brought to the listener's attention. This is due to the sound of hiss turning on and off, an effect appropriately called breathing. In order to avoid breathing, it is helpful to reduce the player's dynamics so that they don't confuse the gate with constant level transitions. A compressor/limiter is a good tool for evening out the dynamics before the signal enters the noise gate.

An attenuation control can also help overcome the breathing effect. It determines how much the input is attenuated when the gate is closed—that is, the gate need not shut all the way, all the time. By setting the attenuation to an amount below the maximum—say, around 10dB or so—the hiss will still be there, although it will be reduced. Paradoxically, since the overall noise level

remains more constant (rather than full-on when the gate is open, full-off when it is closed), it becomes less noticeable.

Some attack transients may cause the gate to open with an audible pop, and some instruments may produce inconsistent attack levels, causing the gate to open sporadically. Such problems can be overcome by varying the gate's attack time so that its envelope is optimized for any given input. The attack time control can also be used to contour a sound. For example, you can take a harsh, heavy attack (such as a Rhodes piano sound) and give it the softer rise of a violin. Slower attacks also work well when gating the reverb assigned to your keyboards. In fact, gates are very much a part of today's reverb effects. For instance, if you put a lot of reverb on a percussive keyboard part, route the reverb through a gate, and then set the gate's release to be short and the attenuation at full tilt, you can create an explosive effect very much like the famous Phil Collins snare drum sound.

Once you join the Hiss Patrol, you'll find unwanted noise even in unlikely places. Some digital keyboards in particular generate an alarming amount of hiss. Some even have noise gates built into their output stages. They are set for slower release time, though, and breathing can again be a problem, so you still need an external gate. Using two noise gates in series isn't such a bad idea either. Although it may seem a little extravagant, sometimes the envelope of even the fastest release may be too slow. By adding a second gate, you may be able to tailor the envelope more closely to that of the original sound.

Expansion

Valley People was one of the first manufacturers to market a professional noise gate, the Kepex. The name Kepex is short for the keyable programmable expander. A noise gate can be used as dynamic range expander, since the ratio control found on most gates defines a continuum from expansion to gating. Low ratios such as 1:2 and 1:4, for example, are in the range of expansion. Since the gate starts out partially open, the output signal remains at a relatively high level; but it's even higher when a peak at the input tells the gate to open completely. High ratios such as 1:10 and above are considered gating, because the gate begins completely closed, opens in response to a peak, and closes

52

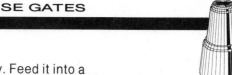

again. If you set the controls properly, the expansion effect widens the dynamic range of the input, so that soft passages or events are softer relative to loud ones.

Tightening An Ensemble

The key input function can help you create a variety of interesting effects, particularly when using high ratios—that is, when you're gating. The key input allows the gate to track the dynamic envelope of whatever material you feed into it, imposing that envelope on the audio input to the gate. This is most commonly used for tightening up an ensemble performance. If you have three tracks of horns all doubling the same line, they may not begin and end the phrase at the same time. The two most ragged tracks are fed to separate gates, and the best track is fed to their key inputs. (The gates must be set to external key mode in order to see the key input.) Of course, the best track is also returned to the console, as are the outputs of the two gates—otherwise, we wouldn't be able to hear our horn section. Now, when the players on the first track begin, the gates open, and when they stop, the gates close. This brings the envelopes of all three tracks together for a tighter-sounding ensemble.

Composite Sounds

The example above can easily be used when recording multiple MIDI tracks doubling the same line. If, for instance, you're using brass sounds from different instruments to make one composite brass sound, it's a lot faster and easier to use one signal to gate the others rather than re-program all the envelopes. If you record each instrument on a separate track, the multiple enveloping can be fixed in the mix. It's in a mixdown situation that most sloppy envelopes are discovered anyway.

Another useful function of the key input is to add liveliness to percussion sounds. The key track, in this case, is a rather dead and unexciting snare drum. We're going to add some excitement by mixing in white noise to lengthen the drum's original envelope. We get the white noise from a synthesizer. (You do still have that Minimoog or ARP 2600 in a closet somewhere, don't you?) Make sure the synth is sending out a steady stream of white noise—try the old pencil-wedging-down-the-key trick, or open

the VFC and VCA fully. Feed it into a noise gate, set the gate to external key mode, and patch the snare track into the key input. Now whenever the snare sounds, the gate will open and white noise will be added to the snare. Set the gate's release time so that the white noise trails off a tad longer than the original snare sound. By adjusting the attack time, you can get the crack of the snare drum without any white noise, and then have the noise come in and trail off later. Add a little reverb, and it's deadly!

A similar setup can be used to add tonality to a tom-tom. Instead of white noise, use a particular pitch, or even a chord, from your synth. Again, you set the gate's envelope controls as your imagination dictates. A vocoder does something similar, but in a more elaborate way. Don't expect a gate to follow the formants and resonances of a vocal track, though. Leave that to a vocoder. The gate only responds to changes in amplitude.

Envelope Mapping

You can also use a gate's key input for arpeggiation effects by using a steady hi-hat rhythm to key the bass line or chordal pads in a song. You'll most likely have to double up two or more gates to really tighten the keyed envelopes in the application. Background vocals can follow the envelope of your Rhodes part during a ballad, if you want to get really far out. If you have an idea, try it! There are no rules in the keyable programmable expander zone.

Quieter Samples

You say you have a sampler instead of a synthesizer? Well, if you're not using a noise gate before the audio input of your sampler, you're missing the trick! When sampling percussive sounds with envelopes that decay naturally, it is important to gate them so that you're not just sampling hiss after the sound dies away. Truncating the end of a hissy percussion sample will only make the hiss more apparent. Set the gate's release to approximate the original sound's envelope. Hiss coming from the audio source should be as inaudible as possible before you sample. If you're planning to loop a sample, gating is not as critical; but I recommend having a gate normalled and ready for action.

By Bobby Nathan

53

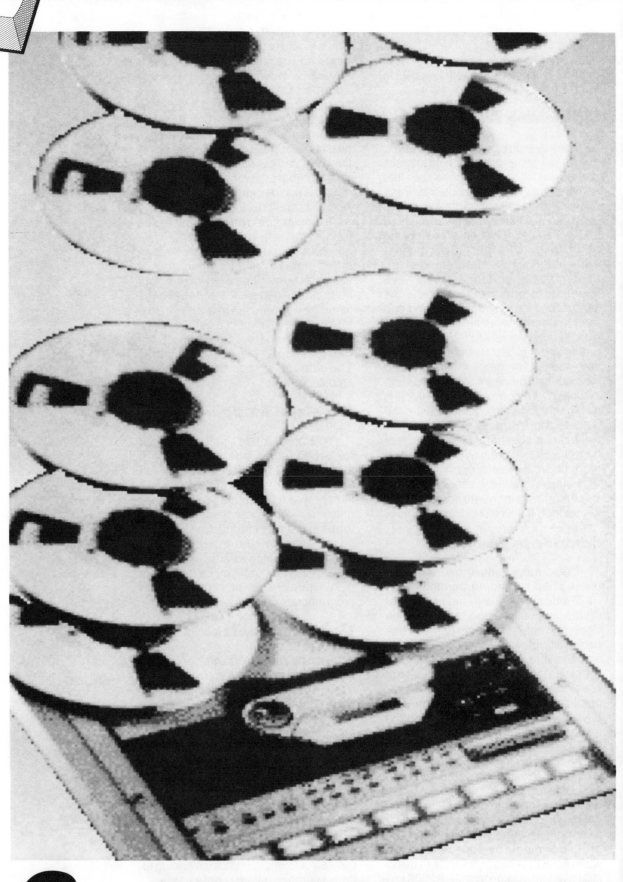

3 SYNCHRONIZATION

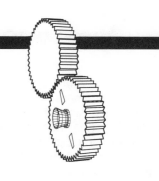

SECRETS OF SYNCING

June 1986

Synchronizing sequencers and drum machines to each other, to tape, and to film is one of those mind-boggling topics that has the power to send many musicians, and even some highly trained technicians, running from the room in screaming fits. The mere mention of terms like FSK, SMPTE, and PPQ can make eyes cross and sweat break out on the forehead, but if you plan on taking advantage of your sequencer and/or drum machine's ability to sync to external gear, sooner or later you'll have to get your head around the concepts of synchronization. By the time you get done with this article, you'll be well on your way to understanding those concepts.

Getting musicians in an ensemble, whether it be a small chamber group or a 100-piece orchestra, to play in time with one another is a problem we're all familiar with. At the heart of it is that each player interprets tempo differently. How different the individual fluctuations in tempo are determines whether a performance is tight or loose. When you hook together electronic gadgets and expect them to play in time with one another, you face the exact same problem, since gear from different manufacturers more often than not interprets tempo differently. Unfortunately, getting different equipment to synchronize isn't a matter that can be fixed by rehearsal. It requires the right outboard gear and the knowledge of how to use it to get the right feel from your music.

Basics

Perform this simple test: Get two stop watches (either digital or spring-driven will do), and start them at the same time. Watch the second hands tick. Unless you can arrange for some major divine intervention, it won't be too long before they get out of sync, even if you somehow managed to get them both to start at the exact same nanosecond.

Why is this relevant? The same problem appears when you try to sync up two or more electronic devices. Unless they are both driven from the same clock (which usually means that the internal clock of one device is used as the mas-

ter, while the second device is slaved to the first), there's no way that they will stay synchronized. Without proper syncing connections, even if you start a sequencer and a drum machine at the same instant, one of them will quickly get ahead of the other. If your tune is long enough, you'll find the drum machine playing the chorus while the sequencer is churning out the verse—a situation only a true anarchist could get into.

Sequencers, drum machines, and arppegiators all derive their tempo from electronic clocks. Naturally, there are lots of different kinds of clocks—you didn't think the manufacturers would want to make this stuff too easy, did you? The plot thickens even further when you get into syncing clock-driven devices to a signal on audio tape (not to mention film or video). Several questions

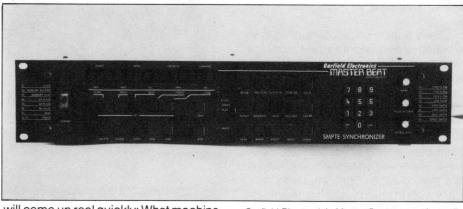

will come up real quickly: What machine do you use as the master and what do you use as the slave? What type of synchronization signals are they sending and expecting to receive? Do you need to turn one or both on before starting the tape sync signal? What level should you record the sync tone at? We couldn't hope to answer all these in the space we have available. What we will try to show you below are some rules of thumb, which when combined with a hefty dose of common sense and an owner's manual or two should get you through the trials and tribulations of syncing.

Syncing Device To Device

Clock-driven devices, whether they are free-standing, computer-based, or resident in an instrument, usually feature a jack for connecting them to some external clock. This jack (which might be anything from a 1/4" phone jack to a 5-pin DIN connector) could be labelled EXT CLOCK, CLOCK IN, or SYNC; you'll have to refer to your owner's manual to

Garfield Electronic's Master Beat can perform all the functions of the Roland SBX-80 (page 10), as well as other sync-related functions.

55

know for sure which is which on your particular instrument.

Which instrument you use as the master clock (the one that drives all the others connected to it) will depend on the particular situation. For example, you might have a sequencer that will record tempo changes and a drum machine that won't. If the tune you're working on requires a lot of rubato passages, you can use the sequencer as the master, thereby getting the drum machine to follow along as the tempo speeds up and slows down. Likewise, if you have a synthesizer with an arpeggiator in it that doesn't send a clock signal out, but will accept a clock signal in, you will have to use the arpeggiator as the slave. Again, common sense will serve you well in these situations.

PPQ Clocks

Early analog sequencers used low-frequency oscillators as their clocks. It was a simple matter to sync up multiple analog sequencers within a modular setup. All you needed to do was use a single LFO as the only clock. When the first digital sequencers came along, they borrowed this LFO-as-clock scheme from their analog predecessors. However, where analog sequencers derived the note duration from what was typically a set of potentiometers, the digital sequencer assigned note duration by dividing each note into a number of steps. The more steps a note took, the longer its duration; fewer steps, shorter duration.

That's a pretty basic concept, but think about its ramifications. One manufacturer decides to assign 48 clock pulses to a quarter-note, another decides on 24 clock pulses per quarter-note (PPQ), and yet another thinks 192 clocks per quarter-note is better. Since they can't agree on a standard, they all go ahead with different PPQ schemes. This is no problem as long as all your gear is made by Mondophlegm Unlimited. But what happens when you try to connect a Mondophlegm Unlimited sequencer to a drum machine made by Crunchy Frogs, Inc.? Chaos at best. Imagine driving a 24 PPQ device with a clock signal from a 192 PPQ system. One would be finished playing the tune before the other even got finished with the first verse!

This is exactly the situation we have with drum machines and sequencers that use pulse-per-quarter-note clocks.

Roland and Sequential use a 24 PPQ clock, Korg devices run on 48 PPQ, Linn products run at 24, 48, or 96 PPQ (some LM-1s feature a variable clock), Oberheim uses 96 PPQ, Fairlight favors a high-resolution 384 PPQ, and the PPG Wave offers a variable clock that includes a 64 PPQ resolution (unusual because it's not evenly divisible by both three and four).

To make matters just a bit more confusing, Roland and Korg both decided to use 5-pin DIN plugs for their clocking signals. That might lead you to think they were compatible, but they aren't.

The first professionally-popular digital drum machine, the Linn LM-1.

Roland's DIN sync is a 24 PPQ system, while Korg's is a 48 PPQ system. We should also warn that you shouldn't confuse a DIN sync connector with a MIDI plug. They look the same, but aren't.

Well, why not just hook a Roland device to a Korg device and program the Korg to play what it thinks are eighth-notes, but what you secretly know are quarter-notes? The two devices should now work just fine, right? Sorry, but we're not out of the woods yet. Roland boxes send (and expect to receive) a run/stop signal. All the other manufacturers use the clock signal itself to start and stop the synchronization. Roland gear only operates in the presence of an additional signal that tells it that it's okay to start running.

To interface devices that run on PPQ clocks, what you need to do is divide the fastest PPQ clock in the system so it will produce clocks of longer duration. To do that, you'll need a clock divider. These come in various shapes and sizes. There are several inexpensive units offered by companies like Garfield Electronics (the NanoDoc), and J.L. Cooper Electronics (the MicroSync).

MIDI Sync

MIDI clocks are fast becoming the standard in synchronization between sequencers, drum machines, arpeggiators, and outboard effects, if for no other reason than that there is an agreed-upon specification and one standard connector provided for the job no matter whose product it is. But of course, it's not a system without problems. For example, say you're using a sequencer with only MIDI in. How do you slave it to a drum machine and at the same time load the sequence in from a MIDI keyboard? You can't unless you use a MIDI merger device. And what if you want to connect a non-MIDI device to a device that only sends and receives MIDI clock? Again, you'll need some outboard gear—in this case, a conversion box like those made by Garfield, J.L. Cooper, Korg, Roland, and Fostex.

Many MIDI-equipped sequencers and drum machines are now being equipped to respond to Song Position Pointer, a function that allows you to start a sequence from someplace other than the beginning of a song.

Syncing To Tape

Somewhere down the long halls of synchronization, someone thought it would be fun to be able to sync up a sequencer or drum machine to a signal on audio tape. It's a great idea, for lots of different reasons. For example, you can record a drum part with a drum machine, add the bass and rhythm parts on separate tracks, and then go back and re-record the drum part, changing it so that it makes more sense with the new musical elements. By driving a drum machine from a sync tone on tape, you can even leave the drums off the tape. You gain back the tracks you would have lost to the drum signal, and you don't lose those snappy transients to tape degradation. The drum machine can be synced to the multi-track tape and played 'live' during mixdown. You can do the same thing with sequencing.

Of course, the other side of the coin is that you may not have enough mixer channels or outboard gear to be able to mix the live drum machine plus all the tape tracks. And what if you want to record the vocals dry and add reverb during the mix? If you only have one reverb unit, you may not like having to put the same reverb time on the vocals

56

as on the snare drum. Likewise, if you've only got one keyboard, driving it from a sequencer synced to the tape may limit you to only one tone color, which certainly isn't ideal.

The most obvious way to get a clock-driven device to sync to tape is to record its clock signal straight onto the tape. Sounds simple enough, but unfortunately, it doesn't always work. Many devices, such as E-mu drum machines, use a simple square-wave clock, and at slow tempos this tone can be so low in pitch that it won't record accurately on an analog tape recorder. This makes syncing to tape tricky at best. Syncing a square-wave pulse clock to tape works best at higher tempos.

FSK

One way of getting around this problem is a sync tone called Frequency Shift Keying (FSK). With FSK, an audio signal is recorded onto tape rather than a low-frequency square wave. The audio signal alternates between two pitches; in effect, it acts as if it is being frequency-modulated by a square wave. The pitches alternate at whatever the clock rate is set to. When a FSK tone is played back, the slave device 'hears' the alternations between the two pitches, translates these back into a clock pulse, and presto—the device is synced to tape.

Or is it? That depends on how well you managed to record the sync tones on tape. FSK is sensitive to record and playback levels, and tape dropout and noise can have a negative effect on its effectiveness. And a tape splice will make FSK useless. You should be prepared to play with getting your FSK tones on tape the right way. Another minor problem you might encounter is that a FSK sync track can't be sped up or slowed down too far before it will be rendered unreadable by the slave device. A pulse sync track, on the other hand, can be doubled in speed, or halved, and will still do its job.

And as with pulse clocks, not all FSK is created equal. Oberheim, Yamaha, and Roland use different audio frequencies as well as different clock rates, which means their FSK tones are only partially compatible with one another. Some Yamaha and Roland FSK will sync successfully, but because Roland starts with a higher pitch than Yamaha, speeding the tape up even slightly if it has a Roland sync tone, or slowing it down

slightly in the case of a Yamaha sync tone, can prevent a device by the other manufacturer from reading the sync tone. The LinnDrum and Linn LM-1 use different FSK systems, so here's a case where instruments from the same manufacturer won't work together. We've even heard that early Yamaha QX1 sequencers are not compatible with the new QX1s as far as syncing is concerned. When in doubt as to compatibilities, consult your manuals. When that doesn't work, call the manufacturer.

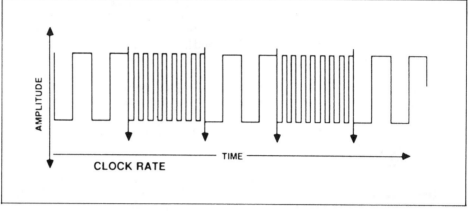

An FSK tone alternates between two set frequencies at a given clock rate.

Applications Tips For Recording Non-Digital Sync Tones

Many tunes don't require tempo changes. But what if you're working on one that does, and your drum machine or sequencer won't record tempo changes into its memory to execute on playback? Try performing the tempo changes live while recording the sync tone on tape. Then, when the sync track is played back, your machine will respond by changing tempo, just as if the tempo changes had been programmed.

Many pro studios always leave a buffer track between a sync track and any audio tracks, because of the possibility of bleed-through. It's nice to have this luxury, but if you're working on 8- or 4-track format, you won't be able to afford it. Still, if you plan on going into a pro studio, be sure to take this into account when you're making up your track assignments.

You should also take into account whether the instrument sends out another clock signal when it's being synced to the external clock signal coming off the tape. If it won't you'll have a tough time syncing, for example, a drum machine to tape while driving a sequencer from the drum machine at the same time.

What do you do when you want to drive two or three or five or ten machines from tape simultaneously? Go crazy and use up ten tracks for all the different tape sync signals? It's far more economical to get one of the FSK-to-whatever converter boxes out on the market, such as the Garfield Doctor Click 2.

Recording FSK or clock pulses onto tape should always be the first thing you do if you're going to be syncing to tape. The procedure is fairly simple:

(1) Run the FSK or pulse clock output of your device to the appropriate input on your mixer or tape recorder. If possible, bypass any noise reduction and EQ on the mixer, to minimize coloration of the signal.

(2) Adjust the record level. Remember, FSK is sensitive to levels, so this step is going to take some experimentation on your part. You may have to try recording at several different levels to get one that is right for the slave device to read.

(3) Punch into record mode and wait at least five seconds for the tape transport to stabilize.

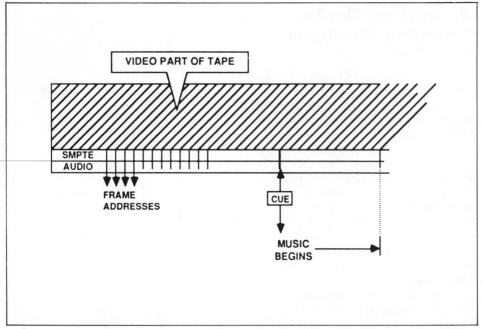

SMPTE time code is often recorded, or "striped," on a single audio track of a video tape. A Roland SBX-80, Garfield Master Beat, or other SMPTE-based device can be set to start when the tape reaches a pre-programmed cue point.

(4) Hit the play button on your device to record the sync tone onto tape. Remember that you can perform tempo changes manually as the tone is recorded to tape, if your sequencer or drum machine won't let you program the tempo changes you need.

(5) Put the device in external clock mode and feed it a signal from the tape track. Play the entire song through while listening closely, to verify that there is no hiccoughs in the rhythm.

Click Tracks

Back in the days when music was made by banging rocks together, people used metronome clicks and click tracks to keep a handle on tempo. Click tracks can be thought of as conductor tracks, which the player monitors while recording, but which are eliminated from the final mixdown for obvious reasons. There are any numbers of ways in which a click track can be produced. One is to simply play a rough version by hand of the song being recorded. You could outline the melody and certain key harmonies, making sure you keep the tempo exactly where you want it throughout. Or you could record something that sounded like a metronome click by setting up such a sound on a synth keyboard. You could use an LFO-generated click and modulate the LFO frequency with the voltage from a keyboard in order to produce varying tempos. Whatever method you use, the result is more or less the same: you get a track that you can use as a rhythmic guide throughout the piece.

Click tracks are rarely used to sync electronic instruments up to tape, but it has been known to happen. Devices like Roland's SBX-80, the Chroma Polaris, and Garfield's Doctor Click will allow you to translate a recorded click track into a synchronization signal.

Syncing To Film

Syncing sound to film has been a concern ever since the first talkie. Even today, after the godsend of SMPTE time code, it's still possible to hear bad examples of sound-to-film synchronization. Just think about how many times you've seen a film where the actors' mouths move before you hear the words they've spoken. Such goofs can be a lot of fun. Just imagine how you could mess with the minds of your friends at a dinner party by taking your TV's audio output, feeding it into a DDL, and putting a 250-millisecond delay on the entire soundtrack of whatever they decide to watch (claiming of course, to hear nothing wrong at all). All kidding aside, film is an exacting medium when it comes to time. Film is capable of repeating the same actions in exactly the same amount of time, every time. It's very important for film composers to be able to hit exact points of a film with music of an exact length.

There have been all kinds of methods for doing just that, ranging from the approximate to the precise. Click tracks in film work can be built around particular scenes that the composer wants to fill with music. With this method, the composer constructs a map that precisely locates all the actions of the film. Then the positions and lengths of these cues are used to plot a constant tempo for each section of music. The click track is assembled from these pre-calculated tempos. To speed this process along, people have come up with digital metronomes and complex reference books that tell a composer exactly how many measures of music at a specific tempo will equal a particular number of frames of film.

SMPTE

In 1967, The Society of Motion Picture and Television Engineers (SMPTE —pronounced *simptee*) came up with a timecode based on the 24-hour clock. The code is divided into hours, minutes, seconds, frames, and subframes. Since there are a number of different standard speeds for film and videotape, there are a number of different values for frames in SMPTE. Video uses "drop-frame" SMPTE, where each frame is 1/29.97 second. European Broadcast Units (EBUs) require a frame based on 50 cycles per second, so every frame is 1/25 second. The so-called standard SMPTE frame is 1/30 second.

SMPTE timecode can be used for a number of purposes. Pro studios use it to lock tape recorders together. This is done by recording SMPTE onto one track of each recorder. Their tape drives are then servo-locked to those timecode tracks. When one machine starts, the other starts as well, and they stay synchronized. The same trick can be done with a multi-track recorder and a videotape recorder. Again, SMPTE is recorded (or striped) onto both machines, and their tape drives are servo-locked to the code, keeping them synchronized. Don't however, think that you can just stripe SMPTE onto two tape machines and have them magically lock together. You'll need to have a device that will lock the motors together, and another device to read the code. Some semi-pro recorders are built to accept servo-locking signals without modification. Others require modification. The same holds true for pro video recorders. If you're interested in servo-locking your home VCR, we'd suggest checking with a manufacturer of SMPTE-locking gear and/or VCRs to see if such a modification can be made to your machine.

In addition to making life a little easier for film composers and letting pro studios put two 24-track machines together to get 46 tracks (you lose two to the SMPTE code), SMPTE allows you to do some heavy-duty synchronization between sequencers and drum machines. The one thing FSK and click-track systems don't allow for is starting a sequence at someplace other than the beginning. SMPTE allows you to begin anywhere, since it is always referenced to time. Of course, that kind of power ain't exactly cheap, and you'll need the right outboard gear to convert SMPTE to the various other sync formats your instruments will need to see. Devices like Roland's SBX-80, Friend Chip's SRC, Synchronous Technologies' SMPL Lock system, Fostex's 4050 autolocator, and Garfield's Master Beat enable you to convert SMPTE to other sync formats, including MIDI and PPQ clocks.

When converting to a MIDI format, these devices calculate the relationship between SMPTE time and musical measure numbers (the tempos and time signatures for each song must be entered into the translation device). By doing this, the sync device can tell the MIDI sequencer or drum machine to start and stop at given measure numbers. The catch is that the MIDI device(s) must have the Song Pointer feature—most new sequencers and drum machines implement this feature.

One main purpose of SMPTE sync is, of course, to enable you to sync to film. It makes life much easier for sound effects people who want to be able to hit all kinds of weird non-rhythmic visuals. Everything from boots clanking on metal flooring to multiple gunshots in a battle scene are made much simpler if the sound effects man can lock into and trigger off of SMPTE code. A couple of software companies are promising SMPTE compatibility for their sequencers. The E-mu Emulator II and SP-12 drum machine already read and write SMPTE. Look for more instruments and devices to include SMPTE hookups, as prices come down. It's definitely going to be making its way into the keyboard universe, though there is a new but related standard. . . .

This very important development is the introduction of MIDI time code. MTC's essentially a means of sending

SMPTE information through MIDI cables in a coded form. MTC can be used for syncing MIDI devices which are designed to generate or read the code. The greatest advantage of MTC (over the SMPTE/Song Pointer method) is that devices can be synchronized to start at any time and not just at the beginning of a bar—be sure that more and more devices will recognize MTC as time rolls on, so to speak.

Real World Problems

Most of the synthesizers in use today take advantage of microprocessors to do everything from tuning and recalling stored patch information to scanning the keyboard and responding to information coming in from external devices. One side effect of this is that each microprocessor has to do many different tasks. Unfortunately, a computer can only do one thing at a time, so decisions must be made by the instrument's designers about the order in which it will do things when push comes to shove. Basically, one task must be interrupted so that a second one can be dealt with. Some of these interrupts cause delays that have no effect upon the user. Other interrupts create audible delays that can affect the synchronization between two or more devices. These delays may or may not be bothersome enough for you to worry about. Some of them may be constant and predictable enough that you can devise fixes, but others may not.

If you are running into problems with delays caused by the response times of your various instruments, the first step to fixing the problem is to measure the constant delays in your system. The instruments we'll test in this example are a drum machine and a synthesizer with an on-board sequencer, but bear in mind the same method can be applied to any combination of equipment.

(1) Put a sync tone on tape.

(2) Program the drum machine to play a quarter-note click. A cowbell or clave sound would be ideal, but any fairly sharp sound will work.

(3) While playing the sync tone into the drum machine, record a quarter-note pulse from the drum machine onto a free track.

(4) Set up a sharp percussive sound on the synthesizer, and record an auto-corrected quarter-note pattern into the sequencer.

(5) Play the sequencer from the sync tone and record its click on another empty tape track. Then compare the two click tracks by playing them both back and listening to them together. Repeat this test with each of your instruments and compare just how long it takes them to respond to the sync tone. You may find that some of them respond faster than the drum machine click on the tape, while others respond slower.

(6) Insert a digital delay between the earliest of the clicks and the output stage of the mixer. While listening to these clicks and also the set of clicks that are furthest behind them in time, adjust the digital delay until the two rhythms are exactly synchronized (if you can get access to a dual-trace oscilloscope, you'll be able to line the clicks up more precisely).

(7) By checking the digital delay's front-panel LED display, note the amount of delay it took to get the earlier of the two click tracks in sync with the later of the two. This is the amount of microprocessor delay for the instrument that made the later set of clicks. Using the same technique, make a list of the amount of delay present in each of your instruments.

That's how you figure out the amount of delay. Here's how to compensate for it:

(1) Record a sync tone on tape, as before.

(2) While syncing your fastest device to this, record a quarter-note click to tape delayed by the maximum microprocessor delay of any of your instruments *plus* 10 milliseconds. The extra 10 milliseconds gives us some room to play with. Some sounds take longer to develop and must be played a bit ahead of the beat.

(3) Connect a delay line between the sync tone from tape and the sync input of your sequencing device (or drum machine). The DDL will be used to move the sequencing device forward and backward in time as compared to the quarter-note click. If the maximum microprocessor delay for your instruments was 20 milliseconds, then you should have delayed the quarter-note click by 30 milliseconds.

(4) When it's time to record instrument A, look up its delay on your chart. Let's say it has a 10-millisecond delay. 30-milliseconds total of delay minus 10-milliseconds machine delay leave 20-milliseconds, so set the delay line to 20-milliseconds and you'll be very close to exact synchronization.

Microprocessor delays that aren't constant can sometimes be minimized by using a slightly different approach. A large system that is being run entirely from MIDI can exhibit some of these non-constant delays. MIDI is a serial format—data packets are sent one after another. A large number of very dense sequencer tracks playing at the same time can fill a computer's output buffer or an instrument's input buffer and affect the synchronization of the system.

If you encounter this problem, try muting all but one or two of the sequencer tracks and playing back only these tracks while you record one or two of your synthesizers. This may speed up the effective rate of data transmission. Or, depending on the design of your sequencer software, it may not. Some sequencers may be able to ignore data on muted tracks completely, while others have to cycle through this data silently, which could take just as much time.

A Final Word

Syncing is one of the most complex areas of music production. Whenever you find yourself in a situation where you'll be using one of the various forms of sync we've covered here (or even some new type that hasn't been thought of yet), take your time, test the system and your equipment as thoroughly as you can, and revel in the fact that we've come as far as we have and needn't sync to tape by banging two rocks together.

By Terry Fryer
and Dominic Milano

SYNC TONES AND CLICK TRACKS

January 1985

Given the complexity of today's multi-track recording technology, the first step in recording is usually putting some sort of synchronization signal on tape. If you own a drum machine or sequencer and a tape recorder, the following information should help you get more out of your equipment. If you don't own the equipment but plan to make use of it in a recording studio, again this should help you.

One of the commonest ways to sync drum machines, sequencers, and synthesizers to tape recorders is with a sync tone. The LinnDrum, Oberheim DMX and DSX, Sequential Circuits Drumtraks, Polysequencer, and Model 64 sequencer, Roland TR909, MSQ700, Microcomposer 202, and MPU-401, E-mu Drumulator, Yamaha RX-15 and RX-11, MXR Drum Computer, PPG Wave 2.2 and 2.3, and Oberheim DX (with a mod) can all generate a type of sync tone called FSK. FSK (frequency shift key) is a method of encoding the clock timing output of a device in the form of two different tones. These tones have been modulated so that their pitch is noticeably different from one another (an octave apart for instance). Most FSK schemes work so that when a device accepts an FSK input from the tape (or from another device) and decodes it, each time a different pitch is perceived an internal clock pulse is generated, which then governs the speed with which the machine operates.

One problem that many musicians have run into is getting two machines built by different manufacturers to sync to one another's sync tone. Not all FSK tones are alike. Another problem is that some drum machines and sequencers don't use FSK at all, so that users must buy an interface device (such as the Doctor Click, the Byter Interface, or the KMS-30 MIDI synchronizer) to convert one type of timing signal to another. But the biggest problem is knowing what procedure to use when recording sync tones and click tracks.

Whether you are recording on a 4-track or a 24-track, recording a sync tone is much the same. Before attempting to record your sync tone, make sure the heads are clean and properly aligned. If you lack the skills or the proper test tapes and calibration gear needed to do an alignment, be sure at least to stick to the manufacturer's recommended tape type. The level you record sync at is most critical. Poorly recorded sync (too hot or too low in level) will most assuredly have dropouts (missing FSK pulses) and will be totally unusable.

In the studio, consoles and tape recorders operate at ±4dB, while semi-pro gear operates at a -10dB level. The best level at which to record sync tone in a professional studio is around -10dB. On semi-pro gear, -3dB seems to work best. Never use noise reduction on your sync tone tracks. On many semi-pro recorders equipped with dbx or Dolby you don't have the option of turning off

the noise reduction, so some experimentation with different levels will be necessary to tell you whether your drum machine will read sync that has been encoded with noise reduction. I have used a LinnDrum and a DMX with a Tascam 244 Portastudio, which has dbx, and the -3dB level seems to work fine. Never equalize or compress your sync tone track when recording it, either. If at all possible, patch directly into your recorder, bypassing your mixer. This will ensure a good clean signal to tape. To adjust the level, use the input level control of your deck.

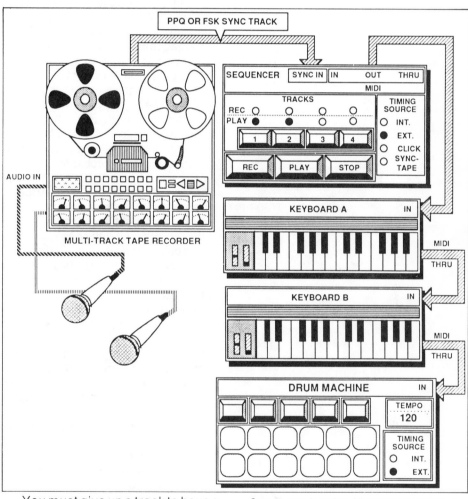

Sync-to-tape in action. All sequenced and drum machine parts can be "driven" from a single sync track on the tape recorder, leaving the remaining tape tracks free for vocal, acoustic instrument, and other non-syncable parts.

You must give up a track to have a sync tone on your tape; sync tone cannot be bounced onto one track with audio tracks. This might seem like a great limitation for a 4-track user, but if your sync tone is recorded properly, your drum machine and sequencer do not even have to be on the tape. You just have to start the song from the top every time you play it back. If you are using an 8-track, you can record the drums on another track in mono and listen to this track during overdubs. Then use the drum machine in sync with the tape when you do the mix. The advantage is clear—there is nothing like the crispness of first-generation drum sounds in a mix.

As to what track to choose for the sync tone, I would suggest an edge track. Theoretically, edge tracks on any multi-track recorder should not be used for high-frequency data (such as sync tone). but the studio standard for sync tracks and SMPTE code tracks has been track 1 or track 24. If you are using SMPTE, the adjoining track (23) is sometimes used for a sync tone or click. Never record program material with high-level, high-frequency transients on the track next to your sync track. Tambourine and hi-hat recorded at hot levels on adjacent tracks are prime offenders in causing drop-outs on sync tracks due to crosstalk. This holds true even on sync tracks that have been known to be good until a high transient sound was recorded on an adjacent track. Semi-pro recorders have lower levels of crosstalk rejection, so extra care must be taken to avoid this problem.

The next step is to choose your tempo with care. Once you stripe the tape with a sync tone, you will not be able to change the tempo of the song later, unless your deck has vari-speed capability. When you are laying down the sync tone, don't record the audio from your drum machine or sequencer at the same time. By recording the sync tone first and then on the next pass playing it back into the drum machine to record the audio, you will be accomplishing two major things. First, you will be verifying the sync track's integrity. Many people who record sync tone and audio simultaneously aren't going back to verify their sync, and when they come back later for an overdub, either the sync is no good because of drop-outs, low level, or noise reduction interference, or there may be a constant lag between the already recorded audio and new audio which is synced to the tone on tape. If you print the audio of your drum machine at the same time as the sync tone track, you run the risk of having lag on your overdubbed tracks. In the studio it is a rule that the sync tone or click track is always recorded by itself on the first pass, while the audio is recorded on the next pass. This way, if there is any lag, all the tracks will have the same amount.

Up to now, we have been talking only about sync tone. At Unique Recording Studios, with so many different manufacturers' drum machines and sequencers

to choose from we have made Doctor Click part of the procedure. The process is very similar to recording a sync tone, except that you are recording a square-wave pulse trigger. This square-wave trigger sounds like a click track and thus has an additional use. It serves as a metronome for the musicians, since we usually record it at a quarter-note value. We've found that a quarter-note click is truly what Doctor Click wants to see to generate all its available clock outputs (12, 24, 48, 64, 96, and 384 pulses per quarter-note, plus eighth-note, eighth-note triplet, sixteenth, sixteenth triplet, and so on.) Unfortunately, Doctor Click is too expensive for many semi-pro users. If you are using the Mini-Doc, Nano-Doc, FSK or MIDI adapters, or the Byter Interfaces, you cannot use a quarter-note click to drive them. They would prefer a 96 pulses-per-quarter-note FSK (Oberheim standard) sync tone. Although they will work with the slower FSK (48 or 24), it is always best to divide down from the master sync tone rather than multiplying up.

With the advent of the MIDI clock, many of the newest drum machines and sequencers (e.g. Yamaha's RS-15, RX-11, and QX-1, Roland TR909, MSQ700, and MPU-401, the LinnDrum 9000, and the Emulator II) will be most dependent on the sync tone track. The best part of the MIDI clock is that it is a standard. You will need only one interface to read the sync off the tape and translate it into MIDI clock. The newer sync tone tracks will offer the user the ability to sync the device to tape in a SMPTE transport fashion. The user will be able to fast-forward, rewind, stop, and play the tape from any point within the song and the device (provided it is in song playback mode) will slavishly stay in sync with your 4-track, 8-track, or whatever. Roland's SBX-80 Sync Box can read a quarter-note, eighth-note, etc., click from tape and generate either 12, 24, 48, 96, or 120 pulses per click or MIDI quarter-note. The SBX-80 can keep your MIDI clock devices in sync with a tape recorder by reading a SMPTE track (there is a SMPTE generator/reader built into the SBX-80) or a click track. It's a great system, but you have to give up two of your tape tracks, one for the SMPTE code and one for the sync or click. This is not very economical track-wise if you are recording on a 4-track, but as I mentioned above, your drums and sequenced synthesizers don't have to be on tape.

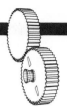

Whatever sync system you use, just be sure the sync track is recorded first and is verified!

By Bobby Nathan

SMPTE AND DRUM MACHINES

September 1985

SMPTE is good for lots of things besides synchronizing tape to film. It can be used as a clock to drive drum machines and squencers in order to give them a more human feel.

There are a number of SMPTE clock devices currently on the market. It was during an Arthur Baker remix of the Rolling Stones' "Too Much Blood" that we came across the fact that you can give devices with electronic clocks—drum machines and sequencers—a more human feel by using SMPTE to shift the tempo around from beat to beat. Here's how we stumbled on the idea:

Arthur wanted to sync up sequencer and drum machine overdubs to a tape which already had live drum tracks and no sync tone. On this session, we were lucky because Charlie Watts had played a steady quarter-note four-on-the-floor kick drum throughout the song. Had there not been a quarter-note instrument on tape already, we would have had to record one on an empty track. This would be accomplished by first printing SMPTE on an empty track, and then tapping a quarter-note click track and printing it on another empty track for the entire length of the song. The click track could have been a drummer playing a wood block or cowbell, or a drum machine's cowbell, clave, closed hi-hat, and so on. One of the tricks to recording click tracks is that if your timing isn't right on the money, you can slow the tape down to half speed and tap in the quarter-note click track with a half-note feel.

After we had the SMPTE sync box programmed to read the SMPTE from tape, we were able to sync up the necessary sequencer and drum machine overdubs. When the session was over, I started experimenting with the SMPTE sync box. I used the song that was still programmed into the sync box from the Baker session and wrote a quick pattern into a drum machine. The feel really came to life. I found that using the live drummer's soul to run the drum machine was so much more realistic that it was hard to believe we were listening to a drum machine. This is what led me to experiment with programmed tempo changes with the SMPTE sync box. I came up with all kinds of different feels. One in particular was produced by programming the third quarter-note of each measure to be either slightly faster (for a dance groove) or slower (for a ballad) in relation to the overall tempo of the song. For example, if the song was at 120 beats per minute (BPM), I'd make every third quarter-note 127 BPM.

Since all the SMPTE sync boxes will display the BPM for each quarter-note, you can analyze a live drummer's feel or soul. Here's what we learned: A live drummer will usually lean into the chorus and lay back a little for the bridge. Live drummers very rarely ever stay at a constant BPM throughout a song. All right, so you already knew that, but if you use one of the SMPTE sync boxes to program the tempo of your song from scratch, your sequencer and drum machine programming will really come alive.

Another interesting effect can be created by randomly choosing tempos that vary around the base tempo. For instance, the base tempo might be 124 BPM, but two measures of quarter-notes might have BPMs that look like this: 124, 120, 122, 127, 123, 121, 125, 122, and so on. When you get to the chorus, you can change the base tempo to 128 BPM. You can then make your own random tempos around the bass tempos of the chorus.

Another way to achieve this live feel is to manually tap in the tempo for the entire tune. Try getting together with your drummer and laying down the song on keyboards while he taps along into the sync box. If no one else is around, put your sync box on the floor and use your big toe to tap the tempo in while you play along. What we really need here, I think, is a foot-controlled square wave momentary switch.

What this all boils down to is the use of SMPTE sync boxes as tempo programming tools. The concept requires that you program your sequencer or drum machine first. Then program your sync box. Check your tempo feel by playing your sequencer and/or drum machine in external clock mode with the sync box as the master. You don't need to sync to tape until you are sure that the feel is right.

Another SMPTE tip is to use the display function of your sync box. After a song has been recorded into the sync box, the internal microprocessor becomes a sort of SMPTE-to-beats-per-minute computer. This can be useful if you want to sequence a synthesizer line at just the bridge of a song. You can figure out the necessary offset and program the sync box to start the sequencer's clock at the desired downbeat. If you fast-forward to measure 21, beat 1, which for this example represents the bridge, your display should tell you the SMPTE time at that downbeat. If you subtract the SMPTE time of measure 1, beat 1 from the bridge SMPTE time, you come up with the amount of offset. Next add this amount to the existing offset. Remember if you have started the SMPTE 15 seconds before the start of the tune, your initial offset should be roughly 15 seconds.

Some sync boxes have additional cue tracks that can be recorded on after the song has been programmed. A good use for these cue tracks is to take live drums and retrigger sampled or other sound events. If you've ever attempted this, you know that there is a delay or lag from when the trigger is sent to when the sound is produced. By recording the cue tracks into the SMPTE sync box memory, they can be offset and programmed ahead of the beat to compensate for the individual lag of whatever device you are triggering. This is a very useful technique that can be used during mixdown as well as during the tracking of a tune. If you set the cue tracks to be late, you can trigger the instrument to have an echo effect. The advantage is that there is no signal degradation, because the instrument is being triggered live to the track by the cue track.

If you are working with certain instruments that have lag when triggered from live sources, be sure to make a note of their offsets.

By Bobby Nathan

USING SMPTE INTERFACE DEVICES

February 1985

SMPTE timecode is starting to play an increasingly important role in syncing sequencers and drum machines to multi-track tape recorders. This month, we'll take a look at what SMPTE (pronounced simp-tee) is and show you two devices used to generate and read SMPTE timecode.

In 1967, the Society of Motion Picture and Television Engineers (SMPTE) came up with a timecode based on a 24-hour clock that could be used to sync soundtracks to motion pictures. Like a clock, their timecode is divided into hours, minutes, and seconds. Seconds are divided into frames and frames into subframes. There are a number of different values for frames, due to different film media requirements. The so-called standard is set at 30 frames per second. Video uses what's called drop-frame SMPTE, which is based on 60 cycles per second, where each frame is 1/29.97 second. European Broadcasting requires a frame based on 50 cycles per second. This European Broadcast Unit runs at one frame every 1/25 second. Film runs at one frame every 1/24 second.

SMPTE timecode is used to synchronize two multi-track tape recorders to each other. In professional studios, what's commonly done is that two 24-track machines will be used together to get 46-track capability. You might ask what happened to the other two tracks, since 24+24=48, not 46. The missing tracks are used up with the SMPTE code.

Running two multi-tracks in sync is just one of the possible musical applications of SMPTE. Imagine what you could do with a sequencer or drum machine that could be synced to tape, so that they would start and stop at any point corresponding exactly with the music already recorded on a multi-track tape. Imagine being able to fast-forward and rewind a tape and still have your drum machine come in at the correct measure. Imagine a sequencer that could be made to follow a click track or a previously recorded live drum track, complete with tempo variations and live feeling. The Roland SBX-80 and the Friend-Chip SRC are two SMPTE interface boxes that can be used to give you just those capabilities. The devices themselves differ in function and price, but they both perform similar tasks. Let's take a look at their operation.

The Roland SBX-80 Sync Box is capable of generating 30-frame-per-second SMPTE code. To start, you print or stripe your multi-track tape with the SMPTE code. This is accomplished by first recording SMPTE at –3 on a semi-

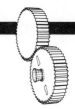

pro recorder (where 0 equals –10dB) or at –10 on a pro recorder. Print the SMPTE for at least one minute longer than your song. At 20 seconds from where you've started printing SMPTE, start printing a clock reference on another audio track of the recorder. For most purposes, a quarter-note click in the appropriate tempo is adequate. Note that all this takes place *before* any music is put down on tape.

After you've striped the click on the tape, you're ready to record a song into the SBX-80. The real beauty of the machine is that when you record a song, you are storing the relationship between SMPTE and the tempo of the song by reading the click track from the tape recorder into the memory of the SBX. Set the SBX to the external SMPTE mode. Then press record, and be sure to start the tape at a place before the SMPTE code begins. You have the option of having a two-bar count-in, where your drum machine and/or sequencer will wait two bars before starting. The two-bar count-in is a useful feature, and I recommend using it when you want to have a count-in for live musicians who might be overdubbing to the song on tape.

Operation of the SBX-80 and the SRC is pretty much the same up to this point. However, the SBX can only generate one assignable clock that produces 1, 2, 3, 4, 12, 24, 48, 96, or 120 beats per quarter-note to its single clock output jack. The unit can also feed MIDI clock devices and Roland-type FSK sync devices via two jacks for each. The SRC, on the other hand, is much more like a Dr. Click in that it simultaneously puts out clock tones and click tracks of many different values. Its optional input module also generates and reads FSK sync tone.

The song in the SBX80 can be stored on a cassette tape much the same way you'd store synthesizer programs on cassette. After you've off-loaded your data to a cassette, the click track can then be erased. The SBX-80 and the SRC need only the SMPTE track as their reference.

In the event that you are using the SBX to add SMPTE to a tune that's already on tape, you print SMPTE 20 seconds before the music begins. If you have a click track already recorded, you record it into the SBX-80 after putting SMPTE on the tape. If you don't have a quarter-note click or the drums were recorded by a live drummer, you can tap

along with the music, and the SBX will follow your tap. If you can't keep perfect time with the drummer, try slowing the tape down to half speed and then tap in a half-note click. Unlike the Dr. Click, which looks at every measure, the SBX looks at every single click. Resolution can be increased by recording a sixteenth-note click.

Another interesting use of the SBX is to make the drum machine or sequencer start ahead of the track. After you've recorded a song into memory on the unit, press the SMPTE offset button and note the value in the display. The offset displayed is the difference between where the SMPTE on tape started and the first click of your click track. If you change the offset value to less than the original value, your drum machine or sequencer will start at a correspondingly early time. The SRC also has a variable offset function that defaults to 20 seconds. This is useful, since you need 20 seconds of SMPTE before the start of your song in order to sync up multi-track machines in the studio.

The SBX-80 lets you start your recorder from anywhere within the tune and have MIDI-equipped devices start at the exact point the tape is at. This is like adding tracks to your recorder, because it means you don't have to put sequences and drum machines on the tape. You also get the advantage of having first generation drum tracks in the mix. The SRC doesn't have this feature. However, some MIDI-equipped units, like the Yamaha RX-11 and 15, don't follow Roland's MIDI clock output, so the function doesn't work with every piece of MIDI-equipped gear.

There are quite a few of the SMPTE to MIDI converters on the market, from Fostex, Yamaha, and several other manufacturers. While a growing number of users are employing these devices, we can also expect to see a whole new breed of devices which take SMPTE timecode and translate it to MIDI timecode.

By Bobby Nathan

The Fostex 4050 can generate and read SMPTE time code, and translate time code readings to MIDI measure information—much like the SBX-80 and Master Beat. The 4050 can also be used to program punch-in and punch-out locations for Fostex open-reel recorders.

MIDI TIME CODE

October 1987

Growing—that's what the MIDI spec is doing. Growing into new areas. And that continuing growth is one of the most gratifying aspects of working with MIDI. As sampler technology (which was rare when MIDI was introduced five years ago) became more available, an extension to MIDI was developed to handle the transfer of data amongst different type samplers and computers. This was the sample dump spec.

Shown here, with the Fostex 460 4-track recorder/mixer, is a common sight for anyone who's worked with video: A SMPTE time code "window dub," which gives a visual indication of a video tape's time code reading. This dub displays a reading of "17 hours:26 minutes:35 seconds:17 frames."

As the applications of MIDI have expanded into automation and other usages, it became necessary to describe the settings of numerous controls. This application became the registered/non-registered controller spec, which allows data for over 32,000 different controllers to be sent over MIDI.

Over the last couple of years, it has been obvious that the pro audio and musical instrument areas are developing a large gray area of overlap, due in part to MIDI. Essentially every new reverb and digital delay on the market features MIDI. On some units it is used to control which preset is called up. On others it allows sophisticated control, on a real-time basis, of all parameters of the unit. This trend is now extending into equalizers and small snapshot mixers.

So begins the marriage of MIDI and pro audio. But the one prevasive aspect of pro audio that must be dealt with for the marriage to be successful is SMPTE time code.

A Review. SMPTE time code (which I'll just call SMPTE from now on, even though that's the name of an organization, not the code), is a type of encoded tone that (usually) is put onto one track of a multi-track tape machine. This allows the accurate location of any place on the tape, down to around 1/2,400 of a second accuracy. One use of this technology is to lock the movement of the tape to movement of either another tape machine or video or film. It also allows the convenient description of events in terms of location on the tape, video, or film. These events could be the sound of a gun shot, the change of a reverb setting, or the punching-in of a record track.

The encoded tone that is put onto tape consists of a set of 80 bits (called a frame) that is put down at a bit rate of either 1920, 2000, or 2400 bits per second, depending on whether the frame rate is 24, 25 or 30 frames per second. Twenty-six of these 80 bits are an indication of the frame's actual number, which is put in terms of hours, minutes, seconds, and frames. Thirty-two of the bits are called user bits, meaning that they are open for any usage. Sixteen of the bits are used for synchronization. The remainder are special flag bits.

A frame number might appear as 21:37:29:15, which would be the 15th frame of the 29th second of the 37th minute of the 21st hour. (Notice that we use a 24-hour clock here.) This time usually has no meaning in terms of the time of day. Since the unit that does the striping of the tape is almost always manually settable, the user can have the song (or whatever) start at any time desired.

For some time now there have been boxes that allow the conversion of SMPTE time to MIDI. Once a box of this type is set to start a song at a particular SMPTE time and a particular tempo, it puts out the appropriate song position pointer (SPP) data and subsequent MIDI clocks to a sequencer or drum machine, regardless of where the tape is started. If the song has more than one tempo, a tempo map must be entered into the unit that is sending the MIDI clocks, so that it can follow each change of the song.

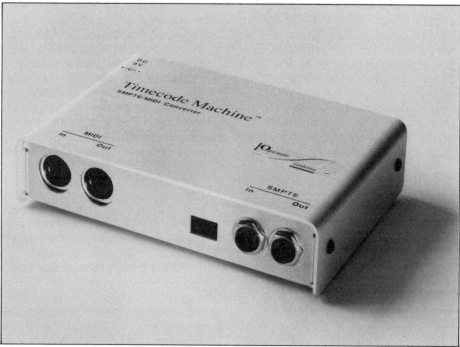

Opcode's Timecode Machine converts SMPTE time code to MIDI Time Code (MTC).

This is ideal, of course, for normal music sequencing, because everything the musician has to deal with is in familiar terms. But it's not ideal for many aspects of music and video/film. For instance, when sound effects are dubbed in, they are rarely identified with regard to tempo, bars, or the like: they are always IDed in terms of SMPTE frame number. And since MIDI control of almost any device such as a tape machine, CD player, or tape cartridge players is now possible via various interfaces, it would be very convenient if we could indicate the punch-in or start point in terms of SMPTE.

Why? Let's say we have a music sequencer synchronized to a SMPTE source (say, a video) via an interface unit. We have indicated that the tempo is 120, 4/4 time. Loaded into the sequencer is the music background that goes with the video. And let's say that we have a sampler loaded with a gun shot, which we want to sound eight seconds into the video. Simple math tells us that we want the MIDI command to go from the sequencer to the sampler at a point exactly 4 bars in. Fine.

Now let's say we make a musical decision to step up the tempo of the background music to 123. Obviously, we want the gun shot to stay at eight seconds in, *not* four bars in. So we will have to get out the slide rule and figure the new cue point for this and any other sound effects. On the other hand, we might find that the work print has been changed and that the gun shot now needs to be shifted back by 35 frames. We would need to figure just what this meant in terms of bars and beats, keeping in mind any tempo changes along the way. It would be far simpler just to add 35 to the frame number and let the SMPTE time directly control the event. These two situations demonstrate some of the problems that can occur at the MIDI/SMPTE junction. It's just a matter of keeping goals and means straight. MIDI clocks and SPPs are great for music, and SMPTE is great for events.

But darned if MIDI isn't straightforward to implement! The amount of extra hardware for the interface is minimal, and may be already present on a given piece of equipment. There are MIDI adapters available for almost any computer, there are MIDI-controlled samplers, reverbs, etc. Wouldn't it be nice if we could describe events in terms of SMPTE time with MIDI? This is what MIDI Time Code (MTC) is for.

Before we go on, please keep in mind that MTC is very new. Even though the term has been bandied about for a bit over a year, the actual approval by the Japanese MIDI Standards Committee and the MIDI Manufacturers Association only took place around April of this year. There are only a few MTC-oriented software and hardware products now, but there are sure to be lots more in the near future.

MTC is *not* meant to replace SMPTE, MIDI clocks, or SPP. MTC is meant to act as a bridge, covering the types of situation that arise at the SMPTE/MIDI junction. The idea is twofold: First, to supply a method of describing the SMPTE time over a MIDI wire. This would inform a master controller (such as a Macintosh computer) where the tape is. It would also inform smart peripherals of the SMPTE time. Second, to have a standardized way of describing a list of events, and transferring this list from, say, an editor program on a computer to a smart peripheral.

The recently terminated LucasFilm Sound Droid project was designed to be a special computer that had a library of sounds on magnetic or optical disk. When used, this $100,000+ system would allow a film sound editor to dub in thunderclaps, space ship noises, and whatever just by punching in the proper code (or using a mouse).

On a far humbler scale, SMPTE, MTC, a personal computer, and samplers can eventually provide many of the same techniques to the video and film world. I really feel it's just a matter of time.

A typical screen from Q-Sheet, an audio/video post-production program for the Apple Macintosh computer. When used in conjunction with a sampler, Q-Sheet can be programmed to trigger various sampled sounds, or "events," to happen at different time code readings. This makes it a perfect tool for adding sound effects to video and film.

There are two main parts to the MTC. First, it provides a protocol for the direct conversion from SMPTE frame number to MIDI, so that any device with MIDI hardware can "know" the real-time SMPTE frame. Second, MTC provides a set-up format for down-loading and up-loading a list of event definitions. (Downloading refers to the transfer from a main computer to a slave device. Up-loading would be a transfer in the opposite direction.) An "event" could be a command to

a sampler to sound a gunshot, or a move of a mixer fader, or a program change command to a reverb unit. A list of these events is generally called a cue list. Traditionally, this is a pencil and paper list, but using computer-based MTC devices opens up new possibilities.

There were at least two cue list programs being privately demonstrated at the June 1987 NAMM Show. Another, not exhibited at the show, is being sold directly to film composers. All of these programs rely on MTC for timing, and some of them can also use the download/up-load part of the specification. Clearly, there will be software support to make this new concept a reality. Let's see how the actual bytes work:

SMPTE Frame Position. There are two ways to transmit the SMPTE frame position from one unit to another. The first is the so-called "full message," and is generally just used to tell a slave unit to go to a time and park there. Or, information could be sent periodically when the tape is in shuttle mode (assuming the conversion device can read SMPTE at high speed). This message would not be used to continually indicate frame number. It looks like this (remember, all notation is in hexadecimal):

F0 7F (chan) 01 00 hr mn sc fr F7

where:

F0 7F is the header for real-time universal systems-exclusive.

(chan) is a special channel number that allows for the unique definition of up to 127 different slave devices. If this message is meant to go to the whole system, an 7F is used as the channel number.

01 00 means this is the full time code message.

hr mn sc fr are four bytes describing the desired hour, minute, second, and frame numbers. Imbedded in the hour time are two bits that specify the number of frames per second (24, 25, 30, or 30 drop-frame).

F7 ends the system-exclusive message.

The second way of describing a frame number is via the short, or "quarter-frame" message. This message uses one of the heretofore-unused system common codes, the F1. Attached to this byte is a single data byte. This byte contains four bits of binary data and three bits that indicate just what the binary data refers to. This data

byte would be printed 0nnndddd, with dddd being the data bits, and nnn being used as follows:

nnn = 0 for the frame-count least significant four bits,
1 for the frame-count most significant bit,
2 for the seconds-count least significant four bits,
etc., until:
6 for the hour-count least significant four bits, and
7 for the hour-count most significant bit. Also buried in this last byte are two bits that indicate the number of frames per second.

These eight messages are sent in order, at a rate of four per frame. Since there are eight messages, it takes a total of two frames to describe the complete frame number. After the frame has been described, the slave device should have the smarts to know what is going on even though it is only getting a piece of the whole picture each quarter-frame. As an example, let's say that we wanted to send the frame number of 02:14:35:20. First, our software would translate into hexadecimal. I'll leave it to the interested student to confirm that this would be 02:0E:25:14. This would split into the following eight messages:

F1 04 (least significant frame bits)
F1 11 (we stuck the "1" on to indicate most significant frame bit)
F1 25 ("2" for least significant seconds bits)
F1 32 ("3" for most significant seconds bits)
F1 4E (etc.)
F1 50
F1 62
F1 70 (ignoring, for this example, the imbedded frames-per-second bits).

What does this cost us in terms of MIDI bandwidth? Since we need to send the two-byte message (640 microseconds) every quarter-frame (8.33ms), we have a bandwidth usage of 7.68%. This is more bandwidth usage than normal MIDI clocks would have, but has the great advantage of specifing actual frame position. Also, a typical system would not have this message being sent over the same cable as MIDI notes, controller data, and so on. It would only be sent from a "black box" SMPTE-to-MTC converter to the host computer that keeps track of the cue list. Or, it would be sent between this black box and any "smart" peripheral that holds its own cue list internally.

Set-Up Messages. An important dimension that the adoption of MTC has brought to pro audio is a specified way of describing events that are SMPTE-oriented (take place on a given frame number). These events may include the sending of normal MIDI commands, such as note-ons, controllers, etc. They could also be tape track punch-in points, start points (such as starting a CD machine), or indeed, anything that might be tied to a SMPTE frame number. The set-up message looks like:

F0 7E (chan) 04 st hr mn sc fr ff sl sm (additional info) F7

where:

F0 7E is the non-real-time universal sys-ex header.
(chan) has the same meaning as with the full message above.
04 is the i.d. for the set-up message.
st defines the set-up type. (for instance, st=1 would mean punch-in point).
hr, mn, sc, fr are the hour, minute, second, frame specification.
ff is the 1/100th of a frame specification.
sl sm indicate the event number, broken into a least and a most significant part.
(additional info) would generally be the MIDI bytes we might want to send at the given event time. Since a MIDI command byte has bit 7 set to be 1, and since we can't allow that as part of a sys-ex message, we split each MIDI byte into two nibbles, and send the least significant one first. That is, if we wanted to send the note-on command 92 37 4E, we would send it as 02 09 07 03 0E 04.
F7 finishes up the sys-ex string.

There are almost 20 types of set-up messages defined so far, and there is allowance for over 100 more to be thought of and defined in the future. If you are interested in the list of set-up types, or want to read up on a couple of other MTC messages that we haven't gone into here, you should contact the International MIDI Association (IMA), which has a 70-page book containing all of the detailed specifications of MIDI, including MIDI Time Code. Contact the IMA (1249 Magnolia Blvd., No. Hollywood, CA 91607) for information on obtaining this book.

By Jim Cooper

69

4 KEYBOARD RECORDING

RECORDING PIANOS AND SYNTHESIZERS

June 1986

When it comes to recording, there are at least two kinds of musicians. There are those who have worked for years to develop an individual sound; when they enter a studio, they expect the tape machine to do no more than mirror their playing. And then there are those who figure that knowing how to play doesn't really matter in the studio—after all, there's so much magic floating around in the control room that everything's bound to come out sounding like dynamite.

What both perspectives leave out is the fact that another human being is involved: the recording engineer. Engineers are musicians, too. While no one ever goes out to see them perform, their work is etched into every record pressed, every television and radio broadcast, and every film with music in the soundtrack. Like other musicians, most of them put a great deal of intensive energy into learning their instrument—the studio in all of its component parts—so that it will respond to the subtleties of their minds' ears. In essence, every recording is at least a duet. A player's performance, no matter how wondrous and technically excellent, won't be reflected accurately in a recording without the collaboration of an engineer whose musical perceptions are sympathetic to the performer's. Likewise, the non-performer who needs the extraordinary powers of the studio in order to realize his or her musical vision must engage the musical talents of an engineer to reconcile vision with technology.

Even as keyboards are becoming ubiquitous in the recording environment, many keyboardists remain unable to answer the studio equivalent of the question, "What are the black keys for?" Yet the recording studio does have its keys, and engineers do pound, tickle, and otherwise caress them. The player is bound to get more out of the studio by being better informed about the technical and musical aspects of making a good recording, and fortunately a number of very experienced engineers were willing to tell us how they go about it. **Howard Johnston**, co-owner of Different Fur Studio in San Francisco, is per-

haps best known for the full-bodied piano sounds on a great many Windham Hill releases. In addition, he has worked extensively with electronic sounds on recordings by the Residents, Mark Isham, and former *Keyboard* columnist Patrick Gleeson. Freelance engineer **Jeff Hendrickson** recently recorded a Lyle Mays' solo album, and has received a Grammy nomination for his hit-making work with David Lee Roth. A staff engineer at Unique Recording, **Tom Lord-Alge**'s credits include Little Steven's *Sun City* project, Orchestral Manoeuvres in the Dark, Diana Ross, and most recently Steve Winwood. **James Farber** currently works for producer Nile Rodgers; together they have worked on albums by the Thompson Twins, Philip Bailey, Mick Jagger, and others. In addition, Farber has recorded a number of jazz artists, most notably Steps Ahead and Stanley Jordan. **Bruce Botnick** has pioneered in recording synthesizers with orchestra in numerous film scores by Jerry Goldsmith. Although he has worked on dozens of scores, including *Rambo* and *The Color Purple*, Botnick is at least as well-known for his work with the Doors during the late '60s and early '70s.

The insights of these five professionals elucidate the connection between technical application and musical effect that is central to the recording engineer's art. At the very least, they should provide some ideas for your next foray into the studio, and, for astute technicians, a few tips on making better tapes at home, whether you're working with piano or synthesizers. It can't be emphasized enough that, as musicians talking about music, every one of them qualified his remarks often with the observation that any point of technique or procedure is subordinate to the needs of each specific musical situation. The ears are the final arbiters of any recording. In the realm of music, there are no rules.

How do you go about miking acoustic pianos?
Botnick: It depends on the size of the piano, how good the sound is, and how good mechanically the instrument is. When you have a grand piano, the classical method is to open up the lid, prop it up high, and put a microphone right where the bar is, up near the top of the lid, so you get the total reflection. You can put two microphones inside the piano, one favoring the higher strings

71

and the other favoring the low strings, right where the strings cross. Then there's another method, having one microphone in the high area and one down at the bottom of the piano. There's a multitude of ways to mike a piano, but if you stand in front of the piano and you like the way it sounds from a particular place, place the microphone there and then listen to it inside the control room. Don't always resort to EQ to solve problems—generally, good mike placement will do the trick. Move the microphones around, or change microphones, until you are as close as you can get to the sound you want. *Then* go for the equalizer. Most people don't take the time to place the microphones properly, or to use the right microphones, and as a conseqence they're only getting about 40 percent of the sound that they could.

Lord-Alge: I like to get a nice bright piano, so I take two of the brightest microphones I can find, which around here are the AKG414s, to get a nice bump on the high end. I usually put one right above where the hammers sit, about six inches above the strings—as close as I can get. The closer you get, the brighter the sound. I put that one in the middle, and then I throw one down on the lower part. That technique is for a more rock-and-roll approach, or a dance approach. If you have a whole band in there, you're going to want to isolate the piano by covering it up with a heavy cloak. If you sing while you're playing the piano, I would recommend putting a cloak over the top of the piano and just draping it down in front, so that you can't see the inside of the piano. It's also a good idea to put a cloak on the floor, because a lot of piano players have a tendency to tap their feet.

Farber: I usually use a pair of high-quality condenser mikes. Often I end up with AKG 414s, but I couldn't say where they should be placed without hearing a specific song. You have to consider what kind of sound you want, how much stereo separation you want, and so forth. If you're miking in stereo, the main thing is to make sure it sounds cool in mono. If it seems like there's no bass when you flip it to mono, play with the phase button—but chances are that's not the problem. You've got to move the microphones around.

Why check it in mono if you're going to be listening in stereo?

Farber: What if it's played on the radio, and it's broadcast in mono? But even if you're listening in stereo, it still won't sound right if it's out of phase.

Lord-Alge: Phasing matters because if you have it wrong, the low end won't sound right. Certain notes will cancel right out. When the mikes are out of phase, there's also an illusion that it's wider than it is. I can tell that something's out of phase if it sounds really wide.

Hendrickson: For Lyle Mays, we used a couple of Schoepps mikes. One was pointed right toward the V of the frame, the metal part on top of the soundboard, and the other was at the low end. The high-end mike was pointed away from the low-end mike. It's hard to explain the exact location, but it just turned out amazing. When you place the mikes away from the hammers like that, it tends to mellow the piano out a little bit, which is better for jazz. You don't go for a lot of the attack; you go for clarity and smoothness, so you can really hear a performance. We had the piano uncovered. He has his own piano, so that was sounding great to begin with. We used a couple of mikes in the room to add fullness. When you close-mike, you don't get all the rich tones that you would if you brought the mikes up farther from the soundboard. Close-miking is more directional, so the tones are really directed in a certain area. When the mikes are farther away, they reflect the overall tone of the whole piano. Pianos are pretty dull for the most part, so usually I EQ in some top end and a little bit of midrange, if it's needed. Once in a while I'll compress them. If you listen to a compressed piano alone, sometimes it sounds like crap, but in the overall spectrum of a mix it works out great. The way I evaluate any sound is to listen to it in the track. I never listen to anything by itself, except for drums.

Johnston: I find there's a big difference in the sound between where the player sits and how the piano actually sounds. If you do an XY over the hammers sometimes you can make a bad piano sound good.

Could you explain what you mean by XY?

Johnston: There's a lot of ways you can do XY. Basically, you make an X out of two microphones, maybe Neumann KM84s or AKG 452s, crossing them halfway. How narrow or how wide you spread them affects the sound, but basically it looks like a cross. It's a bright and percussive sound, and sometimes you can defeat some of the negative things that come with a room, or a piano that may not have a tremendous tone unto

itself. Sometimes we'll even mike a good piano that way too, to get a certain sound. Two microphones in an XY over the hammers, in the middle of the piano, with one pointing toward the low end and one toward the high end, is a really good position. It's an easy way to get a stereo sound on the piano without any phasing problems. It doesn't have some of the soul that other ways of miking have, but it's a nice, clean, clear, bright signal, and whenever you check the phase, 90 percent of the time it's almost exactly right.

Do you use this same technique to record a solo piano, as opposed to piano in a group?

Johnston: Well, for solo piano I would use five to six microphones around the room, some close in and some farther away. If it's a duet, too, you might do that to get the room sound on both instruments. But if you were doing a trio with drums, you'd have to tighten up the piano sound. Particularly for rock-and-roll piano, sometimes you have to baffle the piano off, cover it to keep the other instruments out, and put maybe two microphones inside.

Does that compromise the sound?

Johnston: Yes, that compromises it a lot. The lid's not meant to be closed. Whenever you close the lid at all, the phase inside the piano gets funny because of all the reflections inside, and you get resonances. Microphones tend to pick up a boxy sound when the lid is closed, even with the short stick. So what I like to do is this: if you want a nice, big piano sound, play the piano part on a synthesizer going direct for the basics, and do the piano as an overdub. Then you can open the lid.

When you have five mikes set up for a solo piano recording, what approach do you take to mixing all of them together?

Johnston: Certain mikes will have certain characteristics, and for some songs you might emphasize ones that are farther away, or ones that are brighter, or ones that have more low end. If you're doing an entire album, you change it from song to song. The basic sound pretty much stays the same, but you'll emphasize certain microphones or de-emphasize them, change the EQ if you're using EQ, and certainly change the reverb. The way the musician plays the piano changes, so the microphones react to the sound differently. If you didn't do it on purpose, you'd do it anyway.

So there's no one piano sound

you're going for?

Johnston: No, that's for sure. Everybody plays differently, and everyone hears differently. If you had two piano players in the room, and one was going to record and the other was just there to play while you get sound, there's only so far you could go. No matter what, the other player's touch will be so different that sometimes you'd swear it's a different piano being played. There is no one sound; usually you change it from song to song, and certainly from player to player.

Do you ever use effects on a piano?

Johnston: Well, pianos are a sacred domain, so to speak. If you're doing solo piano, usually the player is judged by their ability to master the instrument. I've done delays and things like that on piano—there are always weird things you can do—but the application is very small. I think the creative use of delays is good to do with synthesizers. Not that that's unique by any means, but there's a real art to making it work. If you throw delays up, you've got to make sure they're working together.

Can you give me an example?

Johnston: I did an album with Ira Russell for Windham Hill called *Transit*. On a couple songs we used sequences. We had a Prophet 600 and a Yamaha DX7, and they were playing a similar pattern. So I'd put the Prophet on the left and maybe harmonize it on the right, and take the DX on the right and chorus it on the left. Then I'd find some longer delay that was in time with what they were playing, and run both the Harmonizer and the chorus into that delay, and record that on both channels. That kind of treatment wouldn't do for a lot of things, but it gives you this thick, complex, stereo sound with lots of personality in it.

Hendrickson: Stereoizing a synthesizer sound can make it more apparent, and it makes you want to listen more, whereas a synthesizer in mono may be too dull to notice. I'll spread a mono sound with a Harmonizer [pitch-shifter], detuned just a tiny bit, or spread it with a delay, or spread it with a Harmonizer and put a delay in the middle to create some kind of ambience. For a lead synthesizer, you want to make some kind of effect so that you really hear it, so it really sticks out in the mix, because that's what it's there for. I may put a lead sound up the middle with a short delay softly out to the side, and a tight chamber to make it sound like it's in a small room. On the

Howard Johnston at Different Fur Recording.

73

other hand, a pad is more of an ambience type thing, so I may use a longer chamber to make that a softer sound, so it blends in more. You may not even be aware of it unless it's taken away. For a rhythm part, I may just pan that off to one side. If there's a rhythm guitar panned to the other side doing something opposite, or even playing the same rhythm, if they're really playing off of each other, right there that creates an ambience all its own.

Farber: Sometimes I put a synthesizer bass in the middle with a stereo pair of Harmonizers, where the one on the left is tuned ever-so-slightly sharp. I'll add that effect to widen and make it sound bigger. Compression usually helps bass sounds, too. On a lot of synthesizer sounds, compression helps. It makes things punchier.

Johnston: A little pitch shifting and a little delay always helps the sound. It makes synthesizers sound a little more real, because their pitch is just too perfect. If you have a couple of string players, and everybody is playing in tune, their attacks are just a little different and their pitches are just slightly different. That's what makes four violins sound like four violins. You may develop a synthesizer patch that'll be the equivalent of four violins, but you can't get that same effect. A little delay, or chorusing, or something like that helps to get a little more complex information in there.

Farber: A delay to your reverb device is always a great thing to give an added dimension. There's a delay before you hear an echo which tells you that the room is a certain size—depending on the delay time, it defines the room size. Sound travels at 300 meters per second, so you can figure out how long it should take before you hear the earliest reflection, dial up a delay time of that length, and create a room size that way. A lot of times I'll use an invisible kind of delay, which repeats in time with the music. You can calculate the delay time in milliseconds per quarter-, eighth-, or sixteenth-note if you know the tempo of the song in beats per minute. Or you can just send some steady pulse, like the snare drum, to the delay unit, and fiddle with the delay time until the regenerations are happening in time with the drum. The effect is kind of invisible, but it makes things sound deeper.

Hendrickson: There are so many different things you can do with delays. You can make a stereo-type delay, between 10 and 40 milliseconds, panned

opposite the undelayed sound. Probably every engineer puts some kind of delay on vocals. The best way to know if they work is to try different ones on everything, and one will hit you the right way. That's usually the way I determine what my delay is going to be.

Farber: If you take the same synthesizer sound and put it in two different songs, you would treat it completely different. You have to listen to how it's fitting into a particular song.

Lord-Alge: Stereo chorusing is one of my favorite effects for synthesizers. Any synth that was recorded in mono will come alive, and spread out so nicely, if you add a stereo chorus. My favorite is the AMS DDL [digital delay line], which is a $10,000 piece of gear, but a lot of the

Tom Lord-Alge at Unique Recording.

cheaper ones are real good. Bell sounds love to swim, so I use a lot of reverb with them. When you have a bell that's dry, when you hit it, it just goes, "ting." But if you put it in a two- or three-second-long reverb, it just comes to life. I put a real quick reverb on synthesizer horns, a real tight slappy reverb that takes the sound and blurts it for a second and makes it thicker. I'm always trying different things, even if it's something unheard-of. You just go for it and experiment, and if it sounds right, then that's it.

Do any unheard-of things come to mind?

Lord-Alge: On some keyboards I like to try backwards echoes. I turn the tape over so it plays backwards and print the reverb on another track. Say it's a horn blast; I'll put reverb on that horn blast backwards, so that when you play the tape forwards it gives you a sucking effect. You'll hear this thing swelling up, and then you get the regular blast. Right

now I'm working on the Steve Winwood project, and I did that in one of the mixes. This one part of the song would go by, and there was this little hole that was just begging for the synthesizer to have backwards reverb on it. So I did it, and sure enough it really brought the song home.

Do you ever record effects to the multi-track?

Lord-Alge: We've got 48 tracks, and with 48 tracks I don't really delve into printing effects. For people with 4- or 8-track, I would say to experiment and see what you can get. I would definitely print effects with a 4-track, if I knew they were going to be right later on. I wouldn't do it with a vocal, but with synthesizers, if you know of an effect that you definitely want, by all means print it. It's a commitment you have to make, something you'll have to decide right then.

Do you ever find that the direct sound is right just as it is?

Lord-Alge: Yes. Sometimes it's just right the way it is, no processing, no anything. If you come across that, don't ever mess with it. If it's right, right away, then just go for it. Why mess it up if it sounds good?

Do you prefer to record synthesizers directly, or do you sometimes mike them through an amplifier?

Lord-Alge: Sometimes when I take a direct sound, I'll split the signal and run it through an amplifier. Then I'll mike the amplifier, and put a mike in the back of the room, so you get the direct, the amp, and the room. It comes out with a really nice sound sometimes. I'd recommend it any time you can get a big room. It's almost like reverb, if you have a room that's big enough.

Hendrickson: If I want a real controlled sound, I usually just take it direct. If it's really a pertinent part, like a rhythm that needs to have an emphasis, sometimes I'll mike it and then I'll take a direct signal and mix the two. I might effect one of them, maybe delay it, so you can definitely hear it. Often effects can make a sound harder. A lot of times when you use a direct sound, even if the sound is hard, it softens it up much more than an amplifier would, especially when you distort the amp.

Farber: The only time I mike an amplifier is if I'm doing a live band and I want to make it sound like the band is onstage. Otherwise I do everything direct. I guess most amplifiers don't sound that great to me.

Lord-Alge: I don't think I would use

74

as much of the sound from the amp with a synthesizer, but I would definitely experiment with mixing the direct signal with the sound from room mikes that are set up ten feet to 30 feet from the amp. It sounds more natural than adding reverb. On a lot of old records, if you listen real carefully you can hear the room, especially on drum sounds.

A lot of Keyboard Magazine *readers have drum machines.*

Lord-Alge: Right. I'll have a drum machine running through the speakers in the studio, and I'll put two mikes up to get the sound of the room. That's how you can make drum machines sound like real drums sometimes. Obviously, not the feel, but at least you can get the sound.

Hendrickson: I've done that at home. I have this real live kitchen. I put the amplifier in the kitchen and put some mikes some 15 to 20 feet away, or even in another room, so you get a distant effect. The mikes can be facing the amplifier, or away. It doesn't make any difference—it's whatever sound you're into. If you want a longer delay, face them away.

Farber: If you can make an echo chamber out of your bathroom, that's going to be the best space in the house.

Bruce, you like to mike synthesizers in a room.

Botnick: In the optimum situation, it's possible to balance the synthesizers in the room as part of the orchestra. I take a direct signal, which I will put up against the sound from the room, for presence. I do this with Jerry Goldsmith, who is an innovator in this style of recording. Most people use only the direct sound because they don't want any leakage, but the fact is that they don't know how to balance the synthesizers with the orchestra. By playing it in the room, and having Jerry balance it with the orchestra, it has size, it has depth. If you're playing a lower synthesizer part, lower frequencies take a longer time, and thus more distance, to develop properly. If you take it direct, it isn't developing.

Where do you mike the amplifiers for this kind of application?

Botnick: I don't place any microphones on them; I treat them as if they're violins, violas, cellos, or woodwinds. Mainly I use overall microphones, three at the front of the room, with occasional sweeteners—one above the violins, one above the violas, one above the cellos, a couple on the double basses, and two

on the woodwinds. If you have a synthesizer section, let's say five or six synthesizers, you could very easily put up five or six guitar amplifiers, preferably tube amplifiers. And, of course, they have to play dynamics with the conductor. That gives me dimension—distance from the overall microphones to the sound out of the instrument—so the sounds are rounded, they have size, you can touch them. Then, if you take the direct signals for presence—say you have a stereo instrument like the Yamaha GS1, and you bring that up against the overall sound, then you have the presence, and yet the dimension and depth of the microphone sound. You have a much bigger synthesizer sound, and it blends better with the orchestra. If you've got acoustic instruments in the room and you put something synthetic up against them, they don't really blend because one's in one room, and the other's in no room.

Can individual synthesists use this technique to do multi-track recordings of themselves?

Botnick: Absolutely. When I did the score to *Runaway* with Jerry, which was an all-synthesizer score, we recorded everything direct; but sometimes when we were mixing I would feed that sound into the studio and bring it back on a microphone. Again, that gave it size and room-tone. I recommend that highly to anybody recording synthesizers.

Does this replace a digital room simulator?

Botnick: No. That's another sound. A digital simulator is exactly that. It's still direct. There is *perceived* depth, but there's always that ultimate in presence without any dynamics—and what we're talking about is dynamics. When a synthesizer decays, when you release a note, if you're direct, you hear it released exactly as it's designed in the instrument. When it's played into a room from a speaker, the room itself is also resounding. If you play a $B\flat$ into the room, and the room happens to be receptive to that frequency and enhances it, the decay of the $B\flat$ will continue longer than the actual synthesizer played. It's only milliseconds, but it does go on longer and you get an enhancement of the sound. If you move the microphone farther away from the loudspeaker, you get natural delay in the room the farther you go back.

Do you have any favorite effects for giving a direct signal some depth?

Botnick: I try everything. I'll try a

standard acoustic echo chamber with delays on it—delaying the signal going in, delaying the signal coming out. I'll equalize the chambers. I'll use the Yamaha REV1, AMS 16 RMX, or Sony DRE2000, and heavily modify the programs in there, or even write my own programs, shaping the equalization, the decay, and the predelays. You use every tool at hand to make a synthesizer sound acoustic, because we still hear acoustically. We don't plug directly into the tape machine and hear without any loudspeakers—you don't plug a wire into your brain. Often one reverb doesn't do everything: you may use an acoustic chamber, say on drums, for the roundness and the rise time, and you may use an EMT plate on the snare drum because it has a real crack, and then you may use an AMS digital reverb to get the snare's crunch, and then you may use an EMT set at a very low delay time on the tom-toms.

Do you try to keep each of those reverberant fields distinct?

Botnick: No, they tend to blend into one reverberant field.

Farber: Five years ago you had one EMT plate, and that was it for your whole record. Now, six or seven digital echo devices, four plates, and three live chambers aren't enough. Record listeners these days expect to hear things certain ways, and you've got to be contemporary with that if it's a contemporary song. Often we'll use a long chamber to make the vocals sound intimate, and a gated room sound to make the drums sound huge, and that makes something sound intimate and huge all at once. Once again, it's a matter of setting up various sounds on your different devices and trying them. If one or two of them seem to go in the general direction you want to go with that instrument—whether it's an electronic snare drum, a real snare drum, or a synthesizer—then you go with them. If they're close, but not quite what you had in mind, you make adjustments until you get what you want. I'm a very non-technical engineer. I don't usually talk about decibels and waveforms. If it sounds good, then it's the right thing.

Hendrickson: A longer chamber tends to soften things, in my opinion, and using a shorter chamber on a different sound at the same time separates the two sounds much farther than if I had the same chamber on both.

Do you have any favorite effects for drum machine sounds?

Hendrickson: Nowadays, everybody's using gated chambers and gated rooms for drums. To me, that's getting sort of old. But there's always an instance where you can use it, and I do it too. There are some things you can do besides just gating the chamber to the snare. I'll key a miked room to the bass drum, and key the room to the snare, so you have the room open up on the bass drum, and have the room open up on the snare drum, to create a distinct rhythm. Sometimes you may have a hi-hat rhythm, or something like that, that plays a major part in the song, so I'll key a keyboard pad off the hi-hat rhythm. That way you get the notes in the pad playing in a hi-hat type of rhythm.

Farber: I've gated a pad to a snare drum to make the backbeat huge. Sometimes a pad is just clogging up the song, so I'll gate it to the snare or hi-hat.

Do you ever use a gate to fix a noisy synthesizer?

Farber: As a last resort, but if there's too much noise, I'll suggest using another axe. Often I can back off on the filter to the point where it doesn't disturb the sound, but gets rid of the annoying noise. But if you can't hear it in the song, I wouldn't worry about it if you hear it by itself.

Lord-Alge: Depending on the sound, I try to roll off the high end so that it won't be hissing all the time. If it's just a sound that happens in a couple of spots, you can mute that channel on the console, or on the tape machine, or just pull down the fader, until that sound comes in. Usually, when the signal comes in, the hiss isn't that bad; it's just when the signal's not going that you'll hear all the hiss. You can use a gate, which closes and doesn't let the noise through when the signal's not there.

Do you end up gating out digital noise when you're working with digital synthesizers?

Lord-Alge: Oh yeah, a lot of the time. Especially with brass sounds and bass sounds. When I record them, I'll roll off a little bit of high end. I come across this all the time with DX7 bass sounds: You want to get it bright and warm, but when you boost the high end, you get all that hiss, just from the instrument itself. Instead of boosting the high end, instead I boost up more in the 3k to 4k range, which is an upper midrange. If you just add a little bit of that, it usually works really well, and then you can roll off the top end so that it's not quite as noisy. The main thing is to get it to tape as clean as

you can get it, because if you have it on tape really clean, half the battle's won. You're saving yourself a lot of work later when you mix it down; then, if the stuff is all noisy and hissy, you're going to go crazy. If I have 46 tracks that are hissing, you can imagine how much noise that would be, so I try to put it on tape as quiet as I can. I always record at an optimum level—the safest level you can record on any tape machine is 0VU. On the machines we use, I can get away with just slamming it for certain things, not for lead vocals, but say for guitars, or just about anything that doesn't have a lot of transients. You have to record something that has a lot of attack, or is very percussive, at a lower level. Something like a hi-hat should be hitting at –10dB; any higher and it'll leak across the tracks.

But isn't level a relative thing? You can calibrate one meter so that it reads zero at one level, and you can calibrate another so that zero is an entirely different level.

Lord-Alge: I'm referring to home equipment now. If I'm ever in doubt about something, I'll record it at zero. On almost any tape machine, that level is good.

Hendrickson: I usually have the tape machine aligned so it's recording five or six dB hotter than normal. There's a certain point where the tape saturates and won't take any more signal, and it starts compressing. To me, it makes the sound much fuller and more punchy. You can do it at home with any tape, but in equipment made for home recording the electronics won't hold up as well as they do in the studio. You may get distortion instead of tape compression, but there will be a certain amount of tape compression if you don't go overboard.

Do you equalize synthesizers?

Hendrickson: Unless the sound is really dull I try not to use any EQ on synthesizers, because the sound is already there. If the player knows his instrument and he hears something a certain way, I usually don't have to mess with it. As far as EQing in general goes, once you get things sounding a certain way in the mix and they fit together, you just know where to go, or you search for a frequency if you're not sure where it is. You just tweak the thing around until it sounds right. Somebody can say, 'oh yeah, it needs a little bit more 6k,' but until you tweak it there you never know. Sometimes I go overboard just to find out if it's right or wrong—if I know there's

a frequency in there that I don't like, I put the level all the way up on the EQ and poke around until that frequency sticks out. Then I back it off.

Johnston: Acoustic instruments are not flat instruments. They all have personality. The way people play them brings out certain frequencies. Synthesizers, in my opinion, sound better if you EQ them, even in some places where you think they might not need it, because it skews the frequency response just a little bit.

Botnick: I think equalization with synthesizers leaves a lot to be desired, because synthesizers, in their basic form, sound right to begin with. If you start equalizing, you're changing the balance of the chordal sound. You're going to bring out certain notes over others. It's not the same as when you equalize an acoustic guitar, when you want to make the overall instrument brighter, because what you're really equalizing is the percussiveness of the attack. Or, in the case of an acoustic piano, you're enhancing the brightness of the hammers striking the strings.

What about using an aural exciter to add brightness to synthesizers?

Botnick: In *Runaway*, we used an aural exciter on the synthesizers and it really made them come to life. If you wind up with, say, 30 tracks of synthesizers, and they're all direct, and you mix them together, you get all these overtones sitting on top of one another and they don't mesh very well. We found that by using the aural exciter we were able to give the synthesizers *air*, the air you hear in an orchestra that's flowing freely around the instruments. A lot of times we have to get that by adding lots of reverb—not to the point where it's ringing, but to the point where the instruments are flowing.

Hendrickson: I used an aural exciter once, but to me it was like a bunch of distortion. I decided that I didn't need any more distortion than I already had on my tapes. A lot of guys swear by them, though. I'll probably try one again in the future. I give everything more than one chance.

Lord-Alge: I never use them. If you want the honest truth, I think they're a big load of crap. I really do. They don't do anything for me.

What advice can you give players that would make life easier in the studio?

Lord-Alge: Be friendly with the engineer, and let him know what you want, especially if you're getting a head-

Bruce Botnick.

77

phone mix. Let the engineer know how you want to hear the song, how the mix would make it easier for you to play the part—because you could be struggling, and all you'd have to do is say, "Put up the kick drum, I'm having trouble with the time." Keep the lines of communication with the engineer and the producer open. It makes things much easier.

Hendrickson: I find it helps a player's performance to get the mix to sound like they're ready to perform, so they get excited about it—maybe not a final mix, but good enough so they can groove on it. If there's no chamber on anything and everything is real dry, then there's just no excitement to it, and the only way you can get excitement is to turn it up to 120dB. You have to try to get

Jeff Hendrickson.

a feel going for the song, so the guy who's playing gets a feel. After that, it's up to the keyboard player. The better he knows the instrument, the better it's going to sound, and the more comfortable he's going to be in the studio. The best sounds I've ever gotten came from guys who knew their axe up and down. They knew the programs, they knew how to play, they had a lot of confidence, and the sounds come out much better because of it. There can be a lot of players in there, and no matter what I do, i can't make them sound good if they don't play well.

Farber: To me, the most important thing about recording synthesizers is not so much what I do, but having a player I can communicate with. Communicating with him to make the sound right can make my work minimal. If the sound isn't getting into the track right, I can say, "Can you open up your filter a little bit more?" instead of just cranking up the

10k. If he's playing a bass sound and it seems to be going in and out of phase, I'll ask him to try putting the voices in unison, or mono, or whatever the setting is on that particular axe, to see if that makes it more solid. Basically, that's the key in recording any of this kind of stuff. It shouldn't be a lot of work or a lot of tricks—the sound you want for that song should be coming out of the instrument. You should hire someone who's in tune with you, someone who can get those sounds. Then it should fit automatically, and whatever effects you decide to add can only enhance it.

You play some keyboards yourself. Does that make any difference in your approach to recording them?

Farber: Sure, because I've owned

synthesizers, and I've studied electronic music composition. It helps me to communicate better with synthesists, and to know what's possible. Usually, as an engineer, I don't like to distract a musician from what he's doing, and I don't like him to distract me; but sometimes we can help each other out. Sometimes I'll wind up playing something, and sometimes I'll hand the faders over to a musician, if he wants to try something that he might have a better feel for.

Lord-Alge: The main thing is to get the performance on tape. "Always In Record"—that's my motto. I've gotten some of my best stuff, especially on this Winwood project, because I would put a blank track in record while he was messing with his sound, or while I was getting my mix together. Sometimes we got solos out of that, or a part would come out of it. I think that musicians should tell the engineer, "If you have a blank track, put me in record while I'm messing around," because things come out of it. Ideas just come and go. I've seen it

happen a million times—they missed it because the tape wasn't recording. Always keep the tape machine in record—that's what it's there for.

by Ted Greenwald

STUDIO PROFILES

June 1986

It began innocently enough: After the session was over and most of the band had gone home, the keyboard player would take his axe into the control room, plug it directly into the board, and whip off one last track. From an odd overdub now and then, this grew into a more regular practice, and soon the keyboard player was setting up in the control room as a matter of course. Soon the drummer got a drum machine, and brought it in with the keys to sync it to the sequencer. Then the sax player got a pitch-to-MIDI converter and plugged into his bandmate's DX7. One day the engineer, wondering why the control room felt so crowded, looked up from the console, over the stack of synthesizers, past the table littered with MIDI accessories, out through the glass at the recording studio—and realized that the other room was completely empty.

Studio players caught in the whirlwind of commerce have had to assimilate constant changes in keyboard instruments for at least two decades, while the recording facilities themselves could afford to stand back and watch. Developments in MIDI and synchronization technologies, however, are having such a drastic impact on music production that recording studios are beginning to step to the tune of keyboard players.

While small, limited-access studios are springing up right and left in the fertile ground of audio and video production, the first generation of professional keyboard-oriented studios is still nested in the living rooms and garages of the most successful players and producers, and germinating in the profits of a few top recording companies. Several large-scale facilities are, at this moment, in the design or construction phases. A few fledgling operations have already appeared, though, to point the way to the future. Four facilities in particular, illustrate the kinds of impact that keyboards are having on the professional recording environment. Unique Recording in Manhattan has had great success in the field

78

of popular records, while at the same time making a point of accommodating keyboard players. In Los Angeles, MIDI-Land has expanded the personal keyboard studio concept to serve the film and television scoring community. In the field of advertising music production, Ciani/Musica Studio and Shelton Leigh Palmer & Co., both in New York City, have taken their own high-tech approaches to recording keyboards.

A studio built around the new technology must adapt traditional styles of music production to the expanded capabilities that it makes available. This raises a number of issues of design, both technological and logistical. Audio signal routing, for example, is a complex matter in any modern studio. The addition of MIDI, however, with its serial nature, its master/slave relationships, and its unique opportunities for processing, clouds the water considerably. This and other themes crop up repeatedly in the studio profiles which follow: the integration of computers into the studio, the merging roles of keyboard player and recording engineer, the interfacing of various synchronization codes, the replacement of audio recording with MIDI data storage, and numerous others. In the studio of the future, the power and flexibility of keyboard technology will be fully integrated on an ongoing evolutionary basis.

Unique Recording Studios

Unique Recording Studios in Manhattan, owned and operated by *Keyboard* columnist Bobby Nathan, is one of the most dramatic examples of how keyboard technology is affecting professional recording facilities. Unique is a hit-making, record-oriented operation, and as such can't afford to ignore instrumentalists playing guitars, drums, strings, winds, and so on. Nonetheless, ever since Unique's inception as a rehearsal studio, Nathan has recognized the tremendous power of electronic keyboards, and has steadily incorporated them into his operation. Recently Unique opened a new room, MIDI City, dedicated to recording MIDI instruments.

While mountains of keyboard technology line the walls of MIDI City, the space is remarkably uncluttered. "The room was designed for keyboard recording," Nathan explains. "It has a large control room, so there's lots of space. It

can easily accommodate 25 or 30 synthesizers, and there's still room to set up a bunch of tables full of interface boxes and sequencers. In a lot of other rooms, the synthesist has to set up his racks in front of the console—he's standing under the speakers, and he has to run around the room just to get past the board." Direct boxes are built into the walls so that unbalanced synthesizer outputs can easily be routed to the console from anywhere in the room. "That does away with a lot of unnecessary wires," says Nathan. "It's set up so that if a keyboardist wants to play with guitarists or bass players, they can all play in

The Solid State Logic 4056 console in Studio B, Unique Recording, New York City.

the room together. There's even room for a Simmons kit, and instead of the drummer listening through headphones, he can listen to the monitors and hear it the way the engineer and producer are hearing it." Acoustic recording hasn't been ignored entirely; it has simply been relegated to a small booth situated in front of the console, where the studio room would ordinarily be.

While the console, monitoring system, and racks of outboard gear permanently occupy their traditional position at the front of the room, the remainder of the equipment in MIDI City is in constant flux. "If you come in tomorrow, the setup will be totally different," Nathan asserts. "People think that a MIDI studio should be set up a certain way. That might be fine if you're a group and you need a consistent arrangement.

79

We've found that there's an infinite number of setups, as far as which master keyboard someone will use, which slaves, which sequencer." At this point, MIDI splitters and switchers are brought in as they're needed, although Nathan has plans to build MIDI ports into the walls.

An infinite number of setups may well be possible at Unique, which owns virtually every popular make and model of synthesizer and sampling keyboard except the Synclavier and the Fairlight CMI, some of them in triplicate to satisfy demand. They're all available with a booking in one of the three main rooms. A full complement of MIDI accessory boxes is also kept on hand to satisfy any need that might come up. None of this equipment belongs in a particular room, Nathan explains: "Everything's floating around between all the studios." In addition, Unique maintains a collection of modular and otherwise "obsolete" instruments, including such rarities as the Movement Drum Computer. "It came out in Europe at about the same time the Linn LM-1 was getting popular here. Its specialty is that it has both digital and analog sounds," Nathan says. Available to clients on a rental basis, these antiques are not only kept in working order; they're also retrofitted with MIDI. "Every synthesizer we own has to have MIDI," Nathan insists. "That's been our tradition."

Another of Unique's traditions is that each engineer knows at least the basic programming functions of every instrument in the studio. "We have seminars with our own staff," Nathan reports. "When we get a new piece of equipment, the engineers who have learned it first show the rest of us. That keeps us abreast." Competition, as it happens also plays its part in keeping everyone informed. "If you want to be on top of it as an engineer, or an assistant, or a programmer, you have to be able to handle the new gear. And you can be on top of it today, but if you miss one NAMM show, where will you be tomorrow? I don't have to hand out responsibilities. The people on the staff take it upon themselves to know how to use this stuff."

Not all of the work at Unique is done in the recording studios. There's also a small preproduction room down the hall from MIDI City. While its technological aspect is certainly less flashy, not to mention more cluttered, than the state-of-the-art control rooms, Nathan emphasizes the importance of its role in his production concept. "We try to push people into doing some planning ahead of time, to do all the programming before they walk into the studio," he says. This room is where the planning and programming take place. "There's always something that's going to change at the last minute, but if they do their homework up front, recording is a more pleasurable experience for them. A lot of people will come in here with the engineer and an outside programmer to start working on the track. LinnSequencer, Total Music, the MSQ-700—they can come in here and set up whatever they need. A guy may have written some music at home with the MSQ, but he doesn't have all the synthesizers he needs. He can come here and get a pretty good idea of what it should sound like."

Equipped with an IBM computer (Unique's other computers float), the pre-production room is ideal for sequencing. "We've got the Octave Plateau sequencer, Roland's MPS, Personal Composer, Texture, Sight and Sound's MIDI Ensemble, and lots of other programs," Nathan points out. "I keep them all on a hard disk, so I don't have to worry about any of the programs being lost." Even with such an extensive collection of sequencing programs, Nathan isn't ready to give up on magnetic recording tape. "At this point, MIDI recording isn't as flexible as multi-track. You can still lock up the sequencers with the tape in order to use all the signal processing gear coming out with MIDI implementation."

The preproduction room is also intended as a reference room for the studio's library of synthesized and sampled sounds. "Our library of DX7 sounds has 4,000 patches, and it's growing at a ridiculous rate. Just to blow through them is time-consuming," Nathan explains. "We have them all categorized—say, string sounds, there's 800 different ones to choose from. Why should you do that while you're paying the full studio rate?

"The whole era of recording has changed," he continues. "These days you don't have to go for ten takes before the tempo is right, just to get a basic track for doing overdubs. In many cases now the tempo is determined in advance, the drum sounds are picked, and you can transfer the basics for a whole album in one day." Nathan's entire operation, from MIDI City to the programming room to the other studios, is geared toward adapting traditional recording practices to these changes.

"We're preparing for the future," Nathan asserts.

The particular future he has in mind is a concept he calls "the MIDI band": a group of instrumentalists, each performing on controllers adapted from their traditional instruments just as a MIDI keyboard is based on the piano, all generating MIDI data streams in real time. "With all the sequencers, there's not as much jamming as there used to be. As MIDI devices become more sophisticated, the MIDI band is definitely going to come along. It's sad to say that this whole sequencing/drum machine thing has gotten in the way of people playing together. Just because keyboards have MIDI doesn't mean you have to sequence or quantize." As if to soothe those who feel alienated by the music world's current fascination with electronics, Nathan offers assurances that "live music is not dead. Live drums are not dead. Acoustic piano is not dead. The Rhodes might be questionable—but there are a lot of things that still need to be played by live musicians."

In addition to its effects on musicians and the ways they interact, MIDI is having a direct influence on recording procedures at Unique. "The general rule has always been, 'Don't record the effects until the mix.' We've had to change that, because all of the new MIDI effects, specifically the Yamaha REV7, the Lexicon PCM-70, the Yamaha D1500, the Roland SDE-2500, the Roland SDE-2500, and the MXR D12, can be switched very creatively by the players. You can even program a sequencer to do a patch change on every eighth note." The ubiquitous nature of MIDI has also prompted Nathan to install 48-track capability in all of Unique's rooms: "We've found that with MIDI, people don't want to make definite decisions. Since we have a lot of synthesizers they can't find elsewhere, they would rather record it all now. Then later, if there's a question, they've got it all on tape.

"We have a game called MIDI Roulette," he jokes. "Take any five synthesizers, MIDI them together, and bring up a string patch on each one. You've got a killer sound that no one synthesizer can compete with. Then you can change the balance of the five faders at the board. There's an infinite number of possibilities."

With so much equipment on hand, Unique's engineering staff has come to rely on sampling technology to simplify matters. "When we did the latest Cheap

Trick record," Nathan recalls, "we found that we were using a big MIDI hook-up with ten or 20 synthesizers all the time. We'd fade them in at the console, and

one fader might be up just a touch. Even though we have Total Recall automation [which electronically photographs the positions of very potentiometer and switch on the board at any given moment] it would have taken a long time to set up the synths again and recreate it on another day. So we took samples of every sound right then and there."

A Neve console surrounded by MIDI gear at Unique Recording. This photo was taken prior to the installation of the SSL console pictured on page 79.

81

Chris Page at MIDIland, seated in front of his Apple IIe and Macintosh SE computers. The large bank of meters in the background belongs to a Sony/MCI JH24 24-track tape recorder.

If Unique's obvious commitment to MIDI isn't enough, there is one final tidbit of evidence testifying to the tremendous influence keyboard technology is having on hit record production. In order to make way for mounting banks of keyboards and MIDI boxes, Nathan was persuaded to swap spaces between his traditionally cramped control rooms and the larger studio rooms. "We started this MIDI City concept in May of 1985, and it turned out so well that we've already flipped around one of the other control rooms because it wasn't as comfortable for keyboardists," he reports. "We made what used to be the studio into the control room." While Unique has de-emphasized the studio area it has been done away with almost entirely in the other three facilities discussed here.

MIDIland Studios

Chris Page and Mike Lang, two prominent Los Angeles session players, have teamed up with keyboardist/producer/engineer David Hentschel, best known for his work with Elton John during the early '70s and later with Genesis, to launch MIDIland Studios. Their facility is a full realization of the personal keyboard studio concept, integrating a full-scale MIDI keyboard rig with a standard studio control room. In many ways this arrangement is representative of the trend in personal studios built by keyboardists for their own use. "It's

designed, not exclusively for us to work with, but certainly to support our own careers and to make our work a lot easier," Page explains.

"One of the reasons I wanted to design the room was to alleviate the frustration I knew composers were having on scoring stage, integrating synthesizers into a live orchestra," he continues. "There isn't the time needed for programming in a live scoring situation. There isn't time for a composer to get the most out of synthesizers, as far as doubling for colors, and programming the sounds the way that they're responding in the score." One of the chief functions of MIDIland is the preparation of multi-track tapes using synthesizers, to be overdubbed later by an orchestra at a studio better suited for that kind of work. "After all of the scoring dates I've done in the last few years," Page says, "I knew there would have to be rooms like this, where synths could be treated as a separate issue and then married to the orchestra in a scoring situation."

It's equally important that the three owner/musicians have a stable environment suited to their way of working. I've built a room that's familiar to me," Page continues, "because if the ambient area that I'm dealing with remains constant, then my ears will never be confused." Furthermore, David Hentschel explains, "Everything is close at hand. Everything comes up straightaway on the board without having to patch anything in. You can more or less reach the whole console and all the keyboards at one time, which is one of the most important things in working quickly. You don't

have to waste time on communications with other people; if you have a sound in your head that you want to go for, it's a lot quicker just to tweak the knobs yourself and fly back to the keyboard, rather than trying to explain your idea to someone else. You don't even need an engineer at times."

"Having so much equipment over a large area, instantly available, allows one to keep the spontaneity and creativity," Page adds. "I could not possibly take all the equipment I have here to another studio. It would take far too much time to get it all happening, and to become familiar with the control room, the board, and the engineer."

Like MIDI City, MIDIland is an extension of the traditional control room, augmented by small areas for preproduction and acoustic recording. "There is no actual live area in the studio," Hentschel point out. "It's just like a big control room with no studio area, and it's attached to the side of a house. I've run mike lines to the house for live recording. In fact, we recorded a choir in there the other day."

The board and monitors occupy the front of the main room, while keyboards and other instruments dominate the rear. The master keyboard will eventually stand in the center at the back of the room, but Page, Hentschel, and Lang have yet to decide on the best one. "Mike is using a Sequential Prophet-T8 for the feel," Page reports, "and I'm looking at the Yamaha KX-76." Among their arsenal of instruments, which is made up of the combined setups of the three keyboardists, the most unusual is a Kobal RSF Expander system, and 8-voice analog synthesizer with continuously variable waveforms, for which virtually every parameter is voltage-controllable. The RSF Expander is linked to the newer instruments with CV-to-MIDI converters. "In one back corner we've built a whole electronic percussion section," Page describes. "That consists of a Simmons kit, various Linns, and an Emulator for any extra percussion we need." Tie lines route signals from the back of the room to the board's inputs and the patch bay. "All of our drum machines can plug into the wall and straight to the tape machine. All of our synths can do that too."

"The computers sit right in the center of the back," Page continues. A Commodore 64 handles most of the patch library. MIDIland uses an Apple to run a Greengate sampler/sequencer, which

82

is also dynamically controllable via MIDI, and the studio has just acquired a Macintosh and Opcode sequencing software. Most of the sequencing, however is done with the LinnSequencer, which doesn't require an external computer. "It's still one of the most usable, creative sequencing tools I've ever seen," he reports. "It sits in my rack. It's very easily accessed with my left hand as I'm playing. Using a computer is not quite as fast as having something instantly there, with one hand to work with while the other is playing—but I've only just started working with the Macintosh."

The interface for synchronization between all of the various sound generators, drum machines, and sequencers is the Garfield Electronics Doctor Click, which integrates clock pulses and MIDI, while SMPTE is supplied by the LinnSequencer. "We drive everything mostly from MIDI," says Page, "but we're starting to get heavily into SMPTE." Hentschel amplifies Page's comment: "At the moment, to do offsets we have to delay a pulse going to the Doctor Click by however many milliseconds. With SMPTE it's much easier to enter in an offset. Also, because the Doctor Click is always chasing a click, there are minute discrepancies which you don't get with SMPTE. When you're scoring to picture, if you're using that system, you're locked up to the picture straightaway. You can run all your MIDI sequences straight off the picture if you want to."

The sequencers, both hardware and software, are used more as composing and arranging, rather than recording, tools. "I use the sequencer mainly to hear the parts, but that's not necessarily the way it will be laid down," Page says. Hentschel agrees: "This is a lot quicker than laying down three or four overdubs to check whether an arrangement is working or not." "We're updating all the time as we go," Page continues. "From the press of a button on the Doctor Click, we have all the drum modules and synth modules working together to give us a full orchestral concept before anything goes to tape. I'm not too worried about the sounds at that point."

Page shares Bobby Nathan's opinion that tape is generally a more practical medium than MIDI data for actual production, particularly in a situation with limited slave modules and signal processors. "I'd far rather use the modules for doubling colors, experimenting with trying different sounds together, to respond off of one sequence,

rather than a single sound off of one sequence. When I'm going to commit to tape, I will take each part of that sequence and create the sounds to be as wonderful as I think they can be, which may possibly entail my using all of my equipment on one sound. That needs to go to tape. Tape also gives me a certain flexibility as far as outboard gear is concerned. Once the stuff is committed to tape and coming back through the board, I can process the sounds."

David Hentshel, also at MIDIland, pondering a score. He's seated at a Roland S-50 sampler, and in the rack (from top to bottom) we see an E-mu Emulator, a Linn Sequencer, a Roland MD-8 MIDI interface, Zaphod MIDI switchers, Yamaha TX7s, a Roland Jupiter 8, and a Yamaha DX7. Behind David is a Hill Multimix console and a Roland MKB-1000 controller keyboard.

In keeping with this method (that is, applying signal processing during the mix), a portion of the studio's signal processing gear is mounted beside the mixing console, accessible from a patch bay. Some outboard boxes, however, are mobile. "I have a rack that travels with my synthesizers, which of course has some processing gear in it," Page explains, "so I can commit processing to 24-track tape as I'm programming a sound, which I like to do."

Programs created at MIDIland, at least those for the DX7, are stored and indexed using Mimetics software for the Commodore 64. "I spent three months organizing about 5,000 sounds," Page recalls, "and there are lots more I have yet to go through." The computer's MIDI output is connected to a switcher box for routing to the DX7 and TX modules. Page's library of samples is equally large, but hasn't yet been computerized. "I've been collecting samples for about four years now," he says. "I got very established with the Emulator. Mike is getting a compact disc for his Emulator II that has the equivalent of 1,105 disks worth of ROM."

For Page, having all of these sounds on hand allows the MIDIland team to work with synthesizers in an orchestral context. "This facility allows the synthesizer to have the power of the orchestra—not to replace an orchestra, but as an orchestra in itself, for composers recognizing that the sounds made possible by the technology are far cleaner than they've been able to achieve with live recording situations.

Ciani/Musica Studio

Suzanne Ciani at the Synclavier.

Of the four studios profiled here, Suzanne Ciani's takes the most radical approach. Like MIDI City and MIDILand, Ciani/Musica Studio subverts the traditional control room concept in order to grasp MIDI technology by the horns, but its design goes a step further in adapting the recording environment to the creative needs of keyboardists. Rather than organizing the studio's sound genera-

tion functions around several immobile banks of keyboards, or even a single master keyboard, Ciani's facility accommodates up to seven mobile, independent, and interconnected keyboard workstations. [*Ed. Note: Ciani/Musica Studio has updated and enhanced their equipment since this article was written in June of 1986. Contact them at 30 E. 23rd St., New York, NY 10010 for their current equipment list.*] Like satellites amidst the room's spacious floor, the workstations surround a huge horizontal rack of processing equipment in the middle of the room—an advanced version of Ciani's original "voice box." Two additional rooms, partitioned from the main studio with glass, allow for limited live recording. One booth is designed with drums in mind, while the other is currently occupied by couches for visiting clients.

Signal routing throughout the three spaces and among workstations is so thoroughly integrated as to be nearly invisible, and yet the flexibility exists to send virtually any signal—audio, MIDI, SMPTE—between any of the workstations, the voice box, and the board. In tailoring the facility to the company's very individual approach to music and sound production, Ciani/Musica has devised an arrangement generalized enough to suit just about any conceivable working style.

The workstations are designed to hold whatever instruments are needed for a given project, so their individual setups are, at least for the time being, continually changing. Each workstation provides for a master keyboard, a slave keyboard, and a number of rack-mount units. A custom-designed 10-input mixer is permanently mounted below the main surface. It provides balanced outputs, both direct and its own stereo mix, for routing to the console. A foot-pedal input gives the user control over the overall output levels. The same mixer also provides a headphone mix, so the balance heard at each workstation is determined by the user. "That way you can have one person working on a sound while another is recording a track, completely independently," explains Robert Kahn, one of Ciani/Musica's team of writer/programmers.

A MIDI switcher is mounted below the mixer, allowing the user to bus MIDI signals among the various workstations. "If I wanted to play a slave instrument across the room from this station," Kahn points out, "I'd just select station number

84

one as the master, and station number two as the slave. Then at the other station I would select station zero, which allows it to receive the data stream. Anything that's MIDI can be controlled by, or can control, anything else, anywhere in the room." Selecting a station as the master automatically unselects it as a slave, in order to avoid feedback; a station can also be disassigned entirely. LEDs indicate the data stream's status as either outgoing or incoming.

Finally, a box located at the foot of each workstation routes audio and digital signals among them. "Each box has 12 audio outputs, ten of which normal the mixer's direct outputs to the patch bay," Kahn explains. "Then there are two isolated digital lines, which can carry SMPTE, FSK, sync pulses, and so forth." In addition, four pairs of auxiliary buses are normalled to send the station's mix to the console, and to receive mixes from other workstations.

Only four workstations are usually set up at the moment, but that could change. "Right now we have all this new equipment, and a whole new studio, so we're constantly trying things out," Kahn comments. "This weekend, one of our staff people was here doing drums, so we set up a drum station. He had Roland pads set up, and he was flying stuff back and forth between the Synclavier and the TX816. While all that was going on, someone else was in the drum booth programming the Linn 9000 and Prophet-5. That's a completely different situation than if we write a jingle, and we come in at 10 A.M., and we're supposed to finish by 4 P.M. Then the workstations would have to be worked out in advance. Eventually we'll get to the point where one setup will work for everything."

Like the MIDILand staff, Ciani's team is divided about which is the most effective MIDI keyboard controller. Fortunately, since a different one is available at each workstation, it's not a crucial matter.

After the workstations, the most prominent feature in the main room is the expanded voice box, which lies perpendicular to the console like a high-tech casket. The side that faces the mixing board sports a huge patch bay, giving the engineer access to virtually every audio signal in the studio. The narrow box is brimming with a collection of horizontally-mounted signal processors that changes virtually every day. "It's built with the express purpose of changing," Kahn says. "We keep all our

processing here: digital reverbs, delays, chorus, flangers, sampling, Harmonizers, gates, stereo processors, equalizers, and so on."

The voice box, in its current form, has its roots in the working method Ciani developed when her studio was in the living room of her Manhattan apartment, and she was carrying her equipment to sessions around town. Kahn explains its genesis: "The original voice box was a road case lying on its back with a little 8-channel mixer in it. If you were working with the synths on one side of the room, you would roll the box over, plug everything in, take the stereo output from the mixer into the main patch bay across the room, and from there to tape. There were guitar cables, and later MIDI cables, everywhere. It was decided that, one, the wires had to go, and two, the voice box had to stay. Since it was becoming the real central item in the studio, eventually the idea arrived to let the voice box sit, and have the synths roll around instead."

The production method evolved in Ciani's living room also influences the handling of another crucial issue for the new generation of recording studios— the importance of tape recording. Since the voice box is used in the actual creation of individual sounds, the signal processing performed with it must go directly to tape. "We print with effects," Kahn states. "Because of the emphasis on sound design, on the character of the sound, processing is an integral part. It's not just three synths and reverb; it's maybe one synth and five effects. Instead of fixing it in the mix, you get the sound you want and go on. So tape is really central."

The Ciani/Musica staff, like Page, Lang, and Hentschel at MIDILand, uses MIDI sequencing primarily as a compositional tool. In fact, they're intrigued by the different kinds of music they come up with when using different sequencers.

When it comes to producing a finished product, their method is unique in that the final mix is built up one sound at a time, rather than mixed as a whole from a number of pre-existing tracks. The workstation outputs are normalled to the channel inputs on one side of the board, feeding the multi-track, and the tape outputs are heard at the faders on the other side of the board. As each individual sound/part is finished and committed to tape, it is added to the mix using the playback faders. "By the time you're done recording the tracks," Kahn

The control room at Ciani/Musica, showing an Amek Angela mixing console. The box in the right-hand foreground houses signal processing gear, and the roll around pedestal supports the remote control and autolocator for the Otari MTR-90-II 24-track tape recorder (not pictured).

explains, "the mix is finished. It works great, because you're never creating sounds that will step on each other.

"Let's say we're listening to a mix that's not final," he continues, illustrating the inadequacy of conventional multi-track techniques. "There's a delay somewhere that you know you'll want, but you're not printing it. You might record another sound that's filling up the space that should have been taken up with the delay." Most of this work is done by an engineer, but not necessarily. "It's possible to work without one, if you bring the multi-track over and put your workstation close to the board," Kahn says. "It's not too bad once you get everything set up where you want it."

SMPTE is Ciani/Musica's preferred synchronization method; two master devices are involved. "The Timeline Lynx locks up the tape machines to SMPTE," says Kahn, "It's a kind of 'set-it-and-forget-it' thing. The Garfield Master Beat reads SMPTE and converts it into anything you want, so it needs to be available for patching. Through SMPTE we'll tie together the console automation, the Synclavier, the Linn 9000, tape, video, and—using the Master Beat—any MIDI device."

Since Ciani/Musica produces music primarily for television ads, most of the music syncs with a video image. The video player, operated by remote control, is kept hidden behind the console. Its output can be monitored via a large screen hung on the left-hand wall, or from a smaller TV screen. Both screens can be set to show a computer display as well. The large screen can be seen

clearly from anywhere in the main room; it's intended primarily for film scoring, although it is also used to display computerized information, such as waveform editing, to an entire production team.

Surprisingly, there's no place in the room set aside specifically for computers. If a computer is needed, it's simply brought in to fill the gap. At the moment, most sequencing is performed on dedicated machines, although the company is on the lookout for the right software. Ciani/Musica's programmers don't use voicing software: "There's no time and no need," Kahn asserts. Patch libraries, though, are stored on disk. "If there's something specific we need, and we can't make it up on the spot, we can always bring in a computer—but I think we work a little differently from other people. People talk about getting their libraries together, about having access to five zillion voices. Our needs come up as we write a spot. One thing needs to sound like broccoli bending, so we'll make it up right there. It's not a matter of having catalogs—it would take too long to find the right category, and then the right voice, and then it wouldn't be right anyway and we'd have to change it."

Although the studio was completed only recently, there's already a need for expansion. "When we designed the workstation mixer, we figured ten inputs would be ample," Kahn recalls. "Then all of a sudden there's the TX816. That leaves room for the DX7 and the 360 Systems MIDIBass. We designed the switcher back in August, too, and already we've outgrown it." A workstation designed specifically for drum machines is in the works; it will be interfaced with the drum booth so that a live drummer can easily trigger electronic drum sounds. There's some talk about upgrading to 48 tracks of tape, and installing some pre-MIDI synthesizers. "They aren't used that often," Kahn comments, "but it's nice to have them around." The good thing is that every week the machines are becoming smaller—just look at the TX816. We'll have room to grow because everything's contracting."

In addition to the studio's technical aspect, they insist that "an important part of the design is aesthetics. It's real critical that the environment here be conducive to work, so a great deal of attention was put on color, the sculptural quality of the glass, hiding the wires, the sense of space. People don't usually think of decoration as part of the design of a studio—this may be the first studio to be designed by a woman. And it may be one of the first examples of the way studios will be designed in the future. This is clearly a different way to do things. Just as the things that are happening with MIDI weren't necessarily envisioned when the specification was designed, the studio is designed to incorporate the possibilities of MIDI that we don't even know about yet."

Shelton Leigh Palmer & Co.

Their diverse approaches notwithstanding, the studios discussed so far all wed multi-keyboard performance setups with the conventional tape recording studio. Jingle composer/producer Shelton Leigh Palmer's high-tech facility differs in that it addresses the coming revolution in recording technology: tapeless recording. Much of the music Palmer records in his own studio is finished at commercial studios better suited for recording live instruments; he works with tape often for that purpose. Many projects, however, can be completed in a sequencer without ever resorting to multi-track tape. "Since the release of NED's newest polyphonic sampling package with beta-test SMPTE and MIDI implementation, we've been working almost exclusively with the Synclavier," Palmer reports. "We also use Octave Plateau's Sequencer Plus software for the IBM. We record to a Sony PCMF-1, which is a digital 2-track that records on videotape. We definitely do 50 percent of our work from the Synclavier to the console, and from there straight to digital."

"We're not totally tapeless," Palmer is quick to point out. "I don't believe it's possible to be totally tapeless, but what's important is to make the distinction, to determine what needs to go on tape and what doesn't." He scoffs, however, at the idea that anyone should avoid MIDI sequencing because of a lack of audio processing gear, at least in a professional setting. "That's obviously bogus, because a REV7, which is one of the most respectable digital reverbs ever invented—you could have ten of them in a room and they wouldn't cost you as much as one Lexicon 224X. You may not want it for your overall stereo reverb, but certainly it has a place as part of a dedicated reverb or effects system. That stuff is so inexpensive, they read MIDI, and they're all over the place. Roland

makes one; Yamaha, ART, even Korg makes one. I don't know if I'd like to cut albums [with stacks of lowcost digital reverbs], but certainly for the commercial productions that we're doing, it's silly to use anything else."

Palmer's entire studio fits into the space of "an average-sized bedroom." (When we spoke, Shelton Leigh Palmer & Co. was in the process of constructing an expanded facility which should be near completion at press time. For the purpose of this article, however, we discussed the company's former arrangement.) In addition to the equipment mentioned above, the basic setup consists of an MCI automated board, monitors, an MCI 24-track tape deck, a signal processing rack, an E-mu SP-12 drum machine, and an impressive complement of synthesizers.

"I work with an engineer who handles all the engineering functions, while I play from across the room," Palmer explains. "The slave instruments are mostly rackmounted. They're all within reach of me, and the recording is all within reach of the engineer." Although it's not the usual mode of operation, Palmer's studio, like Ciani/Musica's, can be juggled around for a single keyboard player working alone. "It's real easy to move everything into a big U all around the room."

Shelton Leigh Palmer, pictured at his Synclavier keyboard. Also pictured are an Apple Macintosh computer, a Yamaha DX7 (top), and an E-mu Emulator II.

Audio signal routing is handled via normalled connections and a patch bay. By Palmer's count, the studio has a total of 107 outputs: "You've got 32 Synclavier outputs, eight TX816 outputs, two different Voyetras in stereo, a DX7, an Emulator II which has eight outputs, eight from the SP-12—it adds up. The important independent outputs are normalled into the board's input faders, where the microphones would ordinarily be. Rather than bring up all eight Emulator II outputs, which are only used in the most complex sound effects jobs, we

The sampling power of the Synclavier is available as a keyboard-based system, or as a keyboardless, Direct-To-Disk, multi-track recorder—as pictured here.

just normal the mixed output. The first eight SP-12 outputs are normalled into the first eight channels as bass drum, snare drum, hi-hat, that sort of stuff; and the first eight Synclavier outputs, as well as the stereo poly [sampling] and stereo FM outputs, are normalled. The non-normal stuff is brought up at the patch bay." MIDI switching is handled by two J.L. Cooper 16/20 matrices. Are 32 MIDI inputs enough? "Actually, inputs aren't the problem—it's the outputs," Palmer answers. "There aren't that many master machines. You could get away with four inputs.

"There are only three keyboard instruments in the room: DX7, Emulator II, and Synclavier," he continues. "Any of those can be the master. But, you see, the Synclavier has eight possible MIDI out buses, so it's like having eight independent instruments. It has two MIDI ins. Each individual MIDI bus output has all 16 channels available. The complexity of it gets mind-boggling, because you can make anything do anything, go anywhere, be anybody. It's pretty strange."

Palmer uses all three master keyboards, depending on the application. "For most work, the DX7 is probably my favorite. It's fast enough, and sensitive enough, to do very percussive sorts of things. As a keyboard it's got its inadequacies, but it's certainly the best of the three that we have. I find myself playing the Synclavier keyboard, although it's

my least favorite, because it's close to all the buttons. We also have a Voyetra keyboard, which is the hippest keyboard we have for the Voyetra because it takes advantage of all kinds of Voyetra things, but it's a compromise. That's why, at the touch of a button, you can play any keyboard."

Even with three master keyboards, and despite the studio's usual working team of one keyboard player and one engineer, the capability exists to have several keyboardists performing at once. "We can have five or six independent MIDI paths going at once," Palmer insists. "In fact, there's an actual MIDI snake in the studio, like your normal microphone snake. You just plug in and you're on MIDI bus 1. The buses can be routed anywhere."

The same kind of flexibility has been built into the synchronization system, which, like much of the electronics and software in the studio, Palmer designed himself. "Everything is reading SMPTE, which is the master code for the entire world at the moment," he explains. "We hope to replace that with VITC—Vertical Interval Time Code—very soon. Vertical Interval Time code is written into the actual vertical intervals between each video frame, so you can work in slow motion and always be in the right place. That's real important. That's where video post-production is going, and that's obviously where audio will follow. You can create SMPTE from VITC, which is neat, because with a little external hardware and software everybody can be told what they're supposed to do, even if they're not capable of reading VITC by themselves. Eventually—which means within the next 90 days—we hope to be joystick-controlled in sub-frame mode with VITC. That will allow us to work in slow motion, to have basic song pointer technology, and lock-up time will be instantaneous."

"One of the things that makes our sync system a little bit different," he adds, "is that whatever machine you're recording on is the master. You tell our computer controller what machine you'll be recording on. If you're recording to tape, tape drives everything. If you're recording on synthesizers, the synthesizers drive everything. It's important because internal clock rates are internal clock rates, and we want to be true to each machine. To get the best possible performance, you have to be sure that a machine is clocking at its happiest rate."

The subject of clock resolution can

be particularly crucial in producing a recording without analog tape. The quantization inherent in digital technology has musical implications that keyboard players in a tapeless situation should be aware of. "The Synclavier strobes at [has a keyboard resolution of] 200Hz; that's pretty fast. The Sequencer Plus strobes considerably faster than that, and thus it sounds more like a tape recorder. Now, I don't know about some people, but I can certainly hear the difference between what I played into the Synclavier and what comes out of it. It's subtle, but it's definite. You put in something with some kind of a groove, and it comes back differently. The Sequencer Plus isn't like that; it's much more like tape. Of course, there's nothing quite like real tape, and that's why, when you're playing a burning solo—even if it's a synth solo—it's probably happier to

all it would do is eat up RAM. So, one rule is to put things that are RAM-intensive on tape, and things like MIDI information into computer memory. I also use tape for things, acoustic or electric, that need heavy signal processing just to be played properly. Sometimes I use tape just to print the signal processing to. Another rule is, if it's going to need to be changed, or if the client is going to make a comment and it's going to be easier to change in memory, then leave it in memory. If not, put it on tape. The key, of course, is maximum flexibility."

Sound effect, and voice-overs are usually recorded live to digital 2-track, and the relevant parts flown (that is, rerecorded) into the Synclavier's sampling facility. Sometime the procedure is a bit more involved: "We just did a project for some calcium supplement, and we needed a vocal group going

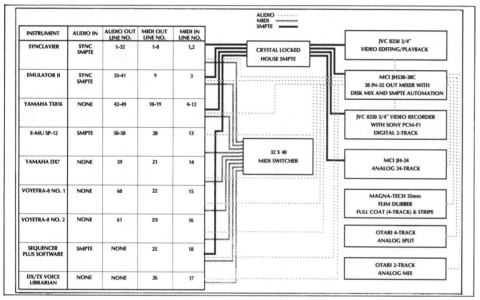

A signal routing diagram for Shelton Leigh Palmer & Co.'s studio, showing audio, MIDI, and SMPTE time code signal paths. Many production studio's have a central "house sync" generator, as depicted.

put it on tape."

"I like to be tapeless when it makes sense to be tapeless," he continues. "In other words, there's no reason to be tapeless for its own sake. It gives you certain flexibilities that tape can never offer. Once things are in computer memory, you can do computer things to them: slow down, speed up, transpose, replace timbres at the touch of a button. Once you put it on tape, it's committed.

"When someone sings and they're a little bit out of tune, you'll sample the whole thing and correct the pitch. But if someone is playing a good, serious guitar solo, what's the point of having that in the computer? That may have some value when digital signal processing gets to the point where you can really do some very fine processing, but right now

"Mmmm-mint!' because it has a minty flavor. We overdubbed one girl doing that eight times on an 8-track recorder, mixed it down into the Synclavier, split it up, put it under different keys, and made it something you could play."

It is in the context of tapeless recording that conventional multi-track techniques will have relevance for keyboard studios in the future. "We're rolling tape all the time," Palmer admits, "and we always have lots of tape tracks lying around. Having 24 tracks takes on a new meaning when you're using one for sync and one for buffer, and you've got 22 additional tracks for a voice-over and a couple of vocals," he concludes. "It's a whole other realm."

By Ted Greenwald

89

MIKING ACOUSTIC PIANOS

October 1985

Every engineer I've ever met has his own way of recording acoustic piano. This may sound like bad news if you're looking for the One True Way to mike a piano, but don't be alarmed. If anything, knowing that everyone has their own approach should lead you to experiment with your particular room and instrument. One reason engineers have different methods is because they record in their favorite studios, which already have a piano in place. Since the grand piano is an acoustic instrument, factors such as the size and treatment of the room, the way the piano itself has been voiced by the technician, and the type of piano sound you're going for (classical, jazz, rock, R&B, etc.) all have to be taken into account. There are so many variables in recording acoustic piano that in many ways it offers as much variety as a synthesizer!

The most important factor to consider is what style of music you're recording. If you try to record rock piano with an instrument that isn't set up for that type of music, it's not going to come off as well. A piano prepared for rock music has had its hammers treated with a substance to harden them, making a brighter, thinner, more percussive sound. Don't try doing this to your own instrument! If you want this sound, hire a piano technician to do the work. Going the other direction, certain pianos have had their hammers pricked with special needle devices to soften them (called voicing the piano). This brings a warmer sound to an instrument that was bright to begin with, and is most often preferable for jazz and classical music. Once again, you should hire a professional to set up your piano.

I would suggest condenser microphones (AKG 414 and 451, Neumann U-87 and U-47 fet [field effect transistor], Shure SM-81) for a brighter more crystalline high-end response. This is suitable for rock and R&B, but can be used for other styles with proper placement. The vintage tube type condenser mikes (Neumann M-49, U-67, and U-47, AKG C-12, and Telefunken 251) found in most studios are well into the $1,800 range and above. They have a more natural-sounding high end and a fuller low-end response than the transistor preamplifier stage of many of the newer microphones. In many ways, tube mikes could be compared to tube guitar amps. Because of the tube, the third harmonic and all the odd harmonics in the piano's sound are emphasized.

Dynamic mikes (Shure SM-57 and SM-58, Sennheiser 421 and 441, Electro-Voice RE-20) are widely used as well, and can give excellent results. As they are transformer-based, they can as a rule accept higher sound pressure levels than tube condenser microphones. Because sound leakage is always a problem when miking acoustic piano with other instruments, either onstage or in the room, pressure zone microphones (such as Crown PZM) have found their niche in piano miking. They can be mounted on the inside of the lid of the piano, and with the lid closed can produce a workable sound with very little leakage.

The next important consideration is what type of placement pattern to use when miking the piano. Many of the microphones mentioned above have multiple polar patterns. In choosing one, you must consider again the musical style, as well as leakage factors and phase cancellation. Phase cancellation occurs when two microphones are placed in close proximity. What happens is that with sound waves of certain frequencies, the peak of a wave arrives at one mike at the same moment that the trough of the same wave arrives at the other mike. When the signals of the two mikes are added together, the peak and the trough cancel out, causing a lack of sound at that frequency. For this reason, setting two microphones close together under a piano lid can give a very unnatural sound.

For rock music, the mikes should be as close as possible to where the hammers hit the strings. Cardioid and hypercardioid mikes work best here, as they are more directional. They pick up less from behind, thus cutting down on leakage. They are also less prone to phase cancellation. AKG 45, 452, and 414 and Neumann U-87, U-67, U-47 fet and tube, and KM-84 are good examples. PZMs are also excellent, alone or in conjunction with cardioids.

For classical and jazz piano, however, omni-directional patterns work best. It is usually desirable to record the room sound along with the sound of the piano. For classical music, it is customary to place the microphones outside the piano on the side of the lid that opens. This allows the piano to breathe. The important thing is to mike the piano from the point in the room at which it sounds most natural.

All right—but where do we put the mikes? Well, as I said above, for rock piano two mikes can be placed close to where the hammers hit the strings. These are usually panned anywhere from hard left and hard right to nine and three o'clock for stereo. But don't forget to switch to mono to check for phase cancellation. The mikes can be at the ends of the piano facing in, or, as I prefer, in the middle facing out. The latter causes less phase cancellation. Of course, if you're going for a very bright percussive sound, you can make good use of a little phase cancellation to thin the sound out. I suggest using AKG 451s with the A51 swivel mounts. The A51s allow the capsule of the 451 to be at a 90-degree angle to the body of the mike. You can use these with the lid down low and the 451s right over the hammers. For added low end, a third microphone can be placed at the far end of the piano, panned up the middle in the mix. A pair of PZMs on the lid also work great in conjunction with the 451s Unfortunately, if you're trying to record rock piano in a room or onstage with loud amps blazing, you're not going to be able to use those omni-directional patterns for a little phase cancellation. In fact, you're going to have to place gobos (go-betweens) around the piano and cover it with blankets. Onstage this is unsightly, so you might want to use the PZMs. Elton John had a custom shell constructed around his piano for live concerts to minimize feedback. You might want to construct a similar shell, but keep in mind that the lights are optional!

In miking jazz piano, whether on-stage or in the studio, you're always going to be recording live group playing. Mike placement is important, because jazz musicians are not interested in headphones. They want to perform as naturally as possible. Try working with fewer microphones, and place them carefully around the stage or studio. This will eliminate more phase cancellation and produce a more natural sound. Of course, the placement should not be taken to the extreme of not being able to hear the piano player. In jazz, a more mellow piano sound is required, so try to mike the piano from the rear as well as the right side. If you don't have expensive tube microphones, try the dynamic mikes. In general, stereo pairs work best

when both mikes are the same, but other combinations do work too. Don't be afraid of trying things. Shure SM-57s, Sennheiser 421s, and Electro-Voice RE-20s all work well together. You can even pair a condenser with a dynamic.

Before you add any equalization from the board, work with mike placement. You may get just the sound you're looking for without adding tons of EQ. It's not that EQ is bad, but any time you put a new device into the signal chain, you're adding noise. Especially in jazz or classical music, noise is not acceptable. During quiet passages in rock ballads, too, noise is the enemy.

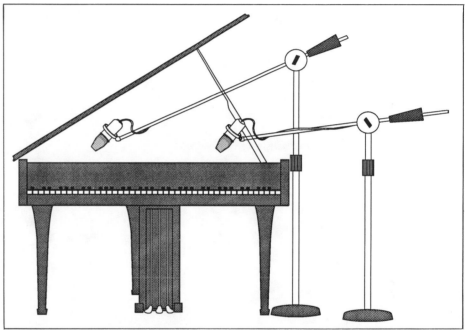

Compression can be used to reduce the dynamic range of the piano. Since this is so wide to begin with, a little compression or limiting can make a piano much more enjoyable to listen to. This holds true for any musical style, and especially for ballads. But be careful. Too much compression can add noise, and if the way you EQ'd the piano added noise, compression may bring this up to a most noticeable hiss. Another effect you might want to experiment with is adding a little chorusing, or Harmonizer at 99 or 101, which will give you a honky-tonk sound without detuning the instrument.

Oh, and if I didn't mention it, be sure the piano is in tune before you start working on the sound. You don't want to have to move the mikes so the tuner can do his job after you've got them set up where you want them.

Miking pianos isn't an exact science—it's a chance for your technical chops, creativity, and experience to come into play.

By Bobby Nathan

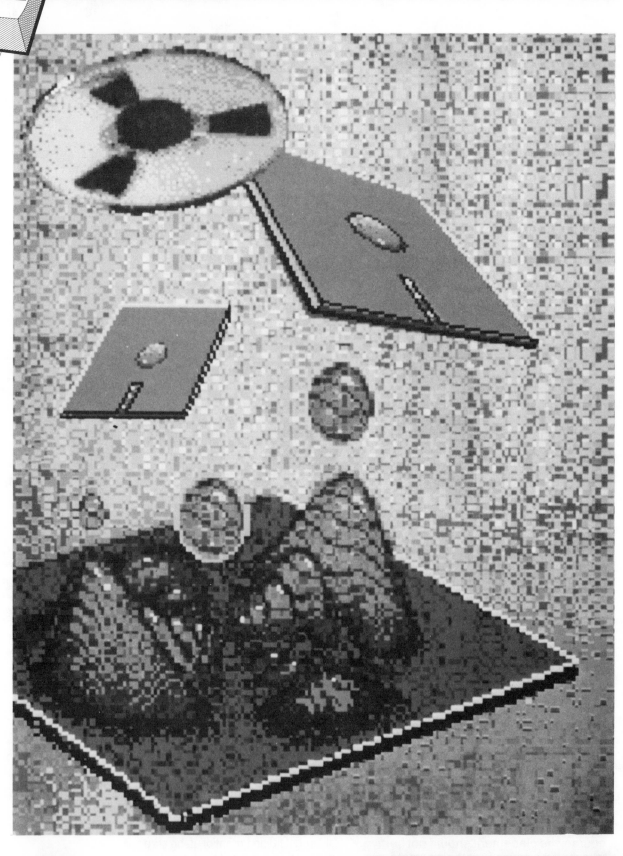

5

ADVANCED TECHNIQUES

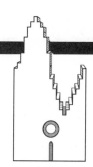

SESSION PLANNING

June 1986

"What do you mean, you forgot your guitar? We're paying $200 an hour for this!"

"Hey, no problem! Let's use that great Van Halen guitar sample you have on the Emulator."

"Well, actually, I left the disks on the dashboard of the Vega and they all melted."

"We could always replace the guitar solo with a drum solo. What do you think, Bhagwan? . . . Bhagwan? My God, Bhagwan's unconscious!"

Sure, nothing this awful is ever going to happen to you in the studio. Or is it? Maybe you'll only lose a footpedal, or have to drive halfway across town in rush hour for a MIDI cable. No mattter what the foul-up, it will cost you money, not to mention frazzled nerves. Ultimately, it may force you to make compromises in the sound of the tape. The lesson: The more you can do to prepare ahead of time for the recording session, the better.

There are lots of things you can do to minimize the inevitable hassles and pitfalls of getting your act on tape. Some of them are just common sense, but some of them you may never have thought of. Every little detail that you can take care of before you go into the studio, when time is cheap, will be one less detail that you have to worry about when the meter is running.

Before you even start looking around for a studio, ask yourself why you want to record in the first place. Demo tapes don't necessarily require as high a level of quality as master tapes for records or cassettes you intend to sell. That doesn't mean it's okay for a demo to sound crummy, but you can get away with a bit more tape hiss, or a string sound that's a bit muffled, as long as the music itself is happening.

Billy Barber, keyboardist with the jazz fusion group Flim And The BB's, advises, "If you're doing a demo tape for a record company, I think it's a good idea to go into a less expensive studio. If you're trying to sell your idea, your sound, I don't think it makes a lot of sense to do a whole album's worth of music and spend thousands and thousands of dollars when the record company may ask you to make a left turn somewhere any-

way. Save the money and concentrate on the non-production things, the things you're trying to sell, like the sound of the band, the sound of the singer, or your instrumental chops if it's a jazz label. Use the time to record ten short numbers so that you get maybe three good ones, rather than recording three full-blown pieces and only coming up with one you can use, which isn't enough to get a record deal."

Once you've got an idea of what you're trying to achieve, and how much you can afford to spend, you're ready to choose a recording studio. You are about to put your musical talent into the hands of someone—an engineer or producer—whom you've never met before. Before signing up to do any recording in a studio, you should feel 100 percent certain about the equipment and the people operating it. Clearly, one of the best ways to find a good studio is to ask around. Chances are, one or two studio names will come up more frequently than others for various reasons—rates, engineering quality, equipment, and so on—and you should look into those first.

You should be able to tell a lot about a studio's quality by the tapes it turns out. Don't be afraid to ask to listen to some previous sessions that the studio has done. Ask to hear material that's similar to what you're planning to do; no matter how terrific a studio sounds with rock bands, it may not be the right place for a solo piano session. As you're listening, don't fall into the trap of judging the music itself. Listen to things like mix levels, clarity, and the use of outboard effects. If these don't sound right on someone else's tape, chances are they're not going to sound any better on yours.

Chris Boardman—a two-time Emmy winner and recent Academy Award nominee for *The Color Purple* who also happens to be the keyboardist with the jazz fusion group Wishful Thinking—has some other ideas for how to evaluate a studio and its staff: "Ask questions. 'How did you mike the drums? How many tracks did you use for the keyboards?' Even if you don't know enough about a given topic for their answers to make total sense, you'll get a feel for whether you're hearing specifics or vague evasions." If you get the feeling that your questions are being dodged, be extremely cautious.

It's a good idea to do some research and familiarize yourself with the kind of gear a studio should have. The studio people you talk to may want to impress you by bragging about their Headbanger 14-Track Digital Master-Blaster. While you won't have to operate the beast, you should try to acquire enough knowledge to tell whether or not it's a quality piece of equipment. On the other hand, it's easy to waste lots of time in the studio playing with high-tech gadgets. In the cold light of day (i.e., after you're out of money), you may start to feel that the tape has too many gimmicky sounds on it, and not enough honest music. Even if all the sounds are great, the time to learn to use a piece of gear is before the session, not during it. If inspiration strikes while you're recording, that's great, but racks of great effects won't turn a mediocre song into a great one. Sometimes a simple setup is best.

The control room of Different Fur Studios, in San Francisco, California. From left to right: Solid State Logic 4056 console, Sony remote controller/autolocator, signal processing racks, Sony PCM-3324 digital 24-track recorder (with Sony F-1 PCM encoders above), and a Studer A-80 MkIII analog 24-track. On the SSL console, from left to right: Yamaha NS10 and Auratone 5C monitors, Lexicon 480L reverb/sampler controllers (x 2), and a Lexicon 224 controller.

Don't forget about atmosphere. If you find yourself uncomfortable in a particular location, you're probably going to feel a lot less comfortable when the red light goes on. "Some people really feel perfectly at home in a really big room," Barber explains, "but other people need a more intimate atmosphere. That's what studios are all about. Studios are in business to let you come in, take a look around, and make sure you're comfortable in the environment. That's as important to the musician as the console and tape machine are to the engineer."

If your music includes a lot of acous-

tic piano, you'll probably want to visit each studio to determine where the best piano is. "Try to determine if the piano in a particular studio is stylistically right for your music," Barber recommends. "Sometimes a 9' is not the best kind of piano for rock and roll. Conversely, there are some pianos out there that are just not long enough or big enough for certain kinds of music." The acoustics of the room are less important, provided that the studio has a good reverberation system. Willie Murphy, a Minneapolis-based rock keyboardist whose most recent release is a self-produced album of boogie-woogie piano, puts it this way: "If a studio has a good recorder and a good piano, you can work enough to get a good sound even if the room is lousy."

Once you've chosen a studio, talk to the engineer ahead of time to plan the session. Give him or her an idea of the music you plan to record and discuss the number of tracks you'll need, whether or not you'll need to overdub, what aspects of the music are most important to you, and so on. You should get clear, concise answers to all your queries. If you find you're being talked into compromises to make your music fit the studio, you may want to investigate another location. Don't try to do a 16-track job in an 8-track studio. If you want to record keyboards that have stereo outputs in stereo, you may need two tracks for each instrument.

There's no worse feeling than suddenly discovering that you need an empty track to record that cosmic explosion on the 500-pound modular monstrosity you carted up three flights of stairs, and then finding out that there are no empty tracks left on the tape. Sure, you can bounce tracks down to make more room, but bouncing tends to degrade the sound quality, and if you're going to bounce, you need to plan for it

ahead of time, so that there will be open tracks to bounce onto.

Few small studios have the space or the technology to record a full-sized drum set effectively. If your drummer just can't play without his gongs and timpani you'll need to find a studio big enough for him. If you're planning to use drum machines and sequencers, let the engineer know, so that a track can be striped with a sync tone, and so that all the necessary sync devices and cables will be on hand. If you're using MIDI sequencing, you may be able to play the sequence using synthesizers owned by the studio. Find out what they have available, and ask whether you need to reserve it and pay a rental fee to be sure it will be on hand.

Once you've found your recording Valhalla, you'll need to examine your wallet or decide which member(s) of your family you're going to sell to finance this audio extravaganza. Depending on the studio and how well known you or your group is, you may be able to get some recording time at a reduced rate—provided you offer something in return. Usually this means a percentage of the profits on your record sales. Don't be offended, though, if your suggestion of recording 'on spec' (speculation) is turned down. Recording studios are in business to make money, and the studio owner may not be as sure of your brilliant future as you are. Willie Murphy reports, "If you've got any kind of a name at all, or any kind of reputation for playing locally, it seems to me that a lot of studios would be willing to consider that now. The studios in the Minneapolis area have gotten very competitive lately, and more and more of them are doing spec-time deals. The less time you need to do a project, the more likely you are to cut a spec-time deal." Twenty-piece bands with nightmares of logistics, and solo multi-keyboard projects that will take forever, are less likely to be appealing on a spec-time basis than solo piano albums. Still, it never hurts to ask.

When you've determined how much time you can afford in the studio, figure out how to make the best use of it. Don't fall into the trap of using up all the money you've budgeted for recording the basic tracks and then finding out that in order to get a mixdown you have to come up with another $500. A good rule of thumb is to allow one third of the total time you have for the basic tracks, another third for overdubs, and the last third for mixdown. This may mean recording fewer tunes but having them all come out sounding decent, so plan on starting the session with your strongest material, and save the marginal stuff to tack on at the end if you have time for it. And while we're on the subject of mixing, plan if possible to book the time in such a way that you can finish the mixing on a different day than you start. Taking home a cassette of a rough mix will allow you to listen and ponder at leisure, rather than being forced into snap decisions.

So now you've picked the studio, got your money together, scheduled the studio time, and you're all set to do the recording—or are you? What about rehearsal? If this is your band's first time in the studio, you're probably not used to playing your parts independent of your buddies. Try practicing parts separately —especially vocals. If you've been practicing the A section, then the B section, and then the C section, make sure to go through the song from start to finish without stopping, before you get into the studio. Sometimes you'll find that the last reprise of the A section just doesn't fall in as well as you thought it would.

Practicing doesn't just mean running through the tunes, it means knowing the arrangement inside out. The studio is not the place to suddenly throw in some new chords that you discovered late last night. Nor is it the place to come to the sudden realization that the bass line sucks and the guitar and keyboard chords are stepping all over one another. Some people like to work this way, but it can get expensive. If you're hoping to get airplay, even dynamite material may have to be shortened or cut. Chris Boardman recommends a five-minute maximum for jazz instrumentals; other genres have their own requirements.

As a keyboard player, you'll have other things to practice besides notes, things like patch changes and movements from one instrument to another. If you're planning to record with a stack of keyboards, take a look at the studio to figure out how they'll all be set up, and make sure you can move around as needed during the session.

If you're singing as well as playing, you may be shocked when you hear yourself on tape for the first time. You may want to do things over just because it doesn't sound the way you expect it to. The cure? Use an inexpensive tape deck, such as a multi-track cassette machine, during rehearsal, to find out how you sound. Using a recorder at home can give you an idea of which

instruments need to be recorded at the same time and which should be overdubbed. It will also give you a feel for playing separately while listening through headphones.

Some people find even more ingenious ways to take advantage of home recording as a preparation for the studio. Willie Murphy uses his home multi-track to record time-consuming sections that he would otherwise be pressed to do in the studio. "I have an Akai 12-track which I can do a lot of the back-up parts at home on. By striping one of the tracks with SMPTE, I can take it into the studio and add the things I can't do at home and have it all sync up. My piano just isn't good enough and I don't know how to mike a piano, so I do those kind of things in a studio."

Be absolutely sure of your equipment. If you have sounds or sequences that you'll need to use in the session, make back-ups of disks, cartridges, cassettes, and so on, just to be sure. And make sure that any sequenced parts or drum machine parts are exactly as you want them. Making a simple edit in a drum pattern while under the pressure of the red light for the first time can give you sweaty palms or worse. If you have any instruments that require special cords, make sure you've got them. "Take some extra ground lifters with you to the studio," Barber suggests. "You may have worked out any ground loop problems in your own setup, but as soon as you move your keyboards around, it's up for grabs again." Things like this may seem too trivial to worry about, but if it takes half an hour to find a simple power adapter in the studio, that cord just cost you half an hour of recording time.

Check your keyboards for extraneous noise. If you want to use that vintage Clavinet for a solo, let the engineer know that you'll need a noise gate for it. If you're using a sampling machine, listen carefully to your samples. A click at a looping point may be barely audible in live performance, but tape is a notoriously cruel medium, where all defects sound worse than you thought they would. If there's any chance that a sample (or anything else) is going to bother you, fix it ahead of time.

Tuning up is mainly a problem for string and horn players, but if you've got several keyboards, make sure they're in tune with one another before you start recording, and with the studio piano if there's any chance you'll be doing an overdub with it. (And you did mention that overdub to the engineer, didn't you, so that he could have the piano tuned? DX7 users, be warned: If you switch out of the function control section while in master tune mode, the data entry slider will change the tuning at any time. Also be aware that if you MIDI a Casio CZ keyboard to a DX, any time you move the data entry slider, the Casio will go out of tune.

Tascam's 238—which records eight tracks on a standard cassette—can travel from live to studio recording sessions with ease. Other features include dbx noise reduction, SMPTE sync capability, and a shuttle control, for cueing tape.

As glamorous and exciting as the studio environment is, and as much as you want your mom, your brother and sister, your sister's cute friend, and the guy who loans your roadie the van to be there and see this wonderful event in your life, try to keep extraneous personnel to a minimum during the session. The more people you have in a room, the greater the chance that someone is going to trip over a cable while you're finishing the best solo you've ever done in your life. No matter how well behaved they are, they're sure to get on the engineer's nerves by talking when he's working on the sound.

Other things to avoid in the studio: Don't alter any volume setting without alerting the engineer. Don't move any mikes without the engineer's permission. Don't tap your foot on the base of the mike stand. Don't start talking until the final cymbal crash has died away completely. And don't send out for pizza without asking the engineer whether he wants any.

And finally, Billy Barber advises, "I don't think I can over-emphasize the importance of having a really strong song. Before you go into the studio, make sure that the core of what you're going in to record, the actual song, is strong enough. If it isn't, you should

postpone the session until you're satisfied with the material. When the tape is running and the adrenaline starts to flow, a strong song will get even stronger. On the other hand, there's no worse feeling than beating your head against the wall with material that just isn't there in the first place."

We can't tell you how to write strong songs, or how to tell if the songs you've written are strong enough. But if you've got good material, and if you can play it well, the ideas outlined here should give you the best possible chance of coming up with a tape that you can be proud of.

By David Frederick

CREATIVE TIPS

June 1986

I'm telling you this at grave personal risk, so listen carefully: There's this deeply secret, unspeakably awful ritual that all writers of ad copy, owner's manuals, and B-grade music articles are forced to go through (all of us; I speak from experience, having worn at least two of those hats). They come and tear you from your home (at exactly 4:40 A.M.), gag you, tie your hands, throw you into the back of a hot pink '57 T-Bird once jointly-owned by Jerry Lee Lewis, John Cage, and Leopold Stokowski (until Stokowski missed one too many payments and the car was repossessed), drive you to a hidden clearing in the woods just north of Tuxedo Junction, New York, and there, at dawn, having strapped you to a woofer the size of King Kong's kneecap and played AC/DC's revisionist cover version of "Waltzing Mathilda" until your brain is rice pudding and you'll do *anything* they say, they give you **The Key**. The one that, when attached to any typewriter or word processor and pressed, automatically spits out the phrase:

"The only limit is your imagination!"

That key. (Music store salesmen have their own version, a microcassette recorder/speaker system which is surgically attached beneath the tongue by a team of renegade surgeons from the Cheyenne, Wyoming Center for Oral Excellence.)

I swear this is true. Just once I'd like to see an ad or a manual or an article or

96

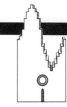

a salesman break free of Them and tell it like it is, like it always has been, like it always will be—*"The only limit to this thing is its hardware, its software, and how much you're willing to sweat!"* Lord, that would feel good.

Actually, when you stop to think about it, what They have been doing all these conspiratorial years is handing us a first-class insult. Even the best, most state-of-the-art gear in the world has sharply defined limits. And these limits—plain as Gibraltar to anyone with some knowledge and a copy of the spec sheet—can't be exceeded, no matter how you try. So every time The Key gets pressed, or your salesman plays his Sony Tongueman, the real message being sent is nothing more or less than "In our opinion, you have a limited imagination."

Do you? Are They right? Have you been depending more on the gear you've bought than the brains you were born with? Let's find out.

True Or False

The following pseudo-scientific quiz will reveal all. Look it over, think carefully, then answer yes or no to each question, but don't cheat by skipping ahead to the analysis at the end of this article! (Advance warning: questions nine and ten have trick answers.)

1. Have you ever done more with a synth than play its presets?

2. Have you ever done anything while recording that made the engineer lift both eyebrows? (No points for single brows; those show doubt, not astonishment.)

3. Have you ever done anything while recording that made you lift both eyebrows?

4. Have you ever played a tape for somebody and found yourself interrupting with excuses for its technical quality or selection of timbres or choice of instruments or (fill in the blank)?

5. Have you ever played a tape for somebody and had *them* interrupt to ask how something was done?

6. Have you ever spent months hungering after *that special piece of gear* only to buy it and then barely use it?

7. Have you ever blatantly violated the original design intentions of an instrument's manufacturer?

8. Have you ever made your own instruments or devices?

9. Do you like what you've recorded?

10. Do you believe in magic?

Personal Confession

The night before my first real session as a producer I was so nervous I dropped a cymbal. On a tile floor. In a crowded donut shop just off Broadway and 51st.

No sound I have ever heard in my life has been louder, or more embarrassing. I was already tense. The cymbal crash made it worse. By the time I got home and to bed, sleep was impossible.

What I kept thinking, over and over, went like this: "Ohmigod these guys in the session tomorrow are so good I mean Adrian has been playing the bass since he was in the womb and he's brilliant and Jeff's drumming makes Adrian look slack and that John, the piano plays *him* and . . . and me, dropout clarinetist from El Dorado High, what can I do? I'm not in their league!" Hard truths, in the middle of the night. And justified. What experience did I have? None! The "producing" I'd done before had been both unofficial and by accident. In the morning I had to steer a mighty ship; the other had been more like getting everyone in a lifeboat to row in vaguely the same direction.

And then, at 4:40 A.M., the revelation.

These guys had been playing their instruments for years. But so had I. They were damned good . . . but so was I.

The only difference was in instruments: Mine was my brain.

Do you realize what a miracle we have stashed away behind our eyes? Check out the specs: Our brains, just under three pounds of convoluted grey sponge with a consistency remarkably like runny lasagna, are made of roughly

Automating your studio's controls is one way to free up your creative talents. The DMP7PRO program for the Macintosh computer can enhance the automation process for the Yamaha DMP7 mixer (page 22), by offering instant visual references to settings, group combinations of controls, and more.

97

ten billion neurons—to put that in perspective, consider that you, me, and eight other folks have as many brain cells between us as there are stars in the galaxy. Furthermore, each of those cells is cross-connected to as many as 30,000 of its fellows, all or some or none of which it can play telephone with, and at these connections there is a little electro-chemical "spark gap" governed by the actions and reactions and re-reactions of different neurotransmitter chemicals. Twenty years ago medical science knew of seven neurotransmitters; ten years ago the count topped

New Age musician Michael Stearns in his home studio. Amidst a plethora of signal processing gear and accessories, pictured left to right are a TAC Scorpion 32-input mixing console, an Otari MTR-90 24-track recorder, an Otari MTR-12 2-track, and a Serge modular synthesizer.

100; conservative estimates today admit there could be more than 1,000, each serving a unique purpose. The upshot of it all is that inside our skulls we have parallel-processing networks which put the grandest supercomputer to shame. Our brains are the ultimate synthesizers of possibility, the bottom line of every signal-to-noise ratio (stand in an anechoic chamber for a time and you'll hear the high-pitched electrical whine of your own nervous system, cycling); they're the part of us that sets our hardware and software limits. What's more, the operating system is so transparent that most of us, most of the time, forget our brains are even there—which is what I had done right up to the moment it finally occurred to me that ideas were more important than chops.

Now, technique is a wonderful thing. I won't argue that. But it isn't as rare and special a commodity as creativity. And it isn't as important. A sufficiently brilliant idea can always survive, and even tran-

scend, lousy technique. But technique free of creativity is doomed. It might as well be white noise or wallpaper. Or a crate of Sominex. Being blissfully free of ideas, it communicates nothing.

What you must do is strike a balance. Strong ideas and strong technique, together, can—and have—changed the world. For all their power, ideas are remarkably fragile. Especially at birth. Facts and experience and need crash against one another constantly down there in our neurons, turning into unexpected ideas, each idea needing attention to survive. And usually getting precious little of it. They must be listened for, gathered, fostered, carefully tested, and protected until they've proven themselves useful or useless. Technique (or more correctly, the way technique is taught) is often an enemy of this process; instead of being the brush through which an idea paints itself into the world, technique can turn, iron-fisted, and smash down all notions outside a rigidly defined boundary.

Everyone is familiar with the stories: The superb classically-trained flutist who could breeze through any score you handed him, but who froze in the face of a short 7/8 piece that required him to play "out," to improvise; the pianist who insisted that a certain chord sequence could not be played "jazzily" because they were not "jazz chords"; the engineer who kept stopping takes because of what he insisted were bum notes but which were, in fact, simply part of the natural process of reconstructing the "Maple Leaf Rag" backwards as a set of monophonic synth and woodwind tracks (when all the notes were in place, of course, the chords resolved exactly as nilpoJ intended). These were not untalented people. They just couldn't seem to keep track of the *idea*.

That was the kicker, there in the pre-dawn darkness. I suddenly realized that having and communicating ideas (as a writer, artist, and occasional performer) had been paying my rent for some time, and in the studio things would be no different. Wherever Adrian and Jeff and John took the tunes, if I sweated I could stay ahead. Which is exactly what happened. We hit the studio, I held the target in their sights, goosed their technical skill and ideas with my own until they hit the target square, and we went home with oxide we could be proud of. I haven't dropped a cymbal since. Except deliberately.

Creativity In Recording Is . . .

The first anything, whether or not it works: the first time someone leaned against a tape reel and flanged a track. The first heavily gated reverb on a snare drum. The first Minimoog bass line. Don't be content to follow old paths. It's where people have never looked that you find gold.

Taking chances. There's a lot of pressure against this in recording studios, what with ticking time and draining money. But dare when you can, in both playing and ideas; every trick or take that works is worth a dozen that fail, and enlarges the arsenal of creative tools you bring to your tasks. Home equipment is a must if you are serious about taking risks, because at home you can take chances at minor cost to your ego and wallet. Tradeoff: With the pressure off, you might not push yourself as hard, or as far, toward the limits of your technique, thinking, and equipment.

Capitalizing on happy accidents. Keep your ears open! Most mistakes are just that, but a few are miracles in disguise. All of us work within the limitations of our thinking or our technique, so things which are totally accidental break open doors to new territory. A misprogrammed drum machine can hand you a startling rhythm. You might forget the changes, but play anyway; the worst that can happen is you have to go back and try again. A bad punch-in can alter the shape of a phrase for the better. The trick, ever and always, is to do whatever is necessary to follow the mistake up and make it seem a natural, inevitable part of its surroundings. So what if the chorus riff of your platinum single started life as a screwup? It's a great story for the interview in *Rolling Stone*.

Faking people out. Limitations are always there, so a prime spur to creativity in the studio is figuring out how to sneak around them. The sound effects men of old radio shows were masters at this, conjuring armies out of spring-mounted boots, forest fires out of cellophane, and Martian cylinders out of opening peanut butter jars in a close-miked toilet bowl. Recording engineers also have a hatful of tricks, from games with vari-speed to constructing fluid synthesizer solos out of 27 different takes to using digital delays to push back in time a track that wasn't played with quite the right feel. In fact, there's unquestionably a trick for every circumstance. It just has to be worked out.

Finding the right sound. Start with loosely-defined boundaries, and narrow the focus. Do you need a dry sound? A wet sound? What emotion should it convey? What "color" is it? Short? Long? Soft? Angry? Buzzy? When you're really out there, it's tough to find the right words for what you want, which is why you end up saying things like "I don't know, I think we need something *squeegly* here." Creativity is finding the perfect *squeegle*, knowing it when you hear it, and capturing it on tape to parade before the whole world.

Hearing what isn't there. Tougher. Very tough. The sonic equivalent of the old line about Michelangelo ("It's very simple," he said, "I just take the chisel to the marble and cut away everything that isn't the sculpture").

Breaking the rules. As a general guide, if someone tells you something is impossible, unlikely, or useless, you ought to try it once to make sure. Especially if you agree with them, if both of you think that way without any evidence, odds are you're overlooking something.

Knowing what rules not to break. Stupidity isn't creative, it's just stupid. Stop short of anything either life-threatening or with results more expensive than you can afford. There are better ways to simulate grenade explosions and small arms fire than miking your local Libyan terrorist.

Not being satisfied. Whatever it is, it can always be done better. Maybe not until next time, but that's the way it goes.

So you've read this far and you're thinking, "Okay, gee, thanks for the philosophical overview, I really appreciate having my horizons broadened and all, but I've got this session coming up next week, and I need some creative ideas! Can't you just give me one or two solid,

practical tips that I can use?" The thing is, if I lay it out for you, it won't be creativity. You'll be using my ideas, not discovering your own. Still, I know some of you are new at this, and probably hopelessly confused by now. So here are some random things that you might try in a moment of desperation, when a tune has gone hopelessly awry, and the only good option seems to be to chop up the master tape and use it for desert topping:

Run an expensive synthesizer through a cheap stomp box, and either overdrive the box or don't feed it enough level. Record something dry instead of

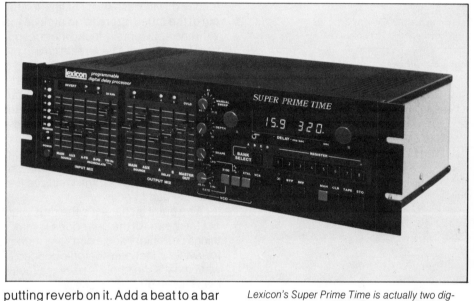

putting reverb on it. Add a beat to a bar somewhere. Change the mix drastically in the middle of a verse. Transpose something up or down by several octaves. Let two time-domain devices get out of sync, and record the result. Set up the graphic equalizer so the sliders make an interesting pattern, and process a signal through it without caring what the actual sound is. Lay down the parts of an arrangement in an unusual order, so that some of the musicians can't hear things they would ordinarily want to hear in order to play their parts. Record a series of random program changes on a sequencer, and play your solo while the sequencer switches the patches for you. Slow the tempo way down, or else crank it up so fast you can't quite play all the notes. Quantize a sequencer track to a rhythmic value that has nothing to do with the beat. Have everybody trade instruments, so they're all playing things they don't know how to play. For one hour, faithfully execute all the suggestions made by anybody in the studio, whether you agree with them or not.

Lexicon's Super Prime Time is actually two digital delays in one, which allows for all kinds of interesting delay, chorusing, and flanging effects.

99

Don't like any of those idea? Fine—make up some of your own.

Creativity in recording isn't copying other people, copying yourself, playing it safe, drowning the track in multiple takes in hope of fixing things in the mix, fear (of anything), or smug satisfaction (even if you have reason for it).

Budgets Great And Small

I remember vividly the day I could finally afford to buy a bunch of synths and PA gear for my band. I laid my money down with sweaty palms, left the din of the music store to go pick up the van, and accidentally found the second-best bass player I've ever heard in my life. He was in the subway. Playing a washtub bass. No kidding. Strings are stings, be they twine or nylon; this man was pouring his soul out through a tin washtub, a broomstick, and cord I wouldn't use to tie a bundle of newspapers, and he had 50 of us standing around mesmerized. When I finally got home with my new synths I realized just how far I had to go.

The point is this—it's the musician not the gear. All the gear does is make things possible. People don't pay money for invisible, inchoate Platonic concepts; what makes the show is having a musician square off and wrestle with that sea of virtually infinite possibility until some small corner of it is made real. For that you don't need the latest and greatest electro-digital-frammistat. Not if you've made your head, heart, and hands strong.

There's never enough money in the budget, or time in the schedule. But if you squeeze every drop from the resources you've got, instead of letting what you don't have get in the way, you'll be kin to the washtub man. And next time out, you'll have a little more. And you'll have earned it.

Answers

Here are the answers to our earlier quiz. Everybody gets an arbitrary score of 440. There are no strictly correct answers—just revealing reflection. Decide for yourself what they mean to you.

1. Have you ever done more with a synth than play its presets? The correct answer is an emphatic yes. Just playing the presets—i.e., performing on a synth as if it were no more than a glorified organ—is a definite early warning symptom of unstimulated creativity. It's not a definitive sign, because you can still be a creative player of chord voicings and lead lines without ever touching the rest of the box. Most doctors, however, feel that years of useful snap can be added to your lifespan and brainspan through proper exercise of sound generating circuitry.

2. Have you ever done anything while recording that made the engineer lift both eyebrows? The answer here should also be yes, with the proviso that your action was legal in the state you were in at the time. This kind of response usually comes from trying wierd things (often the source of happiest accident), like beating on a steel shelving unit for a percussion track, playing organ pedals with your hands or a keyboard with your head, harmonizing the Harmonizer, deliberately erasing random portions of a take, recording a $10 toy with a $400 microphone, and so on. Give yourself extra points if you managed to lift the eyebrows of an experienced (and therefore jaded) engineer. Give yourself even more points if what you did worked.

3. Have you ever done anything while recording that made you lift both eyebrows? For the lucky among us, the answer is yes. This state is the True Zen of the Shining Accident, In Which More Is Achieved Than Ever Expected (Or Intended) (Or Maybe Even Bargained For). Imperial Rome had a phrase for it: Cogito ergo oops.

4. Have you ever played a tape for somebody and found yourself interrupting it with excuses for its technical quality or selection of timbres or choice of instruments or (fill in the blank)? The answer should be no. It's allowable to make excuses beforehand; that's just standard foot-shuffling and insecurity tinged with the occasional trace of false modesty. But during the music, or after? Not a chance! If you feel compelled to apologize for what you did, or excuse it, then on some inner level you know you stepped up to the plate and didn't swing the bat as hard as you could.

5. Have you ever played a tape for somebody and had them interrupt to ask how something was done? Turnaround time. We sure hope your answer here is yes, because it means you at least laid the bat on the ball, even if you didn't knock the sucker out of the park. The appropriate response, if someone asks how you did something, is to tell them the truth. Keeping a technique secret

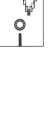

means you'll feel less pressure to come up with something new to top it; this is *not good.*

6. Have you ever spent months hungering after *that special piece of gear* only to buy it and then barely use it? The ideal answer should be no. The honest answer for 99 percent of us is yes. There are always things that get in the way of realizing an instrument or device's full potential, not the least of which is our all-too-human laziness and hunger for easy solutions. Watch for this one and fight it.

7. Have you ever blatantly violated the original design intentions of an instrument's manufacturer? We hope you answered *yes* to this one. . . . The best timbres I've ever gotten with synthesizers came from deliberately violating the "rules" they were organized around. Finding new and unplanned sounds within instruments is very stimulating. Take Bartok's quartets, for example, which require playing techniques that outrage conservative string players (but oh, what gorgeous results!). More recently I witnessed an incredibly effective use of a Kurzweil 250 in which two percussionists physically beat a tattoo on its back lid, using their hands and a rapidly disintegrating bamboo flute. It made one hell of a rattle, just perfect for the track in question. (Of course, you have to decide what it's worth to you. They took great pains not to actually damage the Kurzweil, but the body count on bamboo flutes was terrifying to behold.)

8. Have you ever made your own instruments or devices? This won't be *yes* for everybody, because not everybody is mechanically inclined. But if it's *yes* for you, stand proud. (Me, I started stringing rubber bands between drawer knobs around the kitchen when I was a wee child, stretching them to different pitches and twanging contentedly. As no major symphony orchestra had at that time hired a rubber band man as a soloist, my mother made me switch to the clarinet.)

9. Do you like what you've recorded? The first trick question. The correct answer is *no* and *yes.* You should hate and love what you've created, in a mix that drives you to confusion and agony (and which will annoy your family and friends if you don't shut up about it). Any other response and I'd bet good money you're on the wrong track.

10. Do you believe in magic? The second trick question. Once again, the correct answer is no and yes. Why? Well no, of course you shouldn't believe in magic, because at the root of creative recording is a lot of sweat, tension, angst, and hard work. Nobody is going to wave a wand and make you great. On the other hand, there is *yes.* Better still, *Yes!* Because when your ten billion neurons put their collective mind to the task, and the sounds dovetail and the notes mesh and the juices flow and suddenly there is music where there was only noise and sad disorder, that sudden rush of beauty is the real, true magic, and you are the magician. If you want to be. It's up to you.

By Freff

TAPE EDITING

October 1987
December 1987

Before the development of synthesizers, electronic music was considered any recorded collection of sounds that were modified, by altering the speed of the tape, playing the tape backwards, and other special effects. Known as musique concrète, *its main proponents include Karl Stockhausen, Pierre Schaeffer, and other mid-20th Century composers. Today many musicians*

The headstack of a Tascam Model 32 2-track. Note the editing block beneath the transport controls.

who are creating their own samples use musique concrète *techniques to create varied and interesting samples. One such technique is to splice tape together, so that different musical passages are mixed and combined. This article is an excellent overview of the art of editing, describing basic concepts, as well as modern-day techniques.*

Why do you need to know about tape editing? For starters, if you ever use 1/4"

101

or 1/2" tape, either for mixing or for multi-tracking, you've probably wondered what the best way is to arrange the songs on a reel, or on several reels, in finished order. You've probably ended up juggling reels so you could dub the songs onto a cassette in the proper order. Wouldn't it be nice to have them on one reel the way you want to hear them? Also, extraneous noises almost inevitably end up on tape before and after the song itself. You probably don't want to listen to yourself yelling, "One, two, three, four!" every time you hear the song (unless, of course, it's part of your act). Wouldn't it be nice to remove that kind of garbage forever? And, aside from the practical considerations, tape editing opens up a universe of special effects, many of which you hear every day on the radio (whether you know it or not). Some of them have become popular since the advent of sampling, but can also be done without the expensive instruments, and some are impossible to achieve without cutting and splicing.

The necessary equipment for audio tape editing is inexpensive (excepting the tape deck itself), and the skills can be mastered with just a little practice. Here's what you'll need to have on hand:

• Single-edged razor blades: These can be found in most hardware stores.

• Grease pencils: Preferably white or yellow. These can be found in most art supply and stationery stores.

• Editing Block: You'll need one of these for each tape width you'll be working with (1/4", 1/2", 1", or 2"), or at least for the width you use most often. If in doubt, go for the width that you mix down to. Edital makes a line of blocks with either 60- and 45-degree angles or 90-, 60-, and 45-degree angles. Get the heavy-duty aluminum kind; cheap ones get chewed up after a few splices. You can find editing blocks at pro-audio/video stores, some music stores, and in pro-audio catalogs.

• Splicing tape: Have splicing tape on hand in whatever widths you expect to work with. To state the nearly obvious: Don't use any other kind of tape for splicing jobs—it's likely to gum up your heads, and won't hold as well. Many recording engineers prefer to use multiple pieces of 1/2" splicing tape for 2" audio tape, rather than one- and two-inch widths, because wide splicing tapes are somewhat unwieldy. You can find splicing tape at pro-audio/video stores.

• Deluxe Scotch Tape dispenser:

You will need this to keep your splicing tape ready for use. It's often possible to fit both 1/2" and 1/4" widths at once into a single dispenser. Look at your local stationary supply house.

• Leader tape: I recommend the plastic type, although certain tape deck manufacturers recommend paper leader tape for their machines—check the owner's manual. Of course, you will need leader tape in whatever tape widths you work with. This is also available at pro audio supply houses.

• Blank tape: Have some spare blank tape around to experiment with. Any old tape will do. If you don't have any, buy a reel of the cheapest stuff you can find at your local Radio Shack.

• Of course, you will need a tape recorder. If it has an automatic tape lifter mechanism, it must also have a way of defeating the lifter for editing—otherwise, it's impossible to do precise editing (more on lifters in a moment). In addition, a loud, clean monitor system is essential for checking your handiwork. In the absence of an adequate monitor system, the next best thing is a pair of good-quality headphones connected either to your home stereo or to the tape deck's headphone jack. Keep in mind that cranking the volume way up to hear an edit point, while sometimes necessary, can result in speaker damage and ringing ears.

• There's only one thing missing: Some music recorded on tape. Slap your favorite record album on the turntable and record about a minute of the intro on the blank tape, and play it back to make sure it's there. Now you're ready to start cutting.

Rocking & Rolling. "Hand-rocking" is a basic technique involved in any editing task. It allows you to find the precise spot on the tape to make your cut. It usually takes a little practice, but it's not hard to learn.

Start by playing the tape from the beginning, and stopping the transport as soon as you hear the first note in the song. Then you want to hand-rock the tape back and forth over the tape deck's playback head. Hand-rocking is done by grabbing the supply reel (the left reel) with one hand and the take-up reel (the right reel) with the other, and moving both reels together, a little at a time, alternately clockwise and counterclockwise. Keep the tape taut over the heads as you rock; this keeps the tape in contact with the playback head, allowing you to hear what's recorded on the tape.

Some decks have a tape lifter, which is a network of metal bars that automatically holds the tape off of the heads during fast forward and rewind and when the tape isn't moving. In most cases, you can defeat the lifter by pushing up on a lever situated near the heads. Check to see if your deck has a lifter and a defeat lever, and if so, defeat the lifter now. If your deck doesn't have a lifter defeat, you will have to push the tape against the heads lightly with your thumb as you rock the supply and take-up reels. (If you're in the market for a reel-to-reel deck and think you will be doing any editing, one of the features you should look for is a lifter defeat.)

Once you've mastered hand-rocking, you'll need to become familiar with the layout of the tape heads. Most decks have three heads, arranged from left to right in the order of erase, record, and playback. "ERP" is a handy mnemonic for remembering the positions of the heads. The erase head erases the tape whenever the machine is set to record. The record head records the incoming signal onto the tape. In sync mode (sometimes called "sel-sync" or "simul-sync"), the record head functions simultaneously as a record head and a reproduce head. The head on the right side is the reproduce, or playback, head. When editing, it's necessary to pay close attention to where on the tape you're cutting, so that you don't accidentally chop off the beginning or ending of a note. Thus, the playback head is the most important head for editing purposes. (Some decks, such as the Otari 5050B series, have a fourth head. This enables them to play back both quarter-track and half-track tapes.)

Leadering. One of the most common tape editing chores is head- and tail-leadering a song. There are two reasons to do this: There is usually a count-off before the start of the tune, and in the midst of it a background vocalist is clearing his or her throat and the guitarist is diddling around. None of this goes down too well on Top 40 radio. The second reason is that leader tape is usually light in color, and since the tape itself is brownish, leadering makes it easy to find the beginning and end of a take.

To find the beginning of the song, hand-rock the reels back and forth over the heads. The playback head will reproduce the sounds recorded on the tape, even though the machine's motor isn't running at its usual constant speed.

102

By rocking and listening, you can hear the exact point at which the song begins. When you find that spot, use the reels to pull the tape back just a hair and hold the tape in position over the playback head. Using your white grease pencil, draw a line on the back of the tape exactly in line with the middle of the head. Once you've marked the tape, be sure to check your mark by rocking the tape, again, across the playback head. Watch the mark you've made; the song's beginning should start precisely when the mark reaches the middle of the head. If so, you're ready to cut tape.

Making The Cut. Place your edit block so that the cutting guide goes from the top left-hand corner to the bottom right-hand corner. For most applications, use the 60-degree guide (the one closest to perpendicular). Turn the supply and take-up reels until you have enough slack to put the tape into the block. Then, carefully lift the tape away from the heads, making sure that the back of the tape (with your mark on it) is facing you. Place the tape in the block with its back facing up and the mark you made clearly visible. Line up the mark with the top of the 60-degree angle.

When the tape is in place, hold it there, putting your thumb and forefinger on either side of the area where you'll make the cut. Run the razor blade through the guide with a steady even motion starting from top to bottom, cutting the tape. Next, remove the tape from the block. Put some leader in the block from the left side, and cut it in the same manner. Leave the leader in the block, and remove the excess to the right. Put the tape from the take-up reel (the right-hand reel) back into the block and butt it up against the leader. They should fit together perfectly. If they don't, re-cut the leader to match the tape.

Pull a one-inch piece of splicing tape from the dispenser. (It's a good idea to discard the first few inches of a new roll of splicing tape, where the adhesive may be irregular.) Cut the splicing tape with your razor blade, and put the piece you've cut onto the tip of the left side of the blade. This allows you to use the blade to place the splicing tape on top of the join in the edit block. Put the splicing tape over the join, making sure the two sides are still neatly butted up against each other, and press the splicing tape flat, carefully using your fingernail, to smooth out any air bubbles.

Remove the recording tape from the block, wind a healthy amount of leader

onto the take-up reel, and place the other end of the leader into the block. Cut the leader, and join it to the tape on the supply (left-hand) reel using the procedure outlined above. Now you're ready to remove the tape from the block and thread it through the machine as usual. During playback, the song should begin the moment the leader ends.

Advanced Applications. Once you've mastered leadering, you're ready to try some of the more interesting uses of tape editing. In popular music, it's not uncommon to replace a weak chorus in the final two-track mix with a stronger one. For instance, if all of the chorus sections in a song are virtually the same

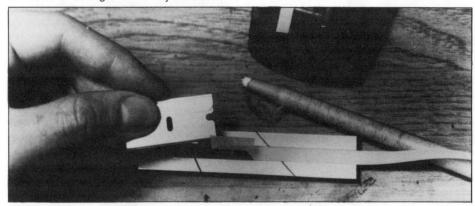

in terms of their tempo, composition, and arrangement, you can replace weak ones with the one that really shines.

The same kind of editing is used to rearrange song sections for a dance mix, to create an interesting intro, and to create dramatic effects such as the stuttering "sci-i-i-ience" in Thomas Dolby's "Blinded By Science." Before you try this "cut and paste" technique, make sure your hand-rocking, tape-marking, and blade-handling chops are in shape.

You can use any song with a good strong beat, but as a reference let's work with "When The World Is Running Down" by the Police, from the album *Zenyatta Mondatta* [A&M, 3720]. You'll notice that the song's third chorus is twice the length of the first and second choruses. Since you, the producer, feel that the song needs to be longer, you decide to replace the two shorter choruses with the longer one. Naturally, the first step is to copy the song to reel-to-reel tape. We'll consider this our "master." Also copy the third chorus, including the few beats before and after it, two more times. These are the pieces we'll be cutting into the song. We'll call them "copy #1" and "copy #2." [*Ed. Note: Since we can't advocate the exploitation*

Once the magnetic tape and leader are cut at the same angle, they can be joined with a piece of splicing tape.

103

of Sting and his fellow musicians, make sure that any of these taped copies you make are for your personal editing experiments only, and not for your friends or for any commercial gain.]

Cue Points. Play the tune through and listen for cue points—that is, musical events that can be used as references for making your cuts. A good cue point is a prominent sound that occurs at, or before, the place where you want to make your splice. Drum hits, brass entrances, and the like work well because they're easy to hear as you hand-rock the tape back and forth over the heads. Cue points have to match between the part of the song you're cutting from and the part you're cutting to. In other words, if you're going to cut the

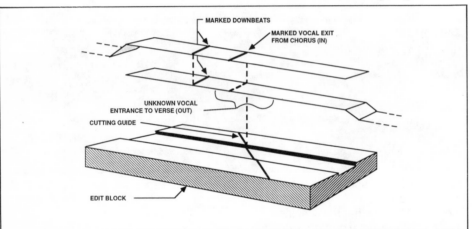

Assuming the tape moves at a constant speed, and that the rhythm maintains a constant tempo, an unknown edit point can be found by comparing the distance between the corresponding edit point and some rhythmic feature that the two sides of the edit have in common, such as a downbeat. The two sides of the edit can then be placed in the editing block together. The marks for the downbeats should be aligned with each other, and the known edit point aligned with the cutting guide. Running a blade through the guide cuts both pieces in the same place relative to the downbeat.

master tape on beat 3 of a given measure, you'll also have to cut the section you want to splice into at beat 3. At the same time, you have to make sure you're not cutting off any phrases that may be playing over the splice. If the brass section's riff ends on the and of beat 3, cutting on beat 3 isn't such a great idea.

In the Police tune, we'll need to find cue points at the beginning and ending of each of the two choruses we're dealing with, both in the master and in copies #1 and #2. The beginning point is called the "in," because it happens as the song is going into the chorus. Likewise, the ending point is called the "out." For the ins, it would be best to use the snare hit that happens simultaneously with the first vocal line of the chorus ("When the world . . . "). This hit begins all of the choruses.

Play the master tape from the beginning, stopping it right at that beat. Now, rocking the reels with the tape deck's head lifters disengaged, see if you can identify the snare/vocal entrance. Once you're reasonably sure you've found it,

rock past it carefully, and then immediately back up just to the beginning of the snare hit. You can rock back and forth a little bit at the hit's attack to make sure you've found the very moment it begins. Use your grease pencil to draw a line right down the middle of the playback head. Now, find the same beat and mark it at the beginning of the second chorus on the master, as well as copy #1 and copy #2. (When in doubt, it's always better to mark the cut a little long rather than a little short. It's possible to cut away tiny slivers of tape to make a splice work, but putting tiny slivers back is next to impossible.)

Now we have to find and mark the outs. There's a pause in the vocal between the last measure of the choruses and the first measure of the verses (and the instrumental break). No additional instruments enter in the meantime, so it's safe to cut on the downbeat following the last measure of the chorus. The thing to listen for is the kick drum. Mark this beat for the first and second choruses of the master. Now, mark the copies. Note that they are followed by eight bars of instrumental material. Since our aim is to make the song longer, we'll leave them in, so mark the downbeat following the eight-bar instrumental section.

Cutting The Tape. Having marked both the ins and the outs, it's time to do some cutting. Cute the in of the third chorus, copy #1. If your tape deck has a button marked "edit," press it, and then press play. The edit button allows the machine's pinch roller and capstan to push the tape forward without involving the take-up reel. This way, the tape will simply spill onto the floor on the right side of the deck. (Be careful not to step on it!) If your deck has no edit button, you'll have to hold the take-up reel (to keep it from spinning wildly) and push up on the tension bar (to keep the pinch roller in contact with the capstan). Then the tape will move properly, eventually piling up on the floor. When you hear the end of the chorus, stop the machine, and cut the out point at the mark you made earlier.

Use a piece of splicing tape to attach the tail end of the section you've just cut out to right side of the tape machine (or somewhere equally convenient, yet out of the way). This makes it easy to find and re-attach it in the right direction. (It's a good idea to do this even with sections you intend to throw away. It may save you if you make a mistake.)

104

Now, spice the tape back together where you've cut the piece out, and rewind to the first chorus of the master. Cut out the first chorus the same way. After you cut off the tail end of the first chorus, attach the loose end coming from the supply reel to the tail of copy #1. Using your hand to spin the reel, rewind the tape from the floor onto the supply reel, and attach the two loose ends. Now, listen to your work. If you've done every thing correctly, copy #1 should occupy the place where the first chorus used to be, and the splices should be undetectable.

Whether or not you hear a problem, go ahead and replace the second chorus of the master with copy #2, using the same method. If that doesn't work, listen carefully to determine whether you can fix the problem by cutting out a beat or two. Failing that, start over. It may take a few tries to get the hang of it, but once you do, you'll find it easy to make "invisible" edits.

Difficult Cue Points. It's important to listen carefully when choosing your cue points. You can't make a good edit without first taking all of the music into consideration, making sure that you're not cutting any instruments off in mid-note, or cutting into a section with a slightly different mix. Be particularly careful when cutting around vocals, synthesizer lines, horn riffs, or strings—you can bet that after a vocal happens, or a horn blast or a synth lick, there will be a trail of reverb. If you cut that trail off prematurely, or cut into it from another section, it will be noticeable. Sometimes this is a hip effect; Trevor Horn used it to great effect in "Owner Of A Lonely Heart" by Yes, at the breakdown where everything drops out but the guitars. Try to anticipate the effect of an edit ahead of time, so you know what you're getting yourself into before you cut the tape. But don't be afraid to try something if you think it might sound good—you can always put the original pieces back together.

Put your producer's hat back on. The edits work, but listening to the song as we've edited it, the eight bars of instrumental after the choruses is a bit much. Let's remove them. Try to find a cue point between the end of the vocal section and the beginning of the verse. If you listen carefully, you'll notice Sting's vocal ad-lib ("whoa-oh") overlaps the downbeat of the first measure of the instrumental section, so we can't cut there. The ad-lib occupies the first half of the first beat of the next measure, so the earliest we can cut is at the second half of that beat. And if we cut any later, we'll chop off part of the vocal entrance to the verse, which happens right on the second half of the first beat. This is what is known as a "tight" edit. Even if you do it right, it will sound as though Sting is getting a little breathless. Let's give it a try anyway.

As we've already seen, the first trick is to find cue points for the ins and the outs—and this is where things get difficult. Finding the place where the vocal enters for the verse isn't too hard, but there's no clear way to judge where to cut after Sting's "whoa-oh." Here's a neat tip that will make such mystery edits a snap: Since the song goes along at a constant tempo, and the tape moves at a constant speed, we can assume that the distance between the downbeat and the second eighth-note in the measure (where we want to make the cut) will be the same for every measure in the song. If we know the distance for one side of the splice, we can measure the same distance for the other.

It's easy to find the downbeat both at the end of the chorus and at the beginning of the verse, because the kick drum makes it pretty apparent. Mark it. Next, mark the vocal entrance to the verse. All that's left, then, is to figure out where to cut off the end of the vocal ad-lib. Put the tape containing the beginning of the verse into the splicing block, and line up the mark for the vocal entrance with the cutting guide. Now, put the piece of tape containing the end of the chorus into the block *on top* of the other. As you put it in, carefully line up the downbeat marks. When you cut through the guide, you'll cut both pieces of tape at once at precisely the same moment in relation to the downbeat. Splice the ends together, and see how it sounds.

Creative Editing. Feeling even more creative? You might consider putting the instrumental sections you just removed into the intro. Or you might add one of them after the third chorus. Try cloning the first verse and putting it after the instrumental section following the third verse. You can keep doing stuff like this until you've extended the song to a length of six minutes or more, or to create a version of the song that's structurally stronger than the original. This is one example of what the art of tape editing is all about.

By Bobby Nathan

105

MAKING DEMOS

May 1985

Whether you've been recording at home or in a state-of-the-art 24-track studio, unless you are signed to a recording contract all of your recordings are considered demos. A demo is a demonstration recording proving to a prospective investor, record company, or whoever that you have a product that is viable for release as a record. I would like to suggest a format for recording your demos so that, when you have been signed to a record label, you won't have to re-record the track from scratch, possible losing the feel that got you the deal in the first place.

A simple 4-track system—such as the AMR Model MCR/4 4-track and Model 64 mixer—can serve as the heart of a compact, high-quality demo studio.

If you are recording on a 4-track and using live drums, print your drums on one track and print the other three main instruments of the rhythm section on the three remaining tracks. If you need additional tracks for overdubs (and everyone always does!), bounce the four tracks down to one or two tracks on another recorder (a 2-track machine or even a cassette deck), and bounce the mix back from the 2-track onto another section of the 4-track tape. This procedure means you won't have to erase the original rhythm tracks. Working with a 4-track always means compromises, but make the best of it. Bouncing form deck to deck will add another generation of tape hiss to your demo, but it will let you keep your rhythm tracks (the "feel") with enough separation that later you can bounce them onto a 24-track and go on from that point, rather than starting over.

If you are using a drum machine, the procedure is different. Print the sync track of the drum machine on one track and the three most important rhythm section instruments on the remaining three tracks. Overdubbing these other

tracks will definitely be a royal pain, because you will have to start at the beginning of the tune every time in order to sync the drum machine. When you bounce the 4-track over to the 2-track, sync the drum machine to the 4-track and record it directly into the 2-track mix. Now you'll have first-generation drums in the mix. Bounce the 2-track back to a blank stretch of tape on the 4-track and proceed as before.

On pages 60-65, I discuss ways of using sync tone, click track, and SMPTE sync boxes to get all of your drum machines and sequenced keyboard instruments into your home demo without having to take up more than one tape track, the one that has the sync tone. Guitar, bass, and vocals can then be recorded on the remaining three tracks. In many cases this will eliminate the need to bounce down to a 2-track and back again.

If you are fortunate enough to own an 8-track recorder, the need to bounce down may be very slight, especially if you also own a sync box for your drum machines and sequencer. The cost of an 8-track recorder, sync box, drum machine, and sequencer may be more economical than owning a 16-track or 24-track recorder. Your mixing console will have to have enough inputs to accommodate the total number of instruments on tape plus what has been programmed into your drum machine and sequencers. You will also have to own enough synthesizers to perform your demo in one pass if they are not recorded on separate tracks. With careful planning you can overcome all these obstacles.

At this point, some of you may be asking, "Why?" The answer is, "To preserve the original groove and avoid having to do the same work twice." All experienced studio artists know how frustrating it can be to try to duplicate a magical performance that you originally recorded at three o'clock in the morning in your home studio in your underwear (only now you have to contend with input from the producer and engineer). I don't want to sound too negative; it's not impossible at all to duplicate the feel of the original demo in a 24-track studio. It just seems a waste of time to have to do the same work over and over again.

I think the biggest problem that most people have recording at home these days is that the sound is not professional. You would be astounded to learn what well-known records were bounced

up from 4-, 8-, and 16-track machines. If your attitude about the equipment you are using is on a professional level, there should be no reason why you can't create tracks at home that can be used on record. Granted, one does need a good recording console, microphones, outboard gear, and a good acoustic environment for recording live drums with ambience. The cost of the above may be quite prohibitive for the small or home studio. But drums are truly the only instrument that requires so much expense. The drum machine has made its mark in the home studio for this reason. And with sampling technology what it is today, you can get around the problem by recording the live drums anywhere and triggering great sampled sounds later.

If you don't intend to use the drum machine in your 24-track recording, it still makes a good guide track. If all the synthesizers have been sequenced and error-corrected (quantized) to taste, then it is easy to turn off the drum tracks and have the drummer overdub to the synthesizer tracks. If the headphone mix is right, the drummer should feel that he or she is jamming with a band; the only drawback is that he has to follow the band and therefore cannot have any influence on the band's performance.

As far as other instruments and vocals are concerned, you would be surprised what can be recorded at home and transferred up to 24-track. Guitar, bass, synthesizers, and vocals especially! If you don't own a great microphone console or compressor, you can learn to record great vocals with moderately priced gear. Later, in the studio, these tracks can be doctored to a certain degree. The quality of the performance always comes first! And recording at home does offer some advantages in terms of psychological comfort. Many musicians never get over the "other side of the glass" phobia in the studio.

If you don't own any multi-track equipment and are recording your entire great-sounding demo on your ghetto blaster, you can try this: Bounce the entire mix of your demo onto the 24-track and use it as a sort of click track. (This technique is used to make a lot of the sound-alike records you see advertised.) As you are overdubbing the individual parts onto the multi-track, you monitor only the track you are actually recording and the original demo mix. When all the parts of the arrangement

have been added, the guide track is wiped, but its original feel has been preserved.

Not all of the methods I've outlined will work for everyone, but if you can grasp one of these ideas and put it to good use, then I've accomplished what I set out to. In many cases, the producer's input at the session can help improve the groove. But it you want to capture the initial feeling that got you the record deal, these tips can definitely help.

By Bobby Nathan

MIDI TRICKS

July 1986

Here are some tips for using MIDI that can save studio time, save money, and hopefully expand your creativity.

Before you walk into the recording studio, make sure that all your programming has been done correctly. Recording your MIDI compositions to cassette is a good way to sit back and analyze your work outside of the MIDI environment. This allows you to hear things differently than you did while you were working. Is the tempo correct? Once you transfer your MIDI sequence to tape, there's no changing tempo. Make sure the song is in the right key for your vocalists, too. A number of sequencers make it easy to transpose an entire song; but it's not possible to transpose without changing tempo once your data has been transferred to a tape recorder, whether it's analog or digital.

Aside from writing your hit song, choosing sounds is often the most time-consuming process of all. Even if you don't have any problems making up an arrangement, finding the right synthesizer patches—sounds which complement each other and yet fit the song itself—is no simple matter. If you wait to do this in the studio, you could blow your whole budget in one shot. When picking out patches and samples, keep in mind that if the vocals haven't been recorded yet, the sound you've chosen may not work with the vocal tracks you add later. Also keep in mind that drum sounds, in particular, have an effect on all the other sounds. For instance, you may have picked your synthesizer patches and samples while listening to a particular drum machine. If, in the studio, you decide to use more ambient drum sounds, all of a sudden your original

synth sounds may not fit. Try to plan beforehand what kinds of stereo panning, volume levels, and ambience you'll use on your drum sounds. This way there's a much better chance that your other choices will fall into place properly.

Of course, even the best-laid plans can change once you get into the studio—which brings us to the next consideration. Let's say, for instance, that you've sequenced and picked all the right sounds ahead of time. You dump the sequence to tape during your first day in the studio, and go home to lay down some MIDI data for the next song. In the more critical light of your second day in the studio, however, the producer decides that the arrangement isn't quite his cup of tea. In this situation, you have a couple of choices. Of course, you could find another producer! But maybe you like your producer, and you trust that he knows best. At this point, you're going to have to go back and rearrange the original sequence data. I hope you still have your original data saved somewhere. What did I hear you say? You wiped the first sequence in order to work on the next one? You don't even have the drum machine data? You'll have to reprogram. Next time, make sure you keep all your data backed up somewhere!

For the time being, however, you're in the unfortunate position of having to reprogram a MIDI composition in the studio. Here's a trick that seems to make things go more smoothly. A lot of programmers transfer their drum patterns into a MIDI sequencer (provided the drum machine has MIDI in/out capability). This can usually be accomplished by setting your sequencer up as follows:

● Pick an unused sequencer track.

● Set that track to receive and transmit on an unused MIDI channel (conventionally channel 16 is the favorite for drum data, but any channel will do).

● Place your MIDI drum machine in external clock mode.

● Place the sequencer in record. Your drum machine should start at the top and play all the way down the entire length of the song. If your sequencer has a keyboard thru feature (MIDI echo), turn it off for this process.

● After the entire track has been recorded, stop the sequencer.

● Set the drum machine to read its internal clock.

● Connect the MIDI output from your sequencer into the drum machine's

107

MIDI input. Be sure that your drum machine is set to receive on the proper MIDI channel.

• Load an *empty* pattern into the drum machine.

• Put the sequencer in play. The drum machine will simply play whatever the sequencer tells it to play, along with the other MIDI instruments reading data from the sequencer, as though you were playing it in real time.

The advantage of working this way is that, whenever you rearrange larger segments of music in the sequence, you rearrange the drum part at the same time. You don't have to re-chain drum patterns each time you repeat or delete a verse or a chorus. If you chop a 4/4 bar in half, you don't have to make up a new 2/4 pattern. And so forth. Many programmers choose to record the drum step by step on the sequencer while composing. It's a matter of taste whether the drums are initially programmed via the sequencer's quantization and looping features or the drum machine's, so you can consider using one or the other, or even both, depending on what suits your needs.

This brings us to another interesting way of programming that has developed at Unique Recording Studios. Because we have so many sequencers to choose from, it has become apparent that each one has features unique (pardon the pun) to itself. Some have different song mode features, some have special cut-and-paste editing commands, others have great step entry, graphic editing, numeric editing, notation, looping, shuffle modes, and what-have-you. What it all boils down to is that, thanks to the standardized MIDI data stream, we can use more than one sequencer at a time for composing and editing. It has already become standard procedure to bounce data in real time from one sequencer to another, with both of them synced via MIDI clock, to make the best of what each unit has to offer. Bouncing MIDI data between two sequencers works like a charm! If two members of your band have different sequencers, get them together and see what you can do with the combination. It's as natural to consider using each sequencer for its strengths as it is to use one synthesizer because it's great for bass lines and another for its Rhodes patch.

I know—you want a practical example. Let's say that, in the interest of freeing up sequencer tracks, you've bounced (or merged) several channels worth of MIDI data to a single track. Now the data for all of the parts is scrambled together on one track. What if, later, you need to edit the bass, which is on MIDI channel 1? Well, you could get a MIDI filter that sorts data according to channel, connect it between your sequencer's output and input, and untangle the mess. Then you can fix the bass part by punching in or re-recording, as you normally would. If you had access to another sequencer, though, you could bounce from one to the other through the filter, which would accomplish the same result. Of course, you could do without the filter if the second sequencer has an unmerge function, or even an input channel assignment (this would cause a given track to record only the data coming in on channel 1). I know of one sequencer that can even take in 16 MIDI channels from a single track and filter each to its own track.

Quantization is another key factor here. Every sequencer quantizes differently, and some are better suited for certain instruments. some seem to work best for bass sounds, some for string sounds, and so forth. Most of the time, fairly superficial considerations—the way the buttons are laid out, the way the displays look, the ease of use for certain functions—cause a musician to choose one sequencer over another. You can bet, though, that the subtle quirks of timing, dynamics, timbre, and user interface will cause that musician to create in a different way. When you get to know a sequencer well enough, you can take advantage of those quirks. You can use one sequencer for its incredibly quick step entry, and another because its quantization function spreads the bass notes out and makes them punch just right.

The same thing has always been true with drum machines as well. A lot of early rap records featured the same cheesy-sounding drums, which led to a sameness in the music. Don't get me wrong—I have nothing against rap, but have you ever noticed that the reason why most grooves have the same feel is because the same machine is playing them? You could sample those cheesy sounds into some other drum machine, and if you programmed the same rhythms into the new machines, the music would definitely feel different.

Getting back to the subject of transferring MIDI sequences to tape, I'd like to stress the importance of a dependable click or sync track. Without the solid

synchron- ization, making even the simplest changes after the fact is a royal pain. Always leave the sync or click track on tape at all costs! I've seen people erase their sync track time and time again, only to pull their hair out during the mix-down session when they realize that a sequence has to be changed.

Once again—save all your data. Even after you've bounced the drum machine parts to your sequencer, you may find good reasons to change the drum part in some way that's fundamental to the drum machine. It may cost a few bucks more in data disks to archive all your work, but you never know when you'll need to dig up that data for a special remix. When it comes to using MIDI in the studio, be prepared for anything.

By Bobby Nathan

BOUNCING TRACKS

February 1987

Here is a simple, low-tech approach for getting ten instrumental parts onto four tracks. The technique is outlined, step by step, in the diagram.

Let's say we already have drums in mono on track 1, bass on track 2, and a mono piano part on track 3. Bring the three tracks into the mixer by changing the source switch on channels 1, 2, and 3 to tape, and route them to track 4. Put track 4 in record, and mix tracks 1, 2, and 3 onto track 4. This is called "bouncing" tracks; that is, the first three tracks are bounced to the fourth.

Your mixer probably makes it possible to bring another instrument in on channel 4 while you're bouncing. If so, you can save a track by recording a take during the bounce, mixing it in with the three tracks all at once. There's no danger in doing as many takes as you need to get the music right, since the first three tracks will play back exactly the same way each time. When you're finished, you'll have drums, bass, piano, and the part you added during the bounce, all in mono on track 4. Tracks 1, 2, and 3 are now free for further overdubs. You should erase them if the overdubbed parts aren't going to play through the entire song.

Overdub new parts on tracks 1 and 2, and then bounce them to track 3. Again, you can add yet another part as you bounce. You should now have three parts on track 3 and four parts on track

4—seven parts in all—with two tracks still available for overdubbing. Two more parts will fit conveniently, but what if you want to add *three* more parts? No prob. Record one on track 1, bounce track 1 to track 2 while adding another, and record over track 1 with the third part. There are now ten parts on your four tracks, but you can still add another as you mix down to stereo. Not bad for a dinky little cassette deck, huh?

Of course, there are some limitations to working this way. For one thing, you're committing yourself to a particular mix of certain instruments early on in the recording process—the mix can't be changed later if it turns out that it's not quite right. There's not much to be done about this; with experience, you'll learn how to judge the proper level of, say, the snare drum, in the absence of other instruments still to be recorded, such as the rhythm guitar. Another limitation is that you can't mix in the kinds of ambience, such as reverb or delay, that in a professional situation are usually added after the tracks are recorded. If you want ambience, you have to record it with the tracks. Along the same lines, the premixed tracks can't be "fixed" later to accommodate changes in the music. Once they're mixed, there's no more punching in and out. And don't forget that in bouncing, the submixes you've created are monaural. Achieving a stereo spread in the drums, for instance, isn't really practical using this method.

The other major limitation is the inevitable increase in tape hiss and degradation of audio fidelity. To some exent, this is unavoidable, but it can be minimized by copying a signal from one track to another as few times as possible. With each recording, or generation, of a signal, its audio quality is degraded. If you follow along with the procedure as we've outlined it, you'll see that the drums, bass, and piano are only second-generation recordings—that is, bounced once. This introduces some degradation, but it's not too bad. On the other hand, the vocal hasn't been bounced at all, which is ideal. All in all, getting ten parts onto four tracks with a maximum of two generations is a pretty good deal.

Another way of minimizing noise is to mute or fade out tracks during silent moments. You can also hedge by recording the first few parts with a bit more high-end EQ than you need. Then, when you bounce, back the top end off a bit. Not only will this restore the tone to

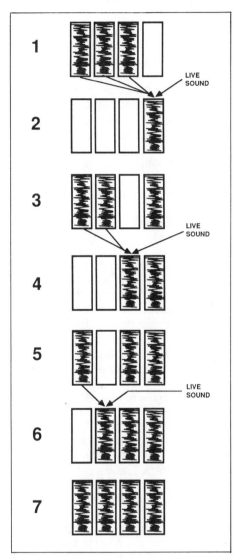

Bouncing tracks greatly enhances your studio's capabilities. Here's how to record ten parts with just a 4-track recorder: (1) Three tracks are recorded, and (2) bounced within the machine while adding another "live" part. The first three tracks are now free, and should be erased. (3) Two more parts are recorded, and (4) bounced to a single track, adding another live part at the same time. (5) Yet another part is recorded on one of the two free tracks, and (6) it's bounced to the other free track along with another live part. (7) The last remaining free track is filled.

where it ought to have been in the first place, but it will cut back a bit of hiss. (You may find that tracks with a little extra high end are less muffled after bouncing, in which case you might want to keep the noise and refrain from cutting the highs during the bounce.)

A common mistake is to fill up three tracks and bounce them to one, fill up two more tracks and bounce them to one along with the previous submix, fill up two more free tracks and bounce, and so on *ad infinitum*. By the time you're finished, the first three tracks you recorded will be third- or fourth-generation, which means they won't sound so great. They will sound muffled and will have lost their punch, and you will have generated a lot of tape hiss, and you won't have gotten many more parts onto four tracks than you would have using the method we described first.

Eight-Track

People who own 4-track decks tend to think that having eight tracks would be heavenly. It seems to be one of the laws of the physical universe, though, that you can never have enough tracks. There are always more parts to squeeze onto tape. Therefore, we're going to see now just how many parts we can get on eight tracks and still maintain relatively high fidelity.

Let's say we're recording an instrumental piece. We have drums recorded in glorious stereo across tracks 1 and 2, bass is on track 3, and a piano part takes up track 4. We put a string pad in the chorus on track 7, and a brass part during the bridge between the chorus and the verse on track 8. That leaves tracks 5 and 6 free, so if all we need at this point is a guitar part and a simple melody, there won't be any need to bounce (re-record several tracks mixed to one within the machine). But this piece is fairly involved (we're artists, for heaven's sake), and we still have to record two guitar parts, percussion, the verse melody, a different melody for the chorus, a harmony part for the chorus melody, and a few tracks worth of effects. What's the best way to go about it?

Bring the recorded tracks into your mixer (switch channels 1, 2, 3, 4, 7, and 8 to "tape" or "mix mode," if your mixer has such switches) and route them to tracks 5 and 6. Now it's time to do the first part of your mix. Pan the tracks in stereo, set their relative levels, and add the appropriate effects. Bear in mind that

you won't be able to change this part of the mix later. Try to second-guess the needs of the final mix. Which parts will be featured, and which will be kept in the background? Is the bass going to be drowned out when you add the other parts? If you give the lead lines heavy delay and reverb, will that nullify the effect of the reverb on the string parts? Will the brass part still stand out during the bridge after the other parts are added? With experience, you'll learn to compensate properly. Just keep in mind that a well-balanced mix at this stage won't necessarily sound right when you've added the other parts.

The next step, of course, is to record the mix onto tracks 5 and 6. Be sure to check it, both on your main speakers and with headphones. Listening through headphones often reveals subtle dropouts and other problems that might go unnoticed on speakers. If the music will be used for broadcast, check it out on speakers salvaged from a cheap television or radio to make sure that everything is well balanced even under less-than-hi-fi conditions. (A company called Auratone makes "crummy" speakers for just this purpose.) If you don't have such speakers in your studio, run off a cassette and check it on a portable cassette player. If you think I'm being a bit pedantic here, you're right. At this stage in the proceedings, it's important to get it right, since you can't change things later.

Once you're satisfied with the pre-mixed tracks, erase the others. You might be punching in and out on them, and sometimes snippets of the original parts will appear between punches, making life hell when it's time to do the final mix.

Now might be the best time to record the melody lines, so you can get a better perspective on how the piece is taking shape. Remember, we've got separate melodies for the verse and chorus. Unfortunately, they butt right up against each other, and the reverb from one hangs over beyond the moment when the next is to begin. Obviously, this will take two tracks (1 and 2). Now bring those tracks into the mixer and route them to track 4. Taking care to balance them with the premixed tracks, bounce the melody parts to track 4 and then scrub tracks 1 and 2.

Now you can give your friend a call and ask him to bring over his guitar. Record the chordal rhythm part on track 1. If it doesn't sound full enough, get him

to play it again and record the second take on track 2. If your tape deck has a variable speed control, slow down the tape a fraction during the recording and then speed it back up for playback. This gives you the same kind of chorus effect you get by detuning synthesizer oscillators.

It sounds good, but there's still something missing. Being a patient sort and a jolly good egg, your guitarist friend suggests that you record another guitar part in a higher register. That goes on track 3, and naturally it sounds marvelous. Time for another bounce: Route the three guitar tracks to track 8, balance them with the rest of the tracks, and press record. An option at this point is to leave the higher part out until the second verse to give the song a bit of a strategic lift. Also consider adding flanging and other effects, but keep in mind that you're committing yourself. Having done so, erase the three guitar tracks and take stock of the situation.

Tracks 5 and 6 have six parts on them. Track 4 has two melody lines, and track 8 has three guitar parts. That's 11 parts with four tracks to burn. It's worth pointing out that all of the parts are only second-generation—that is, they've suffered only one bounce.

Put the percussion parts on the remaining tracks: Congas and claves on track 1—since the congas play only in the verses, you can punch in the claves during the choruses—and cabasa on track 2 (your guitarist friend can pitch in and play a cowbell at the same time). Now record the tambourine on track 3, with agogo bells punched in during the bridge. When you've finished with that, bounce the whole mess onto track 7. This leaves tracks 1, 2, and 3 free for the picked guitar part, the harmony line, and the sound effects (a big gated tom hit right before the first verse, orchestral stabs, glass smashes, and any other clichés you fancy throwing in).

Here's the tally. There are 20 or so parts on tape. Six parts (drums, bass, and keyboards) are on tracks 5 and 6, three guitars are on track 8, six percussion parts are on track 7, two melodies are on track 4, the other guitar is on track 3, maybe more percussion parts on track 2, and effects on track 1. All parts are at worst second-generation, so the fidelity is quite high. You may have noticed that we kept most instrument groups on separate tracks (for example, all the guitars are on one track), which gives us a reasonable amount of control

110

for the final mix. The only real problem is that we've bounced lots of things to mono, so we'll have to use reverb and delay to stereoize them in the mix. Playing around with the pan controls during the mixdown can also give the effect of stereo. An alternative is to bounce together tracks that will occupy the same position in the stereo field—that is, mix to mono the tracks that are to end up panned hard left, and so forth.

We didn't do too badly, but we still could have saved a few tracks. For instance, the guitarist could have recorded his picking part as the other three parts were being bounced. Then perhaps we could have given the guitars a stereo submix. The only trick is planning. Always anticipate what will need to be done, and plan accordingly. Even if you have a 16- or a 24-track machine, you can run out of tracks, so this goes even for larger setups. You can plan more accurately if you record a scratch version of your song first, simply putting all the parts on tape without regard for the number of generations it takes to get them there. Then, you can go back and do it with the proper attention paid to sound quality and other production values.

By Steve Howell

STAYING AHEAD OF TECHNICAL CHANGE

February 1987

No matter which sampler you own, it is a fact of life that in the near future another unit will come along with better fidelity and longer sampling time. People in the industry are working to save us from product obsolescence. For example, a universal sample-dump format was recently defined as part of the MIDI spec, although at present it is far from. universal in its application. Products such as Digidesign's Sound Designer and Oberheim's new DXP-1 are designed to be compatible with a number of samplers. But while technology marches on, standardization tends to crawl through thickets of negotiation, interpretation, and debugging. It will probably be a while before sampling is completely out of the woods. In the meantime, here's some information on

the art of preparing your precious samples for whatever machine comes along.

When 16-bit samplers start to replace your current 8- and 12-bit machines, it won't be sonically efficient to re-sample from an 8- or 12-bit sampler to a 16-, 18-, or 24-bit unit. Don't get me wrong: I'm not advising anyone to wait for a low-priced 16-bit sampler to come along before buying anything! But if you spend time and effort making serious

samples, and the only storage medium for them is the disks from your sampler, you will be on the losing end when you upgrade to a higher sampling resolution.

My main point is very simple: You want to have the sounds you're going to sample in the most pristine condition possible before they get converted into the sampling unit's digital format. The best way, of course, is to record them into the machine live; unfortunately, any distortions introduced by your sampler will forever be a part of the sample, and when you feed that sound into a sampler of higher quality, the new machines will faithfully record those distortions along with the rest of the sound. If you always begin the sampling process by recording your original sound sources cleanly to tape, either analog or digital, you will always be ready for the future.

Digital Or Analog

Which is better? Well, it is a matter of taste. It can also be a matter of cost. Here's how the facts line up:

Even in these digital times, analog recorders are pretty competitive, especially in 1/4" and 1/2" 2-track (1/2-track) formats. Unlike 1/4-track decks (the ones that allow you to record on two ''sides'' of a reel of tape), these machines take full advantage of their

The CompuSonics DSP-1000 digital 2-track recorder uses optical disks to record and play back information. These disks are known as "WORM" disks, for "Write-Once, Read Many times"—as this suggests, they can't be erased or re-recorded.

respective tape widths. The only limitation is that you can't flip the tape over; that is unless you like your samples played backwards. Signal-to-noise ratios for such decks range from 62dB to 78dB—not bad. (Signal-to-noise ratio measures the level of the noise floor in relation to a standardization signal level; the higher the number, the better). Some of the manufacturers making 1/2" or 1/4" decks are Ampex, Fostex, Otari, Sony, Studer/Revox, and TEAC. The prices for analog 1/4" decks range between $1,200 and $7,000, while 1/2" decks go for between $2,500 and $12,000.

Otari's MX-55 2-track 1/4" open-reel analog tape recorder. Many engineers prefer open-reel tape to cassettes, since it can be spliced easily.

Digital machines have signal-to-noise ratios ranging from 80dB to 98dB—as you can see, digital is quieter than analog. The most common machines used for sampling these days include Sony's PCM F-1 digital encoder and a Beta, VHS, or 3/4" U-matic video recorder. Prices on this kind of rig range from around $500 to $1,750 for the encoder (Sony's professional model, the PCM-1630, goes for $22,000) and $375 to $900 for a Beta or VHS deck. A 3/4" deck costs between $5,000 and $14,000. Those of you with cash to burn might consider one of the digital reel-to-reel decks (they use special digital reel-to-reel tape and have the encoder built-in). They range between $17,000 and $25,000, and are made by Otari, Studer, Sony, and Mitsubishi.

Unfortunately, digital still does not sound natural, at least not to my ears. Either the bass is lacking in punch, or the high frequencies sound brittle. But they are quiet. Like sampling technology, digital recording is improving apace and will eventually be perfected. In the meantime, though, we have to deal with the here-and-now, and it makes sense to compare the cost versus the quality of analog and digital formats.

One advantage of analog recording

is that it gives you the ability to leader the start-points of your samples. If you gather representative grand piano samples over the entire range of the instrument and insert leader tape at the start of each note, it will be easier to load them into your sampler. When loading a sample, it is often necessary to try several times until you get the best level. Analog tape transport mechanisms can be rocked to the start of the leader every time, saving you much time and trouble. On the other hand, inexpensive digital recorders rely on video decks, which are tedious to locate to a given point unless you are controlling them with a SMPTE synchronizer.

Another format exists which is often overlooked and yet is quite good and quite inexpensive. It is found in Beta and VHS video decks with hi-fi stereo audio. Video hi-fi's signal-to-noise ratio is better than 80dB. You can get two hours of recording time on a good-quality tape cartridge (up to eight hours, with some loss of fidelity, on some VHS models).

Analog tape costs from $30 to $60 for 30 minutes running at 15 ips, or 15 minutes at 30 ips (the preferred speed for squeaky-clean sampling). Beta and VHS tape costs between $12 and $15 for a relatively high-quality cartridge, and gives you a whopping two hours at the fastest tape speed. The cost of 3/4" video tape is around $30 for an hour's worth. Reel-to-reel digital tape costs from $60 to $75 for a half-hour at high speed.

Sampling Tips

If you are using an analog machine, it is generally desirable to record fairly hot (at a high level). If you record hot enough, a phenomenon called tape compression will occur. Many rock and roll engineers use tape compression in the studio to get a punchy sound (see the article on using compression on page 46). If you are going digital, recording hot is not advisable. There is no such thing as tape compression in digital recording; hitting the tape with too much level will result in a range of disturbing effects that will render your taped samples useless.

Record your samples to tape with whatever effects you'd like, but remember that you won't be able to remove those effects later. It's a good idea to record acoustic instruments in stereo, using two microphones or a single stereo mike. Although stereo samplers

aren't common yet, you can bet that they will be in the future, and many common musical sounds, for example ambience and acoustic piano, are recorded in stereo as a matter of course.

In addition, it is wise to index your samples, so that retrieving them in a year of so will not be too horrendous a job. Assemble all samples on one reel or cartridge (this is another place where analog reel-to-reel tape comes in handy), start the tape counter at 0, play the reel from the top, and note the counter number at the beginning of each sample. Keep in mind that the counter numbers will change if you leader, add, or delete any samples after you have indexed the tape.

Whether you use a digital or an analog recorder, it is always wise to play back what you've recorded immediately afterward. Make sure your recording is close enough to the original sound to satisfy you. Remember: When sampling for the future, your samples will only sound as good as what's on the tape.

By Bobby Nathan

FUTURE DIRECTIONS IN PERSONAL RECORDING

As we peer into our crystal ball to discern the future direction of the personal and small studio, a number of trends emerge from the misty vapors. The connection between audio and video—already underscored by the popularity of music television and the attention now given to post-production "sweetening" of video works—will become even stronger. Digital recording techniques will be the order of the day, in time supplanting even the best noise-reduced efforts of analog methods. Signal processing, or outboard gear, will change radically from the familiar rack-mount devices we all currently hold so dear, and it may become hard to distinguish just where the mixing console, the recorder, and the digital instrument begin and end, as all functions are usurped by computer-based systems of increasing power and decreasing cost. Here's a closer look at what may come to pass in each of these areas. . . .

The Marriage Of Audio And Video

The process of audio and video recording is merging into a single entity, a single discipline. For example, editing techniques that are commonplace in the video world are also applicable to digital audio. An increasing amount of current multi-track work is done to provide music for advertising, music videos, industrial productions, and broadcast features. There's every reason to expect this type of work to continue along its meteoric growth curve in the future, as high-quality audio and video is used to sell everything from Fords to foods.

Synchronization has come a long way in recent times, with the availability of lower-cost units that are reasonably adaptable to the transports of different manufacturers. In fact, it seems likely that synchronizers will become a standard component of audio recorders as well as moderate-cost video production equipment. Because video producers like to relate to their environment through their editing system, audio machines will adapt by standardizing on synchronizer interfaces that emulate popular (i.e. Sony or JVC) video tape recorders (VTRs). Thus an audio machine will be controllable from a video editor *transparently*—appearing as just another VTR to the system—without the inconvenience of interface boxes and external synchronizer devices.

Editing systems will similarly evolve by integrating the functions that are now part of an audio machine's remote control and autolocator. In an advanced system all audio recording functions will be controlled from the same point as all video functions. And there's one very important trend that will burst upon the scene in the not-very-distant future: *Low-cost* video production equipment will become available that will revolutionize the creation of music videos. In fact, the personal recording boom that was set off by Teac/Tascam will be repeated over again in video, starting almost any day now! Audio for video (in perfect synchronization) will be an integral part of this movement, right from the start.

Digital Recording And The Personal Studio

Everybody's been waiting so long for the digital revolution to come about that it may be an anticlimax when it finally

113

happens. Digital recording has taken over a large segment of the professional recording market, so there's no longer any question that it's possible—the question is *when* it will be possible to do it cost-effectively.

The most dramatic development in the consumer world of digital recording is the R-DAT—the *Rotary*-head *Digital Audio Tape* recorder. These devices, using a rotary head with much the same design as found in home video recorders, offer wonderfully high sound quality, and will likely follow the CD player in its downward price spiral. At the time of this writing, however, the R-DAT is embroiled in controversy, since it's considered the *perfect* consumer's copying machine, and there's no reason why one person couldn't turn out an unlimited number of perfect copies of a CD. For the home or professional studio, there's not much question that R-DAT machines already available overseas could take over many of the functions of today's analog 2-track recorders, if only the recording industry can make their peace with copying problems.

While the R-DAT may make a fine 2-track, it's far harder to envision the format becoming a low-cost digital multitrack. The reason is that a number of technical snags are holding up the works. First, any medium that requires a rotating head (such as video machines or R-DAT's) is fundamentally unsuited for multi-track work, because it's prohibitively expensive to devise a method to permit "punching in". Punching-in and punching-out are the processes of entering and leaving the record mode of a single track while the tape is running and playing back other tracks. To make a smooth-sounding punch-in or punch-out at the right place in time, one must be able to accurately judge *when* a machine will enter or leave record—which is very difficult with a rotary-head device, unless complimented by expensive digital editing systems. It's possible to make rotary-head multitrack units for live use, but not ones that allow easy punching on a single track.

So if magnetic tape is going to be the medium of choice, we need to look ahead to the next generation of S-DAT (*Stationary*- head *Digital Audio Tape*) machines to help out. The combination of a cartridge (cassette) format with a stationary head would be readily adaptable to multi-track use, at prices that would bring multi-track digital recording down to earth.

But then again, who said we needed tape, with all its problems of drop-out, accidental erasure, and so on? Taking the long view, it seems inevitable that the rotating media we're so familiar with today will be yet another old-fashioned relic of prehistory in the not-so-distant future, as solid-state memories replace them. Just as today the motionless digital watch has supplanted the familiar moving hands of the clock, digital memory will take the place of the spinning reels.

The Tascam DT-100 2-track R-DAT recorder, with its remote contoller/autolocator. As the DAT format continues to popularize and become affordable, machines such as this one should become common sights in home and professional studios.

At the moment there are all sorts of tapeless digital recorders on the market; they're called *samplers*! Their only shortcoming is that they don't provide anywhere near enough time for recording a typical composition, since their capacity for a single "track" is limited to just a few seconds. A breakthrough in memory density could provide exactly what the audio world is looking for, an inexpensive medium with no moving parts. Nothing could be better for editing and composition purposes, since access to any point in a composition would be instantaneous, and splicing as well as duplicating a section would be trivial.

It's worth noting that the solid-state storage media of the future may well be something other than the chips that now prevail as the item of choice—among the options are organic and plasma storage media.

That's the long view, but in the interim, all sorts of developments are likely to occur that will alter the face of recording. A strong case can be made for optical media as a viable storage possibility for audio. The missing technological link here is an optical format that allows for erasure and re-recording, since there are already a number of formats (including the popular CD) that permit a user to record once and then play back as many times as desired (WORM, for *Write Once,*

Read Many). There are companies on three continents involved in this pursuit, so it can be expected that a workable read/write optical system willappear over the next few years, and that it will be adapted to audio purposes.

Another possibility is the use of hard-disk drives, as is now employed successfully by New England Digital in their tapeless recording system based on the Synclavier. This ubiquitous storage medium has benefitted from ever-falling prices, to the point where it's possible to conceive of a lower-cost digital recording system (based perhaps on one of the super-powered home computers such as the Apple Macintosh II or the Atari Mega ST) that writes directly to hard disk for storage, and then uses tape cartridges for back-up purposes. Right now such systems exist; it's merely a question of whether they will fall enough in price to gain acceptance in the first place, and maintain viability when optical systems get going in earnest.

One thing that will be common to all future recording systems is that noise and tape hiss, for all intents and purposes, will disappear. Through the process of digital recording, it will become harder to make a bad recording. Thus noise reduction systems, at least the current types, will gradually become extinct as the analog recorders for which they were designed are retired from service. Of course audiophiles will find new and ever more esoteric types of distortion to discover.

Remember that for years a handful "golden eared" audio types contended that solid state amplifiers just didn't sound as good as tube amps. They were ridiculed and hooted at by the creators of the transistor amps, until more sensitive tests were devised that revealed all sorts of nasty alterations to the audio signal that solid-state designs were susceptible to. Don't be surprised to see this *same* sequence played over again. This time the subject will be digital audio, sampling rates, how many bits are enough bits, the merits of particular analog-to-digital converters, and so on.

The Demise Of Outboard Signal Processing

Effects are currently a dominant part of the recording scene, sometimes equal in importance to the actual instruments or vocals being recorded. But the prominence of effect devices as stand-alone, outboard devices will decline. Digital

processing is rapidly becoming standard equipment on allsynthesizers, and consoles can be expected to offer a complete range of signal processing in the future as digital consoles come into their own. The reason for this is simple; once an input signal has undergone an analog-to-digital conversion, it requires only clever software to produce the signal conditioning that now may require three or four outboard units.

Specifically, digital compression holds out the promise that dynamic range can be reduced without the distortion and waveform modification inherent in analog processes. Digital equalization offers the ability to change harmonic content without upsetting phase relationships. Every sort of reverberation and delay effect is similarly possible merely by pushing around bits and bytes. Thus manufacturers can offer high-powered units replete with features, yet hold their production costs down by reducing the number of analog-to-digital and digital-to-analog converters (an expensive component, especially for good ones) to a minimum.

The Unified Mixer And Recorder

Audio production machines on the highest levels seem to be erasing the barriers that now separate, the instrument, the mixing console, and the audio recorder. Lucasfilm pioneered this area, creating the Sound Droid, a now-discontinued digital sound production system. The Sound Droid simultaneously provided the functions of a console, a multitrack digital recorder, a digital sampler, and a rack of digital effects. Complete sound effect backgrounds and sound tracks were assembled on this one device, all in synchronization with video equipment. A system with some similar capabilities is the AMS Audiofile, which continues to enjoy growing employment as a complete sound editing system.

Yet another example of a fully-integrated audio production system is New England Digital's Synclavier, which in its costliest incarnation is capable of several hours' worth of digital recording (direct to hard disk). The Synclavier also offers extensive editing facilities, as well as offering a complete arsenal of synthesis tools, including sampling and FM synthesis. The Fairlight system is yet another example of this forward thinking. The relevance of all this to home and personal recording is that there's every

reason to expect this type of all-inclusive audio machine to become far more affordable. This is because CPU (Central Processing Unit) chips are now available for just a few dollars, and they outstrip in capability just about anything that was made a decade ago. The new generation of chips now coming into common use (the 386 and 68020) are making it possible for personal computers to become multitasking; that is, they can now do several things at once.

The idea of simultaneously producing, altering, and recording audio with a single device is a form of multitasking. All it takes is enough processing speed, plenty of memory, and the right software and input/output devices. The hardware is becoming more affordable every day, but it's not to the point where it costs less to make everything digital than to put together an inexpensive 8-track or even 16-track recording system. However, when the complete cost of a personal or small recording studio is considered, it's not uncommon to find $20,000 or more worth of equipment in total. For $20,000, it's already possible to produce one heck of a digital instrument—the future will certainly bring digital instruments of comparable or greater power, at a fraction of the cost.

It's likely, therefore, that the hodgepodge of instruments, effects devices, recorders, and console that now make up the typical studio will be replaced by the audio workstation, a computer-based system that does it all. The key feature of this system will be that the composer/engineer won't have to move between work areas, since everything will be accessed from a single keyboard or ergonomically-designed remote control.

* * * *

All these possibilities point to the last decade of the 20th Century as an exciting time for audio recording. We look back with amusement at the first vacuum-tube computers which occupied an entire room, but had less computing power than today's laptop. When an entire audio/video home recording facility can be controlled from a lap-sized control panel, we may likewise recall the good old days of consoles with lots of knobs, racks full of outboard gear, and keyboard stands stacked with primitive devices.

By J.D. Sharp

115

ABOUT THE AUTHORS

Jim Aikin is an Associate Editor for *Keyboard Magazine*.He has been with the magazine since 1975, during which time he has written features and articles on synthesizer art, performance, and technology. Beginning his musical career as a classical cellist, Mr. Aikin went on to play electric bass in rock bands, and now has an eight-track studio in his home. A noted science fiction author, his novel *Walk The Moons Road,* was published in 1985.

Jim Cooper is the President of the MIDI Manufacturers Association and owner of JL Cooper Electronics. Through his company, Mr. Cooper has been the creator of many music technology devices. His column, "Mind Over MIDI," appears monthly in *Keyboard Magazine*.

Dave Frederick has been involved with electronic music since the age of seventeen, when he studied synthesizers and electronic music production with Allen Strange. While a Product Specialist at Passport Designs, he became an industry expert on MIDI and computer technologies. He was an Assistant Editor for *Keyboard Magazine* and co-authored *Beginning Synthesizers* and *Using MIDI*. Mr. Frederick is currently a Product Specialist and Technical Writer for WaveFrame Corporation.

Freff is a well-known music journalist and *Keyboard Magazine* columnist. He is also a science fiction author and illustrator, and a graduate of the Ringling Bros. clown college.

Terry Fryer is a synthesist specializing in sampling, and a principal in the Colnot-Fryer music production company. He is also the owner of Ear Works, an audiophile sampling service, and is a regular columnist with *Keyboard Magazine*.

Ted Greenwald is a Windham Hill recording artist who had been one of *Keyboard Magazine*'s Assistant Editors. He has a degree in electronic music from Brown University and has done graduate work in film scoring at the University of Southern California.

Steve Howell composes for British television, advertising, and theatrical productions. He also created Akai's sample library for the S900. The tape deck in his home studio has more than four tracks.

Bryan Lanser is the New Product Development Engineer for Otari Corporation. A drummer and keyboardist, he received his EE degree from UCLA, where he also studied film and electronic music. Mr. Lanser serves as the chief engineer and designer for the guitarist/singer Michael Hedges.

Dominic Milano is the Editor of *Keyboard Magazine*. He studied electronic music composition at the Chicago Musical College, and has written numerous articles on synthesis. He is active as a performer, programmer, and design consultant.

Bobby Nathan is the owner of Unique Recording Studios in New York City, one of the first professional studios to become heavily involved with MIDI production. Mr. Nathan has worked with such leading artists as the Rolling Stones, Bob James, Stewart Copeland, and many others—and is also a columnist for *Keyboard Magazine*.

J. D. Sharp is the President of Bananas At Large, an audio/music company in San Rafael, California. Mr. Sharp has wide experience as a recording engineer, producer, and keyboardist and is an active music technology consultant.

RECOMMENDED READING

Acoustic Techniques For Home and Studio, by F. Alton Everest, TAB Books, Blue Ridge Summit, PA 17214.

ARP 2600 Owner's Manual, available from MDS, 4700 W. Fullerton, Chicago, Il 60639.

The Art of Electronic Music, compiled and with commentary by Tom Darter, edited by Greg Armbruster, A Morrow/Quill/GPI Book, from GPI Publications, 20085 Stevens Creek, Cupertino, CA 95014.

Beginning Synthesizer, by Helen Casabona and David Frederick, a volume in the *Keyboard Magazine* library for electronic musicians. An Alfred Publishing/GPI Book, from GPI Publications.

CAMEO Dictionary of Creative Audio Terms, The, by CAMEO (Creative Audio And Music Electronics Organization), Framingham, MA 01701.

The Complete Guide To Synthesizers, by Devarahi, Prentice-Hall, Englewood Cliffs, NJ 07632.

The Complete Synthesizer, by Dave Crombie, Omnibus Press, London.

Computer Music Journal (quarterly), The MIT Press, Cambridge, MA 02142.

The Development And Practice Of Electronic Music, by Jon Appleton and Ronald Perera, Prentice-Hall.

Electronic Music, 2nd edition, by Allen Strange, Wm. C. Brown Company, 135 S. Locust St., Dubuque, IA 52001.

Electronic Music Circuit Guidebook, by Brice Ward, TAB Books.

Electronic Music Production, by Alan Douglas, TAB Books.

Electronic Musical Instruments, by Norman Crowhust, TAB Books.

Electronic Musician (magazine), Mix Publications, 2608 Ninth St., Berkeley, CA 94710.

Electronmusic, by Robert De Voe, EML, Vernon, CT 06066.

Elementi di Informatica Musicale, by Goffredo Haus, Gruppo Editoriale Jackson, Milano, Italy.

The Evolution Of Electronic Music, by David Ernst, Schirmer Books, 866 Third Ave., New York, NY 10022.

Experimenting With Electronic Music, by Robert Brown and Mark Olsen, TAB Books.

Foundations Of Computer Music, edited by Curtis Roads and John Strawn, The MIT Press.

Home Recording (newsletter), GPI Publications.

Home Recording For Musicians, by Craig Anderton, Music Sales, 24 E. 22nd St., New York, NY 10010.

The IMA Bulletin (newsletter), International MIDI Association, 12439 Magnolia Blvd., Suite 104, North Hollywood, CA 91607.

Keyboard Magazine, GPI Publications.

Microphones—How They Work And How To Use Them, by Martin Clifford, TAB Books.

Mix (magazine), Mix Publications.

MIDI For Musicians, by Craig Anderton, Music Sales Corp., Chester, N.Y. 10918.

Modern Recording Techniques, by Robert Runstein, Howard W. Sams and Co., Inc. 4300 W. 62nd St., Indianapolis, IN 46268.

Multi-Track Primer, The, by Dick Rosmini, TEAC Production Products, 7733 Telegraph Road, Montebello, CA 90640.

Multi-Track Recording For Musicians, by Brent Hurtig, an Alfred Publishing/GPI Book from GPI Publications (available Summer 1988).

Mind Over MIDI, compiled by the editors of *Keyboard Magazine*, a volume in the Keyboard Synthesizer Library, a Hal Leonard Publishing/GPI Book from GPI Publications.

Nueva Generacion De Instrumentos Musicales Electronicos, by Juan Bermudez Costa, 7, Spain.

Recording Engineer/Producer (magazine), 1850 Whitley St., Ste. 220, Hollywood, CA 90028.

Recording Studio Handbook, The, by John Woram, Elar Publishing Co., 1120 Old Country Road, Plainview, NY 11803.

Studio Sound (magazine), Link House, Dingwall Ave., Croydon CR92TA, England.

Synthesis, by Herbert Deutsch, Alfred Publishing, 15335 Morrison St., Sherman Oaks, CA 91413.

Synthesizer, The (four-volume set), published by Roland, Box 22289, Los Angeles, CA 90040.

Synthesizers And Computers, compiled from the pages of *Keyboard Magazine* and edited by Brent Hurtig, a volume in the Keyboard Synthesizer Library, a Hal Leonard Publishing/GPI Book from GPI Publications.

Synthesizer Basics, compiled from the pages of *Keyboard Magazine* and edited by Brent Hurtig, a volume in the Keyboard Synthesizer Library, a Hal Leonard Publishing/GPI Book from GPI Publications.

Synthesizer Technique, compiled by the editors of *Keyboard Magazine*, a volume in the Keyboard Synthesizer Library, a Hal Leonard Publishing/GPI Book from GPI Publications.

The Technique Of Electronic Music, by Thomas Wells and Eric Vogel, Sterling Swift Publishing, Box 188, Manchaca, TX 78652.

The Technology Of Computer Music, by Max Mathews, The MIT Press.

Using MIDI, by Helen Casabona and David Frederick, a volume in the *Keyboard Magazine* library for electronic musicians, an Alfred Publishing/GPI Book, from GPI Publications.

The Whole Synthesizer Catalogue, edited by Tom Darter from the pages of *Keyboard Magazine*, a Hal Leonard Publishing/GPI Book, from GPI Publications.

INDEX

From *Keyboard Magazine* Books

SYNTHESIZER BASICS (Revised)

A valuable collection of articles from the pages of *Keyboard Magazine* covering all facets of electronic music. Includes chapters on: perspectives on synthesizers, understanding synthesis, MIDI, sound systems and components, and recording electronic music. Also included are hardware and software manufacturers' addresses, recommended books, and a complete glossary. Contributors include: Helen Casabona, Ted Greenwald, Bryan Lanser, Dominic Milano, Bob Moog, Bobby Nathan, Tom Rhea, and the staff of *Keyboard Magazine*.
ISBN 0-88188-552-5 $12.95   From Hal Leonard Publishing.

SYNTHESIZER AND COMPUTERS (Revised)

A comprehensive overview, useful for beginners or seasoned pros, or anyone interested in the future of music. Includes discussions of digital audio, synthesis, sampling, MIDI, choosing software and interface hardware, and choosing the right computer. Also included is a section on Programming Your Own Software—which leads the reader step-by-step into the world of writing music software, and covers many insider's programming tips. From the pages of *Keyboard Magazine*, with articles by Steve De Furia, Dominic Milano, Jim Aikin, Ted Greenwald, Jim Cooper, Bob Moog, Craig Anderton, and other leading experts.
ISBN 0-88188-716-1 $12.95   From Hal Leonard Publishing.

SYNTHESIZER PROGRAMMING

Don't be satisfied with factory presets! Get the most out of your instrument, whether it's a battered Minimoog or the latest digital dream machine. You can create your own unique sound with the concrete and understandable information in this practical introduction to programming and synthesis. With contributions by Wendy Carlos, Bo Tomlyn, and the editors and staff of *Keyboard Magazine*. Includes specific guidelines for the DX7, Oberheim Xpander, CZ-101, Roland JX8P, and JX10.
ISBN 0-88188-550-9 $12.95   From Hal Leonard Publishing.

SYNTHESIZER TECHNIQUE (Revised)

How to utilize all the technical and creative potential of today's synthesizers, with discussions of Recreating Timbres; Pitch-Bending, Modulation and Expression; Lead Synthesizer; Soloing and Orchestration. Hands-on practical advice and instruction by leading practitioners, including Bob Moog, Tom Coster, George Duke, Roger Powell, and others. Diagrams, illustrations, and musical examples throughout.
ISBN 0-88188-290-9 $9.95 ($12.95 after March 15, 1988).   From Hal Leonard Publishing.

THE WHOLE SYNTHESIZER CATALOGUE

An extensive consumer guide to synthesizers, culled from the pages of *Keyboard Magazine*, the foremost publication of electronic keyboards in the field. Including evaluation and practical analysis of classic landmark instruments, current state-of-the-art hardware, and synthesizer/computer software.
ISBN 0-88188-396-4 $12.95   From Hal Leonard Publishing.

THE ART OF ELECTRONIC MUSIC

The creative and technical development of an authentic musical revolution, from the Theremin Electrical Symphony to today's most advanced synthesizers. Scientific origins, the evolution of hardware, the greatest artists—including Tangerine Dream, Vangelis, Keith Emerson, Wendy Carlos, Jan Hammer, Kraftwerk, Brian Eno, Thomas Dolby, and others —in stories, interviews, illustrations, analysis, and practical musical technique. From the pages of *Keyboard Magazine*, and with a forward by Bob Moog.
ISBN 0-688-03106-4 $15.95   From Wm. Morrow & Co.

BEGINNING SYNTHESIZER

A step-by-step guide to understanding and playing synthesizers with discussions of how to use and edit presets and performance controls. A comprehensive, easy-to understand, musical approach, with hands-on lessons in a variety of styles, including rock, pop, classical, jazz, techno-pop, blues, and more.
ISBN 0-88284-353-2 $12.95   From Alfred Publishing. (Item Number 2606.)

MIND OVER MIDI

A comprehensive and practical introduction to this crucial new technology, including: What MIDI Does, Data Transmission Tutorial, Channels, Modes, Controllers, Computers, Interfaces, Software, Sequencers, Accessories, SMPTE & MIDI, MIDI systems, and more. Edited by Dominic Milano from the pages of *Keyboard Magazine*.
ISBN 0-88188-551-7 $12.95   From Hal Leonard Publishing Corp.

USING MIDI

The first comprehensive, practical guide to the application of Musical Instrument Digital Interface in performance, composition, and recording, including: basic MIDI theory, using MIDI performance controls, channels and modes, sequencers, MIDI synchronization, using MIDI effects, MIDI and computers, alternate MIDI controllers, and more. A definitive and essential tutorial, from the editors of *Keyboard Magazine*.
ISBN 0-88282-354-0 $12.95   From Alfred Publishing. (Item Number 2607.)

Coming Soon:

MULTI-TRACK RECORDING FOR MUSICIANS

How to make professional quality recordings at home or in the studio—comprehensive, creative, practical information including basic theory and up-to-date guidance on the latest equipment.
ISBN 0-88284-355-9 $12.95   From Alfred Publishing. (Available Summer 1988—Item Number 2608.)

To subscribe to *Keyboard Magazine*, write to *Keyboard Magazine*, Subscription Department, P.O. Box 2110, Cupertino, CA 95015

All prices subject to change without notice.